A new phenomenon has emerged in electronic markets. Due to the low transaction costs and the high volatility in these markets many net market makers are using auction mechanisms to buy and sell goods. Recent market studies predict that by 2002 a quarter of all transactions will use dynamic pricing concepts. The design and customization of these market mechanisms involves a number of disciplines including economics, computer science and operations research.

This multi disciplinary book summarizes the introductory economics needed to understand electronic markets and surveys the literature on negotiation and auction theory. It is the first book to combine both the relevant economic and computer science aspects of electronic markets, and the first to describe the variety of new multidimensional auction mechanisms. It uses a number of real world case studies including the trading of financial derivatives.

MARTIN BICHLER is an Associate Professor in Information Systems at the Vienna University of Economics and Business Administration. He is currently visiting scientist at the IBM TJ Watson Research Center in New York. Dr Bichler is Associate Editor of the Electronic Commerce Research Journal, and has served as organizer and program committee member in numerous conferences in Electronic Commerce and Information Systems. His research focuses on electronic commerce infrastructures and advanced market mechanisms.

D0754259

The Future of eMarkets

Multi-Dimensional Market Mechanisms

Martin Bichler

CAMBRIDGE
UNIVERSITY PRESS

PUBLISHED BY THE PRESS SYNDICATE OF THE UNIVERSITY OF CAMBRIDGE
The Pitt Building, Trumpington Street, Cambridge, United Kingdom

CAMBRIDGE UNIVERSITY PRESS
The Edinburgh Building, Cambridge, CB2 2RU, UK
40 West 20th Street, New York, NY 10011-4211, USA
10 Stamford Road, Oakleigh, VIC 3166, Australia
Ruiz de Alarcón 13, 28014 Madrid, Spain
Dock House, The Waterfront, Cape Town 8001, South Africa

http://www.cambridge.org

First published 2001

Printed in the United Kingdom at the University Press, Cambridge

Typeset in 10/12pt Times New Roman   [SE]

A catalogue record for this book is available from the British Library

Library of Congress Cataloguing-in-Publication data

Bichler, Martin.
    The future of eMarkets: multi-dimensional market mechanisms / Martin
Bichler.
        p.   cm.
    Includes bibliographical references and index.
    ISBN 0 521 80128 1 – ISBN 0 521 00383 0 (pbk.)
    1. Electronic commerce.   I. Title.

HF5548.32.B53   2001
658.8′4 – dc21   00-050243

ISBN 0 521 80128 1 hardback
ISBN 0 521 00383 0 paperback

Contents

Figures

Tables

Preface

Electronic markets are breaking new ground in old industries by providing them with a wealth of supply chain information via the Internet. The way that net market makers match buyers and sellers is key to the success of a marketplace and the design of electronic marketplaces has become a million-dollar business. This is a challenging field for both the business and the academic community.

This book introduces a framework of negotiation protocols for electronic markets. In particular, I will focus on multi-dimensional auction mechanisms which allow automated negotiation on multiple attributes and/or multiple units of a product. The findings and analyses should be useful to an audience of scholars as well as practitioners involved in the business of electronic market design. Through this book a reader should be able to understand the multitude of technical and economic issues involved in the design of electronic marketplaces. In contrast to purely economic treatments of this topic, the book combines aspects of both economics and computer science. The book provides a detailed description of the various negotiation protocols, which will be a valuable resource for systems engineers and designers. It also covers the relevant theoretical concepts in this multi-disciplinary field and should, therefore, be of interest to the wider academic community.

It is often difficult to write a book about a fast-moving subject. Describing the past is relatively easy. Predicting the future with reasonable accuracy is possible if the discussion is based on a good understanding of the fundamentals. I have tried to make the description of technical issues as robust as possible without tying it too closely to a particular product or development. Articles in magazines and newspapers can give an up-to-date picture of events. All web addresses (URL) cited in the text have been checked as at May 2000, but may have changed afterwards.

The book grew out of my research at the Vienna University of Economics and Business Administration and at the University of

California at Berkeley. Most of the technical expositions of electronic brokerage described in chapter 2 result from my work on the OFFER project in Berkeley. At that time I became fascinated by auction design and developed the first ideas about multi-attribute auctions. The laboratory experiments as well as the simulation studies described in chapters 6 and 7 were conducted in Vienna. The article upon which parts of chapter 6 are based was published in the *Decision Support Systems* journal. Some of the material from chapters 3 and 7 was published in the *Journal of End User Computing* and *Wirtschaftsinformatik*, respectively. I hope that having read this book you will share my fascination with this exciting research topic.

Acknowledgments

In preparing this manuscript I benefited from the support of many people. My first debt of gratitude is to Hannes Werthner and Hans Robert Hansen for encouraging and helping me through the process of writing the book. Their critical observations have led to numerous improvements. I also owe special thanks to Arie Segev for his generous support during my time as research fellow at the University of California at Berkeley, and to Anant Jhingran for my time at the IBM Thomas J. Watson Research Lab in New York.

I owe a great debt to colleagues and friends who helped me learn and improve the design of electronic marketplaces. First of all, I would like to mention Marion Kaukal and Rainer Klimesch, whose feedback and ideas contributed to important aspects of my research. My thanks go to Roman Brandtweiner, Rony Flatscher, Gustaf Neumann, Arno Scharl, Barbara Sporn, and all other colleagues at the Information Systems Department of the Vienna University of Economics and Business Administration. Claudia Stoiss helped me many times with her patience and understanding. I would also like to thank Judith Gebauer, with whom I have been fortunate to work with at the University of California at Berkeley.

Acknowledgment is due to W.W. Norton, for the reproduction of an extract from H.R. Varian, *Intermediate Economics* (1996) in chapter 4, and to Springer for that from D.L. Olson, *Decision Aids for Selection Problems* (1995) in the appendix.

I would like to recognize the considerable financial support from the Austrian Science Fund and the Austrian National Bank. Finally, I would like to thank Ashwin Rattan and the staff at Cambridge University Press for their support and help in the materialization of this book. Any omissions and errors are, of course, my own.

Vienna, June 2000
Martin Bichler

1 Electronic Commerce and Electronic Marketplaces

> New information technologies like the Internet are allowing a much closer integration of adjacent steps in a value chain. This is affecting firm and market structures and the coordination mechanisms used.
>
> (*Davenport, 1993*)

Information systems and their application play a major role in today's business. In addition to the introduction of new technologies which help to streamline processes within companies, electronic commerce has become the most recent trend. Electronic commerce has been described as "commercial transactions occurring over open networks, such as the Internet" (OECD, 1997). These new information technologies provide new opportunities and mechanisms to cooperate or to compete, taking advantage of computer power, the communication possibilities of the network, and the fact that millions of people and businesses are simultaneously online.

Though only a few years old, electronic commerce (e-commerce) has the potential to radically alter business-to-business, business-to-consumer as well as consumer-to-consumer transactions. For instance, electronic communication between businesses and suppliers via Electronic Data Interchange (EDI) has recently been enhanced by web-based front-ends for the placement of customer orders. Inter-organizational systems, efficient consumer response, and supply chain management are only a few of the challenges that future businesses will have to meet.

The current success of electronic commerce and the creation of billions in market capitalization and revenue is based on fundamental work done in the past in various disciplines. Computer networks, cryptography, databases, and distributed object technology form a mix of technologies and standards for the development of electronic commerce applications (Bichler, 2000b). In particular, the success of the Internet and Internet protocols as an "inter-lingua" between heterogeneous information systems has fueled the enormous growth rates. Network externalities are one way to

1

explain the fact that millions of users worldwide have agreed upon a single network standard, since the utility for every Internet user is increasing, more people are using the Internet.

While computer and engineering sciences have laid the foundation for electronic commerce, electronic commerce technologies are no longer simple efficiency tools that automate various types of transactions. By equipping economic agents with the tools to search, negotiate, and transact online and in real time, various electronic commerce applications promise an unprecedented opportunity to rethink fundamental assumptions about the economic efficacy of markets and open a whole range of new research questions. In particular, electronic commerce techniques are transforming the marketplace by changing firms' business models, and by enabling the implementation of new market institutions.

1.1   Market-Based Coordination

In recent years a particularly influential phenomenon has emerged with regard to electronic markets. Markets play a central role in the economy and facilitate the exchange of information, goods, services, and payments. They create value for buyers, sellers, and for society at large. Markets have three main functions: matching buyers to sellers; facilitating the exchange of information, goods, services, and payments associated with a market transaction; and providing an institutional infrastructure, such as a legal and regulatory framework which enables the efficient functioning of the market (Bakos, 1998). Internet-based electronic marketplaces leverage information technology to perform these functions with increased effectiveness and reduced transaction costs, resulting in more efficient, "friction-free" markets.

1.1.1   Markets vs. Hierarchies

Markets *clear* by matching demand and supply. Sellers are provided with information about demand which allows them to employ capital, technology, and labor, and develop products with attributes that match the needs of buyers. Buyers, on the other hand, select their purchases from the available product offerings after considering factors such as price and product attributes.

A key function of markets is discovering prices and conditions of a deal at which demand and supply clear and trade occurs. Markets are primarily an *information exchange* designed to lower the transaction costs for a deal. Markets can employ a number of mechanisms to match supply and demand. For instance, financial markets use one or more of the several types of auctions to determine prices, such as the "call market" auction at the New York Stock Exchange (NYSE). Other markets, such as the traditional automobile dealership, employ bilateral negotiation between buyers and sellers until a price is agreed upon. In still other markets, such as the typical department store, merchants make firm offers which customers can either take or leave.

This matching establishes a contract between buyer and seller. After a deal is agreed upon, the product being sold must be transported to the buyer, and payment must be transferred. Logistics and settlement require a certain level of trust which protects buyers and sellers. Trust is often provided through the electronic market provider or a third party who issues a letter of credit or a rating of participants. The general institutional infrastructure specifies laws, rules and regulations that govern market transactions. Regulations such as contract law, dispute resolution, and intellectual property protection are typically the province of governments.

Institutional economics has classified different *governance structures*, i.e. ways to organize and conduct economic transactions (Williamson, 1975). These governance structures refer to different types of institutional arrangements within and between firms. One of these coordination forms is the market. "Hierarchies" are seen as an alternative to markets for coordinating the flow of materials and services through adjacent steps in the value chain. The decision between market or hierarchy can be rephrased in management terms as decision between make (= hierarchy) or buy (= procurement on the market) (Werthner and Klein, 1999, p. 143). Many economists have analyzed the advantages of hierarchical and market methods of coordinating economic activity in terms of various kinds of transaction costs (Coase, 1937; Williamson, 1981, 1975).

The price of a product can be seen as a combination of three elements: production costs, coordination costs, and profit margin. *Production costs* include the physical or other primary processes necessary to create and distribute the goods or services being produced. *Coordination costs* take into account the costs of gathering information, negotiating contracts, and protecting against the risks of "opportunistic" bargaining. Finally, the profit margin is what the producer earns. Williamson (1981) was the first to classify transactions into those that support coordination between multiple buyers and sellers (i.e. market transactions) and those supporting coordination within the company, as well as industry value chains (i.e. hierarchy transactions) (Wigand and Benjamin, 1993).

Various factors affect the relative desirability of markets and hierarchies. One of these factors is *coordination cost*, which seems likely to decrease through the use of information technology. Two other factors are *asset specificity* and *complexity of product description* (Malone, Yates and

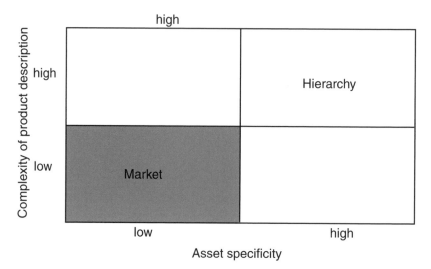

Figure 1.1 Product attributes and forms of coordination.

Benjamin, 1987). The input used by a company is highly asset-specific if it cannot readily be used by other firms because of site specificity, physical asset specificity, or human asset specificity. The term "complexity of product descriptions" refers to the amount of information needed to specify the attributes of a product in enough detail to allow potential buyers to make a selection. Stocks and commodities have simple descriptions, while those of automobiles or insurance companies are much more complex.

Highly specific assets are more likely to be acquired through hierarchical coordination than through market coordination because they often involve a long process of development and adjustment which allows the supplier to meet the needs of the procurer. Moreover, there are fewer alternative suppliers or buyers for a highly specific product. A highly complex product description often leads to hierarchical coordination, for reasons centring on the cost of communication about a product. Figure 1.1 shows that items that are both highly asset-specific and highly complex in product description are more likely to be obtained through a hierarchical relationship.

The shortcomings of market relations to provide sufficient incentives for relationship-specific investments and safeguards against opportunism and quality faults of the participants provide the background for the rise of a third coordination form, namely "inter-organizational networks" (Werthner and Klein, 1999). Networks try to combine the best of both worlds.

The strategic network has been defined as a long-term, purposeful arrangement among formally independent but related for-profit organizations that primarily allow those firms which are part of it to gain or sustain a competitive advantage over competitors outside the network. Although a strategic network is a polycentric system it is, unlike regional networks, strategically led by one or several hub organizations. (Sydow, 1992)

1.1.2 The Impact of Information Technology

Based on the coordination forms introduced in the previous subsection, electronic forms of governance have been established. In a seminal paper, Malone, Yates and Benjamin (1987) described the concept of electronic hierarchies and electronic markets. Electronic hierarchies facilitate a technically enabled, close relationship between companies in a value chain. EDI links between suppliers and retailers in the food industry are an example of hierarchical relationships. These technically enabled relationships often lead to a high level of dependence in asymmetrical power relations. Electronic markets have been defined as institutions in which entire business transactions among multiple buyers and sellers are executed electronically. Online Auctions such as Onsale <http://www.onsale.com> are an example of electronic markets (see section 5.7 for a broader overview). From an economics perspective, electronic markets have fundamental differences from traditional markets:

■ *Transparency*: Electronic markets can be completely transparent owing to marginal search costs (Picot, Bortenlänger and Heiner, 1995). "Market transparency" is defined as the ability of market participants to observe the information in the trading process. Information can be related to current or past prices, offers, volume, and the identities and motivations of market participants. This information in electronic markets is available through advanced search and comparison services.

■ *Size*: An important characteristic of electronic markets is that they are in principle not limited to regional borders, enabling the easy matching of partners from all over the world. This significantly increases the number of potential trade partners compared to traditional markets. It must also be considered, however, that partners may be located in another country with a different culture, other trade customs, etc. which may heighten the complexity of the interaction.

■ *Cost*: The transaction costs for advertising, searching for trade partners and subsequent coordination are generally low owing to a high degree of automation and the cheap connectivity to the Internet (Wigand and Benjamin, 1993). In the early days of electronic commerce (in particular with value added networks and EDI during the 1980s) switching costs

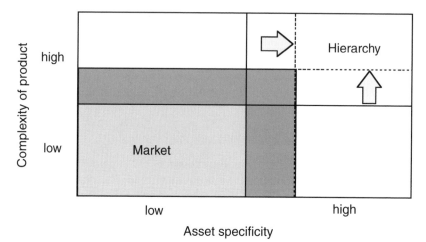

Figure 1.2 Move to electronic markets.
Source: Malone, Yates and Benjamin (1987).

for consumers were rather high owing to significant setup costs for electronic transactions. The costs have decreased as the Internet and its related standards homogenize the access channels.

Although the effects of information technology make both markets and hierarchies more efficient, Malone, Yates and Benjamin (1987) predicted an overall shift towards market coordination (see figure 1.2). The primary disadvantage of markets is the cost of conducting the market transactions themselves, which are generally higher in markets than in hierarchies. An overall reduction of coordination cost reduces the importance of the coordination cost dimension and, thus, leads to markets becoming more desirable. Moreover, low-cost computation favors electronic markets by simplifying complex product descriptions and asset specificity. For example, flexible manufacturing technology allows rapid changeover of production from one product to another. Besides, electronic marketplaces can be accessed by geographically separated buyers and sellers all over the world.

This "move to the market" hypothesis has been questioned by Clemons and Reddi (1994) who instead propose a "move to the middle" hypothesis. This means, on the one hand, a move away from the hierarchical vertically integrated organization to a higher degree of outsourcing, and, on the other hand, a move away from "faceless" market relations towards a situation where the firm relies on a few cooperative partners. These arguments are also based on transaction cost theorizing. The first part of the reasoning is similar to the "move to the market" hypothesis of Malone, Yates and Benjamin (1987). The second part is based on the assumption that long-term relationships provide higher incentives to invest in IT and in the requisite organizational adaptations and learning processes. Long-term relationships also provide some protection against the risk of opportunistic behavior and especially the loss of critical resources (Werthner and Klein, 1999, p. 177). These new forms of coordination combine the competitive power of markets and the integration benefits of hierarchies, and are often called "inter-organizational networks."

The past few years have shown the enormous success of electronic marketplaces on the Internet and illustrate the shift from hierarchies to markets. Bakos (1991) originally hypothesized that, owing to increased competition and less overhead, prices in an electronic market would be lower than in traditional markets. Crowston (1997) and Lee (1998), among others, have empirically tested this reduced-price hypothesis in several situations, but tests have not led to unequivocal results since prices actually went up in an electronic market in some cases. Choudhury, Hartzel and Konsynski (1998) also showed mixed consequences of the usage of electronic markets and suggested that the scope of the electronic market (i.e. which phases of the transaction are supported) is an important variable that has been overlooked thus far.

1.2   Fixed vs. Dynamic Pricing

The previous section described the general reasons for the emergence of new electronic marketplaces on the Internet. An electronic market system can reduce customers' costs for obtaining information about the prices and product offerings of alternative suppliers as well as these suppliers' costs for communicating information about their prices and product characteristics to additional customers. This has implications for the efficiency of an economy in terms of the search costs experienced by buyers and their ability to locate appropriate sellers (Bakos, 1991).

Electronic catalogs were the first step in this direction (Bichler and Hansen, 1997). Over the past few years, companies have put their product catalogs on the web, in order to make them universally available. Most electronic catalogs comprise fixed offers in the form of static list prices. Jango and Bargainfinder (see section 2.2) provide simple catalog aggregation services on the Internet. If the search costs for price information are zero, consumers can be expected to have perfect price information. This typically leads to price wars. Bargainfinder <http://bf.cstar.ac.com/bf> was one of the first experiments with this new kind of competition. Suddenly strong brands became commoditized. Standardized products such as CDs, gas, phone carriers, and even credit card companies had to find new ways of pricing their products. Many economists see product or price differentiation as a solution (Varian, 1996a).

Impeding price comparisons basically means reintroducing search costs. Typically, this can be done by charging different prices to different consumers for the same transaction. Price differentiation achieves this by exploiting differences in consumer valuations (see section 3.2). This discrimination strategy requires detailed consumer information and independent billing. Airlines are an oft-cited example. Currently, it is easy to search for convenient flights but finding the least expensive rate is cumbersome because the number of different tariffs is huge. Complicated pricing schemes for airline tickets defy comparison shopping. Airlines introduced this discriminated price structure (frequent-flyer programs, early reservation discounts, weekend tariffs, etc.) to deliberately reduce market transparency after a phase of open price competition (Picot, Bortenlänger and Roehrl, 1997).

By differentiating products, suppliers can decrease the substitutability of their products and services and customize offers to the requirements of specific consumers or market segments. The more successful a company is at differentiating its products from others, the more monopoly power it has – that is, the less elastic the demand curve for the product is. In such markets (often referred to as "monopolistic competition"), it is possible for providers to extract consumer surplus even among consumers who have perfect price information. Often, suppliers use mechanisms such as personalization, targeted promotions, and loyalty programs in order to distinguish their products from those of their competitors and establish customer relationships. Another very popular strategy in this context is *bundling*, i.e. packages of related goods (such as software suites) offered for sale together.

However, product and price differentiation are difficult in many markets where there is uncertainty about the price of a good or service and there is little knowledge about market participants. This uncertainty may stem from unknown or volatile supply and demand (e.g. bandwidth, electricity), or from the fact that the item being traded is unique (e.g. power plants). Nowadays, many companies are moving beyond *fixed pricing* and online order taking to create entirely new electronic marketplaces. These companies are setting up exchanges for trading things such as phone minutes, gas supplies, and electronic components, a field that is expected to grow enormously over the next few years. Like stock exchanges, these electronic markets must set up mechanisms for negotiating the terms of a contract and for making sure that both buyers and sellers are satisfied. By ensuring that prices match current market conditions, these *dynamic pricing mechanisms* create an optimal outcome for both the buyer and the seller that is otherwise unobtainable.

In general, negotiation is a broad concept and can be defined as "a process by which a joint decision is made by two or more parties. The parties first verbalize contradictory demands and then move towards agreement by a process of concession making or search for new alternatives" (Sierra, Faratin and Jennings, 1997). Dynamic pricing mechanisms such as auctions support contract negotiations in a market. In physical markets, the high transaction costs associated with dynamic pricing mechanisms have limited their application to specific sectors such as finance, commodities, and art. On the Internet, companies such as Onsale <http://www.onsale.com> or EBay <http://www.ebay.com> successfully run live auctions where people outbid one another for computer gear, electronics components and sports equipment. EBay facilitates a consumer-to-consumer exchange, whereas Onsale buys surplus or distressed goods from companies at fire-sale prices and resells them to end customers.

However, up until now, most electronic commerce has involved fixed price transactions. For stable markets or for day-to-day, low-involvement purchases where the stakes are small, the predictability and low transaction costs associated with fixed pricing are more compelling for the consumer. Two trends in electronic commerce are causing a shift from fixed to dynamic pricing for both business-to-consumer and business-to-business electronic commerce. First, price uncertainty and volatility have risen and the Internet has increased the number of customers, competitors, and the amount and timeliness of information. Businesses are finding that using a single fixed price in these volatile Internet markets is often ineffective and inefficient. Second, the Internet has reduced the transaction costs associated with dynamic pricing by eliminating the need for people to be physically present in time and space to participate in a market. The conclusion is that more negotiations can be expected to take place in electronic markets than in traditional markets (Stroebel, 2000). Certainly, fixed pricing will never disappear, but the Internet is changing the balance in favor of dynamic pricing.

This shift from fixed pricing to dynamic pricing (figure 1.3) is expected to be most evident in the business-to-business electronic commerce. Forrester Research predicts that business-to-business Internet auctions will grow to US $52.6 billion by 2002, while analyst Vernon Keenan (1998) forecasts that in the same period dynamically priced business-to-business transactions will rise to US $88 billion, representing 27 percent of the value of all business-to-business electronic commerce transactions.

Nowadays, many other new and interesting market mechanisms can be found on the Internet. Some deploy conventional auction procedures in innovative ways, others invent entirely new matching procedures for products which are either very difficult to describe or which have high trust and security requirements.

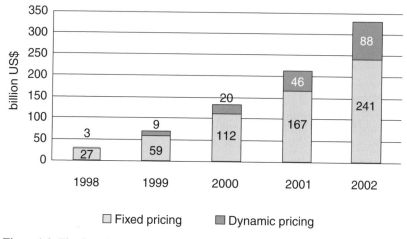

Figure 1.3 Fixed vs. dynamic pricing.
Source: Keenan (1998).

A good example of the innovative use of an auction procedure is Priceline <http://www.priceline.com>. The company lets consumers specify what they want to buy and name their price. Priceline then forwards the bids to participating airlines (or other companies) which can anonymously choose to accept the request or not. The anonymity of the marketplace ensures that suppliers do not jeopardize the prices in their conventional sales channels. Priceline makes its money on the spread between the bid and the lower price of the product. Letsbuyit <http://www.letsbuyit.com> enriches the model by creating a virtual buying cartel (sometimes called "power shopping"). The company gathers a group of buyers interested in a certain product. The bundling of buyer demand allows Letsbuyit to negotiate a better deal with a supplier. All of these examples illustrate that market power has shifted to the buyer side and new electronic exchanges are focusing much more on buyers' preferences instead of suppliers' offerings.

1.3   Advanced Auction Design for Electronic Markets

In section 1.2 auctions were introduced as the most widely used form of dynamic pricing mechanism. In an auction a bid taker offers an object to two or more potential bidders, who send bids indicating willingness-to-pay (WTP) for the object (Milgrom and Weber, 1982). Auctions have been defined as a "market institution with an explicit set of rules determining resource allocation and prices on the basis of bids from the market partic-ipants". (McAfee and McMillan, 1987). That is, any well defined set of rules for determining the terms of an exchange of something for money can reasonably be characterized as an auction (Wurman, Wellman and Walsh, 2000). An auction *clears* when it commands an allocation based on the bids it has received. In the following, auctions will be considered as a particular type of negotiation. In contrast to unstructured bidding, auctions are particularly robust forms of multilateral negotiation: They work well, even in the face of mistakes or irrational behavior by the market participants. In cases where no one person knows the true value and each individual's estimate may be highly imperfect, the clearing price is still an accurate value estimate. The competitive process serves to consolidate the scattered information about bidders' valuations.

Auctions are not a new phenomenon. They were already being used in China in 700 AD to sell the belongings of deceased Buddhist monks, or even earlier in 500 BC for wife and slave auctions (McAfee and McMillan, 1987). Today, auction houses such as Sotheby's or Christie's in London auction off paintings, wine, and other fine goods. In an auction, bid takers can determine a market price for a product without having to set a possibly suboptimal price. As already mentioned, this is also a reason why auctions are a particularly successful negotiation protocol for Internet markets where they account for an enormous volume of transactions.

The English and the first-price sealed-bid auction are widespread auction formats in practice. English, first-price sealed-bid, Dutch, and Vickrey auctions are one-to-many (i.e. single-sided) auctions, between one seller and many buyers (or vice versa in a so-called *procurement or reverse auction*):

- *English auctions* allow back-and-forth offers and counter-offers. The buyer may update the bid; the seller may update the offered sale price. Finally, the highest bidder wins.
- The *first-price sealed-bid auction* is similar; however, bidders are allowed to submit only a single, private bid.
- In a *Dutch auction* the price at which an item is offered for sale starts from a high level and declines steadily until one of the buyers stops the clock and buys the good at that price.
- Finally, the *Vickrey auction* is similar to the first-price sealed-bid auction; however, the winner pays only the amount of the second-highest bid. In this case, neither the buyer nor the seller will have an incentive to lie or hide their strategies (see section 5.3 for details).

In all of these single-sided mechanisms, bidders are uniformly of the type "buyer" or uniformly of the type "seller." Double auctions admit multiple buyers and sellers at once. These mechanisms are mostly deployed in financial markets.

These standard auction formats are primarily a means of negotiating prices. The products in question are pre-specified in all their qualitative attributes at the outset. This has already led to tough price competition among suppliers in many markets. These developments have caused many suppliers to differentiate their products and services and to look for profitable niches in a way that defies comparison shopping by price alone. Nowadays, many goods are wrapped up in service. For instance, when buying a car customers get free servicing, insurance, and perhaps only temporary leasing, etc. In addition to this, as Internet commerce matures beyond books, software, and CDs towards higher-valued items such as financial services and business services, price becomes less important, and negotiation on multiple attributes becomes necessary. Providers will try to educate customers to seek value rather than bargains (i.e. look to find the best solution overall, not just the cheapest). Of course, conventional reverse auctions are far from optimal in these situations, as the customer will be comparing increasingly differentiated products. Therefore, many marketplaces require the design of completely new negotiation protocols.

Various academic disciplines, such as economics, game theory, and organizational sciences have analyzed negotiation processes in different contexts. There have also been several approaches from computer scientists for developing intelligent software agents and protocols for automated negotiation. "Automation" in this context means that a user has only to describe his/her preferences and a certain mechanism will then determine a resource allocation, without any further user interaction.

During the past few years, several researchers have extend the framework of auctions in order to automate multilateral negotiations on heterogeneous goods or combinations of heterogeneous goods. For instance, *multi-attribute auctions* are one approach for supporting multilateral negotiations on multiple attributes of a deal. Throughout the rest of the book, the leading strand is provided by the investigation of negotiation protocols for electronic markets. In particular, the book will focus on the analysis of multi-dimensional auction mechanisms which support multilateral negotiations about complex products.

1.4　The Structure of this Book

Throughout this chapter the move to the market, towards dynamic pricing, as well as advanced auction mechanisms have been analyzed. It has also been shown that there is a need for more complex, multi-dimensional market mechanisms. Chapter 2 will explore Internet marketplaces. The services of electronic brokerages will be analyzed, and an enterprise model and an architectural model of these services will be defined. The chapter ends with a description of a sample implementation and a brief summary of technical challenges in this field.

Chapter 3 gives an introduction to microeconomic theory, and how prices are determined assuming different market structures. In particular, the chapter will investigate differential pricing, and conclude with some of the difficulties of price-setting and the potential for automated negotiation. Of course, the literature on price-setting is vast, and this book can provide only a summary of the most relevant theory in this field.

Market mechanisms are complex economic institutions and a comprehensive analysis requires techniques from various academic fields such as economics, operations research, and computer science. Chapter 4 will take an engineering point of view and examine a set of useful methodologies for the analysis and design of new market mechanisms. Equilibrium analysis, game theory, mechanism design theory, experimental economics, and techniques from computational economics will be considered.

Chapter 5 summarizes the most important research results of negotiation sciences. It will begin with various approaches for modeling one-on-one bargaining and will show the game-theoretical and experimental results of auction theory. Up until now, auction theory has fallen short in explaining the reality of auctions. Therefore, a critical review of the game-theoretical literature on auctions will be provided. Some promising research will be described that is currently underway in the field of multi-unit auctions, trying to extend the framework of theory in order to enable the sale of multiple heterogeneous goods. Finally, the particularities of online auctions will be emphasized and the results of the limited empirical research about this new phenomenon will be summarized.

Chapter 6 describes multi-attribute auction formats and summarizes the results of an economic experiment. These auction mechanisms propose a solution for taking the multiple attributes of a deal into account when allocating them to a bidder. In other words, the mechanism automates multilateral negotiations on multiple attributes. However, the design of these mechanisms poses several practical and theoretical problems. IT support is a crucial pre-condition for the feasibility of these new market mechanisms. In order to make the process more tangible, the implementation of an electronic brokerage system and a number of laboratory experiments which were conducted using this implementation will be described.

Chapter 7 focuses more on the theoretical underpinnings of multi-attribute auctions. It will provide a summary of the small amount of game-theoretical literature in this field, and compare the results of conventional and multi-attribute auctions using computer simulations. A classification framework for multi-attribute auctions where quantity is an issue will then be introduced and a model which analyzes the impact of economies of scale on the outcome of multi-attribute auctions will be described. Chapter 8 summarizes the main conclusions of the book and provides a critical appraisal of multi-attribute auctions and their applicability to the electronic marketplace. Multi-attribute auctions are heavily based on the concepts of utility theory and decision analysis. Therefore, in the appendix (p. 206) a summary of the underlying literature is provided.

Some suggestions are now made which may be helpful to the reader. Chapter 2 gives an overview of the technical issues of electronic markets and may also be omitted by readers who are mainly interested in the economics of electronic markets. The results which are required in subsequent chapters are usually repeated when necessary. Readers with a solid background in microeconomics may leave out chapter 3.

2   Internet Marketplaces – A Technical Perspective

> Internet-based electronic marketplaces leverage information technology to match buyers and sellers with increased effectiveness and lower transaction costs, leading to more efficient, "friction-free" markets.
>
> (*Bakos, 1998*)

This book analyzes a variety of market mechanisms for electronic marketplaces. "Electronic brokerage" is a metaphor for information systems facilitating the matching of buyers and suppliers in an electronic market; and, therefore, these mechanisms are key to the success of an electronic brokerage system. Before market mechanisms are analyzed, this chapter will give an overview of electronic brokerage systems on the Internet, and classify the various services being provided by electronic brokerages.

2.1   The Role of Electronic Brokers

The current state of Internet commerce is a far cry from what an electronic marketplace is envisioned to be. Although a growing number of suppliers, manufacturers and retailers offer their goods and services, in many markets there are no scalable and integrated methods for

■ suppliers to reach customers
■ customers to reach suppliers
■ introducing new products, services, and offers efficiently
■ negotiating, billing, and accounting
■ creating limited, structured electronic marketplaces.

Electronic commerce depends on the emergence of capabilities that empower buyers to obtain all the product data they need to make informed purchase decisions quickly and easily. Traditional physical markets are often brokered by intermediaries or parties that facilitate market transactions by providing brokerage services. The role of third-party intermediaries, linking different parts of a value chain, has been covered extensively by researchers in economics and business. In the 1980s, the question was raised

15

whether the future would hold a place for intermediaries, given that new technologies facilitated direct links between market players, such as manufacturers and the consumers of products, or businesses and their suppliers. Research in this area has been based on a number of theory concepts, such as transaction cost theory (Gurbaxani and Whang, 1991; Malone, Yates and Benjamin 1987), or principal–agent theory (Bakos and Brynjolfsson, 1993) (see also section 1.1). The emergence of the Internet as a business media in the 1990s has refueled this discussion.

Electronic brokerage is regarded as the core concept necessary to overcome the current limitations of Internet commerce and to fulfill the purpose of traditional intermediaries (Bichler, Beam and Segev, 1998a; Beam, Bichler, Krishnan and Segev, 1999). It allows users to be more focused in dealing with information about commercial services in the global electronic marketplace. Brokers are important in markets because search costs, lack of privacy, incomplete information, contract risk, and pricing are better managed through a broker. Moreover, electronic brokers provide a central marketplace and are in a key position to provide many essential third-party services in electronic commerce. They provide the following services to customers and suppliers in conducting electronic business:

- Cost and time savings associated with searching for products and services. It can be expensive for providers and consumers to find each other. Full connectivity in a disintermediated market with m buyers and n sellers would require each one of the m buyers to connect to all n sellers, for a total number of $m*n$ connections (Bailey and Bakos, 1997). A broker could collect full information about the sellers with m inquiries and pass that information to the buyers, for a total number of $m+n$ transactions.
- Complete selection of offers and qualified information about products. When a user wants to make a choice on his own, a broker can collect more information from other sources.
- Better pricing, where a broker can have a better knowledge of what a customer might be willing to pay for specific services. The consolidating capability of the broker leads to better bargaining positions for the customers.
- Establishing confidence when a customer wants to rely on someone's reliability and reputation. The buyer may refuse to pay after receiving a product or the provider may deny responsibility for defective items, etc. The broker can distribute responsibility to all parties, and minimize bad transactions by selecting the best providers and avoiding bad customers.
- Privacy protection. The broker might be a necessary intermediary when either the buyer or the seller wants to remain anonymous.

The above reasons are the basis for the emergence of electronic brokerages. The way these intermediaries will integrate many sources according to their customers' needs will be a key factor for the success of electronic commerce.

The electronic brokers' abilities will be shaped by the technologies employed, allowing them to concentrate on their business needs and not worry about technology concerns.

2.2   Electronic Brokerage Services on the Internet

Currently, most electronic brokers on the Internet (sometimes also referred to as "Internet marketplaces" or "mediating agents") concentrate on the aggregation of information from underlying electronic catalogs. For many of them, information aggregation is static, i.e. the broker gathers the information to create a catalog before the user requests it. However, a growing number of brokers now allow dynamic catalog aggregation where information is gathered only after having received the user request. Since most markets are extremely volatile, it is important to have this flexibility in adapting to the frequent changes in information sources.

Andersen Consulting's BargainFinder <http://bf.cstar.ac.com/> and Netbot's Jango <http://jango.excite.com> are some well known examples of electronic brokers which support dynamic gathering. BargainFinder was the first shopping agent for online price comparison. It requests an item's price from each of nine different merchant web sites using the same request received from the consumer's web browser. Although it was a limited proto-type, BargainFinder offered many insights into the issues involved in price comparisons. For example, a third of the online merchants accessed blocked the price requests (see Guttman, Moukas and Maes, 1998 for a broader overview). Jango searches for products that meet specified criteria and displays hits within a table that permits extensive evaluation. Clicking an attribute sorts the alternatives according to that attribute, permitting an elimination-by-aspect approach. Links display additional attributes and enable more extensive evaluation within alternatives for a chosen product. Jango solved the blocking issue by having the product requests originate from each consumer's web browser instead of from the Jango site. Since then, it has been integrated as part of the Excite search engine (see figure 2.1).

Microsoft's Carpoint <http://carpoint.msn.com> is a good example from the perspective of decision support. It permits evaluation both within and between product alternatives and enables norm-setting by using the "Blue Book," a guide for used car prices, to establish a standard price for a particular model. The comparison feature permits comparison of alternatives in pairs across multiple pre-specified attributes. All available cars for a specified make and model are displayed in a table and can be sorted according to several attributes. Alternatives can be marked for elimination. The query interface also has sliders that enables users to specify ranges rather than point values for price, mileage, and distance between home location and the dealer. Each alternative has a link to the dealer's web site.

Figure 2.1 Screenshot of the Excite ProductFinder.

BotSpot <http://www.botspot.com> gives a comprehensive overview about various kinds of so-called web bots (commercial, search or shopping bots) and their URLs.

So far, examples from the business-to-consumer field have been considered (see figure 2.2). The next two examples describe electronic business-to-business markets (see Gebauer, Segev and Färber, 1999, for a broader overview). During the 1980s and 1990s the predominant form of business-to-business electronic commerce has been EDI. EDI connections tend to operate best in strategic partnerships and specialized relationships, while many new electronic brokers in this field operate in the open sourcing marketplace. So-called "vertical marketplaces" serve a specific vertical industry, such as chemicals or electronic components. Horizontal marketplaces cut across industries and automate functional processes, such as maintenance, repair, and operations procurement (Dataquest, 1999). Electronic business-to-business markets will "re-intermediate" many vertical and

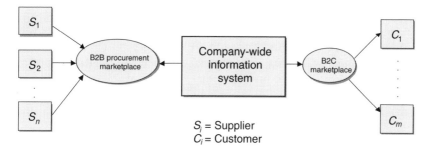

Figure 2.2 Electronic marketplaces in a supply chain.

horizontal supply chains, severely disrupting some but ultimately bringing new efficiency to many others.

MetalSite <http://www.metalsite.com> was initiated by the steel producers LTV Steel, Steel Dynamics, and Weirton Steel Corp. as a neutral market for the metal industry. It offers access to industry news and encourages visitors to interact with each other in discussion groups and via bulletin boards. It is also designed as an electronic outlet for the products and services of the participating suppliers and offers secure online transactions, including online auctions. Buyers submit bids for the online offerings. The sellers subsequently notify them about the success of their bids. Initially, hard-to-sell secondary and excess products such as flat-roll construction steel and cans are included in the online catalog. Future scenarios also encompass prime and made-to-order products as well as other metals such as copper, aluminum, and zinc. The site aims at establishing itself as an independent exchange for metals industry information, product availability, and online purchases.

Another example is NetBuy <http://www.netbuy.com>. It offers services for the distribution of electronic components. Target users are buyers from OEMs (original equipment manufacturers). Founded in 1996, NetBuy attempts to establish a spot market for non-scheduled orders, i.e. unforeseen demand, requiring immediate delivery. This segment covers about 20 percent of the US electronic components distribution market. Relationships between buyers and sellers tend to occur ad hoc. NetBuy's online catalog features more than 300,000 parts from 56 franchised distributors, representing over 1,800 manufacturers. By 1999, the total available inventory exceeded US $2 billion. NetBuy provides prospective buyers with information about prices and product availability for the items that they procure. It also handles parts of the purchase transaction including order management, invoicing, and payment. Throughout the entire transaction process, the distributors' identity is hidden from the buyers. Only when the product is actually shipped are the distributors allowed to identify themselves to the customers. This concept promises distributors an additional, low-cost sales channel which completes their traditional set of channels in a discrete way and helps broaden their customer base.

The foregoing examples provide a brief overview of how the Internet is presently being utilized to bring together buyers and sellers in electronic brokerages. Given the rapid developments in this area, this overview represents only the current situation.

2.3   Software Architectures of Electronic Commerce Applications

Before a framework of general electronic brokerage services is introduced, the following subsections will provide a brief overview of software architectures and technologies used in electronic commerce applications.

2.3.1   Web-Based Information Systems

The electronic commerce applications outlined in this book are being built on the World Wide Web (WWW, web) architecture. The WWW began in 1989, when Tim Berners-Lee (1990) of the European Laboratory for Particle Physics (CERN), proposed the web project for research collaboration. The project quickly expanded beyond all expectations as others understood the potential for global information sharing.

2.3.1.1   The World Wide Web

The web has become an umbrella for a wide range of concepts and technologies that differ in purpose and scope, such as hypertext publishing and the client–server concept. The WWW is built on a number of essential concepts, including:

- A simple network protocol known as hypertext transfer protocol (HTTP) used by the clients and servers, and based on the TCP/IP protocol stack.
- A mark-up language (HTML), which every web client is required to understand; this is used for the representation of hypertext documents containing text, graphics, and other multimedia data.
- An addressing scheme known as a uniform resource locator (URL) that makes the hypermedia world possible despite many different application-level protocols.

The architecture of a typical web-based information system is made up of three primary entities: Web server, web client, and third-party services, such as databases or payment systems. Figure 2.3 shows the numerous pieces that typically constitute this architecture.

The web client resides on the user's workstation and provides a user

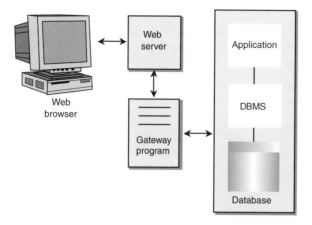

Figure 2.3 Diagram depicting a web-based database application.
Source: Bichler (1997, p. 76).

interface to the various types of content. For instance, if the user retrieves a graphics file from a web server, the browser automatically starts up the browser extension to display the graphics file. Web server functions can be categorized into information retrieval, data and transaction management, and security (Hansen, 1995; Kalakota and Whinston, 1996). An important aspect of web development is application gateways, such as the Common Gateway Interface (CGI), which is a specification for communicating data between a web server and another application. CGI can be used wherever the web server needs to send or receive data from another application, such as a database. A typical use of CGI is to pass data, filled in by a user in an HTML form, from the web server to another application.

2.3.1.2 *Multi-Tier Software Architectures*
Client–server computing attempts to leverage the capabilities of the networks used by typical corporations that are composed of many relatively powerful workstations and a limited number of dedicated servers. Client–server computing has gained popularity in recent years owing to the theory that a model relying on monolithic applications fails when the number of users accessing a system grows too high, or when too many features are integrated into a single system (Lewandowski, 1998). The server proportion of a client–server system almost always holds the data, and the client is nearly always responsible for the user interface. The canonical client–server model assumes exactly two discrete participants in the system. In these two-tier architectures the application logic is either on the client, on the server, or shared between the two. Architectures of web-based

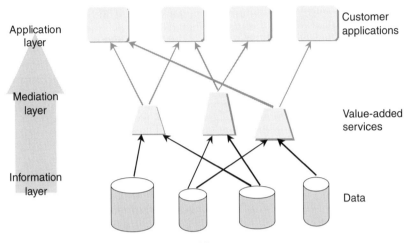

Figure 2.4 Three-layered mediation architecture
Source: Wiederhold (1992); Werthner and Klein (1999).

information systems extend the model of two-tier client–server database applications to a three-tier (and potentially *n*-tier) model, where presentation, application logic and data management are distributed amongst multiple computers in a network (figure 2.4).

Wiederhold described the need for so-called multi-tier, or network-centric architectures:

As information systems are increasing in scope, they depend on many diverse, heterogeneous resources. These resources are typically developed and maintained autonomously of the majority of the applications that use their results . . . When the disparate data collections can be combined, they can support high-level applications such as decision-making and planning. (Wiederhold, 1992)

Wiederhold also proposed a so-called "mediation layer" in order to provide intermediary services, link data resources and application programs. The concept of a mediation layer is very similar to the second tier in a web-based information system.

2.3.2   Distributed Object Infrastructures

The software required to facilitate client–server interaction is referred to as *middleware*; it allows the various components to communicate in a structured manner (Bernstein, 1996). The ubiquitous web infrastructure (including the Internet protocols TCP/IP and HTTP) can be considered as one such middleware platform. Distributed object standards provide another very popular middleware infrastructure. These standards facilitate interoperability of software components in heterogeneous computing environments. During the past few years many approaches have attempted to combine these two approaches into so-called ObjectWeb infrastructures (Orfali and Harkey, 1997). The work done in this field provides valuable ideas for the implementation of electronic brokerage services. This section covers an overview of distributed object frameworks and their use for electronic commerce applications.

2.3.2.1 Object Frameworks

Newer software engineering technologies are based on the principle of making the expression of ideas simpler and more compact. The renewed popularity of object-oriented programming concepts like encapsulation, inheritance, and polymorphism in the early 1980s raised the level of abstraction in problem formulation. The aim of abstraction is to handle complexity. In object-oriented systems *objects* are the units of encapsulation. An object *encapsulates* state (data) and behavior (operations). The operations are the means to manipulate the state. A *class* is a template from which objects may be created. It contains a definition of the state descriptors and methods for the object. *Inheritance* means that new classes (subclasses) can be derived from existing classes (superclasses). The subclass inherits the attributes and the operations of the superclass, but the subclass can define additional operations and attributes. Inheritance facilitates the concept of *polymorphism*, that is, a function call is polymorphic if it may be applied to arguments of different types or classes. A detailed description of object-oriented concepts can be found in Blair, Gallagher, Hutchinson and Shepard (1991); Booch (1991); Rumbaugh *et al.* (1991).

But merely programming with objects does not ensure software reuse (Pree, 1997). With the use of class libraries, reuse began to take serious shape. Domain-specific libraries provide related classes, which can be used as is or can be specialized via inheritance to solve a problem. Object frameworks are one step ahead as they also reuse designs for specific problems. An *object framework* is a collection of cooperating objects that provides an integrated solution (customizable by the developer) within an application or technology. The components of an object framework are not intended to work alone. The distinguishing feature from a class library is that when the library is an object framework the flow of control is *bi-directional* between the application and the library. This feature is achieved by the dynamic binding in object-oriented languages where an operation can be defined in a library class but implemented in a subclass in the application. Because of the bi-directional flow of control the object framework enables significantly more functionality than a traditional library, and also provides large-scale reuse.

A fundamental principle of object-oriented programming is that, owing to the features of inheritance and dynamic binding, a new class can be implemented by specifying only the difference relative to an existing class. With object frameworks the same principle is applied to whole applications or subsystems, allowing the highest common abstraction level among a number of similar applications to be captured in a generic design that can be instantiated for each application in the future. Each product is an instantiation of the object framework and the amount of unique code is proportional to the specific features of the product. In framework development, design reuse is more important than mere code reuse. Creating a new design requires knowledge of an application domain, experience with other designs, and a flair for recognizing and inventing patterns. Framework design is an iterative process, which can take a long time.

2.3.2.2 Distributed Object Standards

Distributed objects that operate in a concurrent and active way have been a research topic in the software engineering community for a long time because the metaphor of communicating objects is very well suited for distribution (Moessenboeck, 1996). Distributed systems standards such as the Common Object Request Broker Architecture (CORBA) of the Object Management Group (OMG), the Java Remote Method Invocation (RMI), or Microsoft's Distributed Component Object Model (DCOM) strongly influence the object frameworks field (Lewandowski, 1998). CORBA is an approach for achieving interoperability among the growing number of hardware and software products available today. It allows applications to communicate with one another no matter where they are located or who has designed them. CORBA 1.1 was introduced in 1991 by the Object Management Group (OMG) and defined the Interface Definition Language (IDL) and the Application Programming Interfaces (API) that enable client–server object interaction within a specific implementation of an Object Request Broker (ORB). CORBA 2.0, adopted in December 1994, defines true interoperability by specifying how ORBs from different vendors can interoperate. CORBA 3.0 refers to a suite of specifications which will add a component architecture and provide better integration with Internet standards.

Object frameworks benefit from distributed object standards in several ways. First they gain high-level language bindings. CORBA separates the interface of an object from its implementation and provides language-neutral data types that make it possible to call objects across language and operating system boundaries. That is, a programmer can combine objects written in different programming languages. Second, an ORB can broker inter-object calls across networks. The programmer does not have to be concerned with different languages or operating systems, since CORBA makes it transparent. CORBA also provides introspection capabilities, as it is possible to query at runtime information describing the functionality of a server object. This allows the discovery of new services and their binding at runtime (Orfali and Harkey, 1997).

Besides the ORB component, the Object Management Architecture (OMA) specifies three categories of object interfaces. These interface specifications represent the functionality needed for a distributed object economy:

- *Object Services* are interfaces for general services that are likely to be used by any program based on distributed objects. They are collections of system-level services like persistence, naming, query, transaction, or security services.
- *Common Facilities* are interfaces for horizontal end-user-oriented facilities applicable to most application domains. They should provide semantically higher-level services than the Object Services. The Common Facilities currently under construction include mobile software agents, data interchange, and the business object framework.
- *Domain Interfaces* are application domain-specific interfaces. Domain Task Forces focus on application domains such as finance, healthcare, manufacturing, telecoms, electronic commerce, or transportation.

An object framework in OMA is defined as a hierarchy of application, domain, common facility, and object service frameworks that are compositions of application, domain, common facility, and object service objects. So the component of a vendor can easily be exchanged with the product of its competitor, as long as it adheres to the OMG interface standard. The payment, shipping, or inventory components of an electronic commerce system can be taken from various vendors and compiled to an electronic commerce application.

2.3.2.3 Electronic Commerce Frameworks

In the past, frameworks were popular in the area of graphical user interfaces, but other domains are coming up as well. There are several research projects developing object frameworks for electronic commerce applications. Many software vendors are also trying to come up with electronic commerce solutions for security, payment, or electronic catalogs.

OMG's Electronic Commerce Domain Task Force (ECDTF) tries to standardize electronic commerce facilities in the OMA. The draft of the ECDTF reference architecture provides an overview about facilities needed in electronic commerce applications (McConnell, 1997). The architecture is composed of three principal groups, namely low-level electronic commerce services including profile, selection, payment and certificate services;

Figure 2.5 OMG ECDTF reference architecture.

commerce facilities supporting service management, contract, and related desktop facilities; and, finally, market infrastructure facilities covering catalogs, brokerage, and agency facility (see figure 2.5).

The following is a brief description of the various parts of the architecture. The OMG is exploring technology for a *Payment facility* that will support and allow the implementation of a variety of electronic payment protocols in a CORBA environment. The *Selection facility* is an object service that provides support for configuration of supporting services across a set of domains. It includes the ability to issue and receive specification of requirements and the ability for multiple participants to negotiate specifications. The *Profile facility* provides a common structure for the semantic data describing products, services, content, and assets. The *Service facility* describes requirements for an object framework in which commercial services can be presented with a declarative interface for consumers, providers and third parties. The requirement specification includes details concerning life-cycle and policy management. *Contract facilities* extend the service specification to include specific requirements related to commercial contracts. The *Object browser facility* provides the desktop facilities in an electronic marketplace.

Catalog facilities provide a framework for portable data stores in which service and contracts can be passed between participants. The *Brokerage facility* requirement specification designates two primary interfaces, namely forwarding and recruiting. Requirements of a forwarding interface include the support for the "advertising" or "distribution" of profiles describing electronic commerce artifacts. A recruiting interface meets requirements "discovery" – i.e. requests for "searches" for content matching a certain criteria. Finally the *Agency facility* supports general requirements for the standardization of a point of presence in a marketplace.

The reference model helps identify the planned and future Electronic

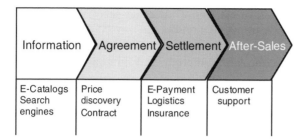

Figure 2.6 Phase model of an electronic market transaction.
Source: Lindemann and Runge (1998).

Commerce Domain Facilities of the OMG (Bichler, Beam and Segev, 1998a). The work provides an overall framework of required electronic commerce components, but is still in its early stages. So far there have been requests for proposals (RFP) for the lower-level facilities, such as an Electronic payment RFP and for a Negotiation and selection facility. Little work has been done in higher levels such as electronic catalogs or electronic brokerage. The next section will provide a more detailed description of the services which should be provided by an electronic brokerage. These services describe the generic functionality of an electronic broker, and are not bound to a distributed object infrastructure.

2.4   Services of an Electronic Broker

The diversity in functional features offered by electronic brokerage services makes it useful to define several criteria for classifying them. In terms of *functionality*, brokers support different phases during an electronic market transaction. Various models describe market transactions in electronic commerce. For example, Schmid and Lindemann (1997) base their classification on four phases, called information, agreement, settlement, and after-sales (see figure 2.6). During the information phase, market participants search for products and potential partners in the market. In the agreement phase, they negotiate the terms of the deal, and agree on a contract. The settlement phase comprises payment, logistics, and insurance, and, finally, customer support is fulfilled in the after-sales phase.

Most brokers on the Internet support the information and partially the agreement phase. Guttman, Moukas and Maes (1998) propose a slightly different model. In their work, they analyze seven electronic brokerage services (called "mediating agents") and show which phases they support. The functionality ranges from product searches and comparison of different product alternatives to negotiating the terms of the deal. Functionality is only one way to classify electronic brokerage services. Alzon *et al.* (1998) describe several additional methods:

- *Provisioning* describes the nature of the content of the trading entity (online information, physical products, or digital products).
- *Payment* determines how the brokerage service is paid. From the user's point of view, there are two main categories, namely one-stop-shopping where the user pays only the broker and separate billing where the end user pays separate bills from the broker and the suppliers. In other situations, the suppliers pay the broker. Moreover, the broker can be paid per transaction or by subscription fees from the participants.
- The *ownership* dimension determines whether or not the mediator is the owner of the content. The distinguishing factor between a broker and a seller is the ownership relationship with regard to the traded product. A broker is supposed to mediate information about trading objects but not own them. The seller is supposed to have selling rights on the traded objects and hence trades with the products.
- Finally, the *technological* dimension determines the underlying techniques used to provide the brokerage services. Many approaches have their roots in distributed systems research, others are based merely on Internet techniques.

As can be seen, electronic brokerage services are complex information systems involving aspects from computer science, economics, and business administration. In order to understand the complexity of a distributed system, the reference model for open distributed processing (RM-ODP) of the International Standardization Organization (ISO) proposed the description of a system from five different viewpoints: enterprise, information, computational, engineering, and technology (Blair and Stefani, 1997). Viewpoints are defined as a form of abstraction achieved using a selected set of architectural concepts and structural rules in order to focus on particular concerns within a system. For each viewpoint a specific model of the system is defined. For example, the *enterprise viewpoint* defines the service from the viewpoint of the organizations and people that will use and operate the service. It summarizes all actors, their domains, their relationships, and their policies. The *computational viewpoint* (*architectural model*) describes the application in terms of computational objects and defines the rules about how these objects will interact with each other, and the *information viewpoint* defines the data structures, interchange formats and the associated semantics of the system.

In order to get an overall picture of the services an electronic brokerage service provides, it is useful to analyze these systems according to the RM-ODP viewpoints (Bichler, Beam and Segev, 1998a). In the next two subsections, a more detailed description of the enterprise viewpoint and the architectural model of an electronic broker will be described.

2.4.1   Enterprise Model

This subsection is concerned with the overall environment in which an electronic brokerage service is operated, and shows how and where the system is placed. The enterprise viewpoint begins with the definition of the actors involved in the service provisioning scenarios. A set of features characteristic for the brokerage service is proposed and relevant scenarios are presented. The overall objectives of an electronic broker are described, including the roles and activities that exist within the enterprise using the system and the interactions between the actors of the system. The roles in the model are restricted to customers, suppliers, and brokerage service providers.

2.4.1.1   The Brokerage Service Provider
The electronic brokerage service provides a trusted conjunction of supply and demand processes. The core services of a brokerage service are various kinds of mechanisms, supporting the matching of consumer interests and supplier abilities:

- Mechanisms through which a supplier can express an ability to provide products and/or services and through which a consumer can express an interest in products and/or services.
- Mechanisms to dynamically aggregate information from registered electronic catalogs, i.e. to enable users to get the appropriate perspective on the supplier domain.
- Mechanisms supporting notification capabilities, i.e. a supplier can supply a description of abilities to a broker for the purpose of propagating the ability to registered consumers who have expressed an interest in the particular ability or vice versa.
- Mechanisms for bilateral and multilateral negotiations about products and services. Negotiation support can be considered the most complex form of matching buyers and suppliers in a marketplace.

Because brokers also provide a central marketplace where many consumers and many suppliers meet, they are in a key position to provide value-added services which are of vital interest to the participating parties. The broker can acquire better knowledge of market demand and supply characteristics. Furthermore, since brokers participate in transactions with different customers and different suppliers they can analyze consumer preferences between products, suppliers, and industries. Some of these value-added services exploit the role of the broker as a trusted third party, while others help by automating tasks during an electronic market transaction:

- Decision support for product comparisons and product selection
- Provision of value-added content (product taxonomies, specification, transaction data, etc.)
- Buyer/seller rating services
- Certification of liability and reliability of participants
- Notary services such as non-repudiation of offers, orders, or contracts
- Support for billing, accounting, and digital delivery
- Advanced payment services such as escrow and financial settlement
- Multiple EDI standards capabilities.

A broker needs to offer various services, depending on the kind of product. As in physical markets, there will be brokers for real estate, for cars, etc. who also need to provide different ways to match buyers and sellers. Of course, the types of participants also matter. For example, there will be different system requirements depending on whether the customer is a professional or a consumer.

2.4.1.2   Customers of a Brokerage Service Provider

The supplier in this model is an entity which offers tradable products to users by means of a brokerage service. For this purpose, it can use the services offered by the brokerage service and provide an electronic catalog as a point of sale. There is no standard definition for an electronic catalog, and the functionality of such catalogs is rapidly evolving, but, at the minimum, it should support listings of products and/or services, price information, and transactions (Segev, Dadong and Beam, 1995). This type of electronic catalog can be registered with the brokerage service provider, in order for the electronic broker to access the information dynamically on customer request. Customers can have contract relationships with the brokerage service in order to meet their requirements. They can register with the electronic broker in order to use its services and become more focused in dealing with information about commercial services in the market.

2.4.2   Architectural Model

The architectural model depicts main functional blocks of an electronic brokerage service. It describes the application in terms of computational components and defines rules on how these components interact with each other. This section will concentrate on the core brokerage services outlined in subsection 2.4.1 and give an overview of their functionality. It will describe the functionality of:

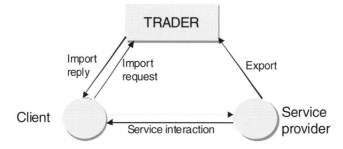

Figure 2.7 OMG trader service.

- the yellow pages
- the catalog aggregation
- the notification service, and
- the negotiation service.

2.4.2.1 The Yellow Pages Service

The yellow pages service mediates long-term market information about the market participants and is similar to the "yellow pages" in the real world. Suppliers and customers register with the yellow pages service in order to participate in the market. The yellow pages service retains participants' profiles including identity, addresses, location, abilities (e.g. line of business, product categories), and their long-term interests and makes this information accessible. The service has to provide a mechanism to register profiles, abilities, and interests; and a mechanism to search for other market participants according to these properties. Functionality like this has been discussed in distributed systems research for a long time, and in contrast to all other electronic brokerage services which will be discussed later in this section, there are open standards for this functionality.

The so-called "trader service" is currently being standardized by the ISO. A trader service is a mechanism which facilitates the advertising and discovery of services in an open distributed system. This standard is also known as the ODP trading function. A similar standard, called the object trader service, was standardized by the OMG. The OMG object trader service provides a yellow pages service for objects in a distributed environment (OMG, 1997) (see figure 2.7).

The service provider registers the availability of the service by invoking an export operation on the trader, passing as parameter information about the service offered. The export operation carries an object reference that can be used by a client to invoke an operation from one of the advertised services, a description of the type of service offered, and information about the distinguishing attributes of that service. This information is stored by the trader. Whenever a potential client wishes to obtain a reference to a service that does a particular job, it invokes an import operation, a description of the service required as parameters. Given this import request, the trader checks appropriate offers for acceptability. To be acceptable, an offer must have a type that conforms to the request and have properties consistent with the constraints specified by an imported service. Traders in different domains may also be federated. Federation enables systems in different domains to negotiate the sharing of services without losing control of their own policies and services. A domain can, thus, share information with other domains with which it has been federated, and it can then be searched for appropriate service offers.

2.4.2.2 *The Catalog Aggregation Service*

"Catalog aggregation" describes the task of consolidating information from a selection of suppliers' catalogs. Electronic catalogs are the point of sales in electronic markets and the aggregation of information in electronic catalogs is an important task of electronic mediators, as it reduces the search costs of customers. The aggregation mechanism relies on bringing a large number of buyers and sellers under one roof, and reducing transaction costs by one-stop shopping. Jango or Bargainfinder (see section 2.2) provide simple catalog aggregation services on the Internet. However, current web-based technology makes it very difficult to implement dynamic information gathering. Brokers face the challenge of writing and maintaining a program that keeps track of the various queries and parses the resulting HTML files individually. New electronic commerce standards and interoperable catalogs are redefining the field (CommerceNet, 1995) (see subsection 2.6.1). They allow the implementation of more efficient and powerful instruments for the comparison of products from different suppliers. Like the OMG trader service, catalog aggregation services can be federated. This leads to a recursive structure where new brokers can build on the knowledge of existing catalog aggregation services (figure 2.8).

Besides the aggregation of product information, intermediaries in a physical market also aggregate supply and demand in a marketplace. Instead of a situation where each customer has to negotiate individually with an appropriate supplier, and each supplier has to negotiate terms with individual customers, the broker aggregates the demand from many customers or the products of many suppliers. This reduces transaction costs and asymmetries in the bargaining power of customers and suppliers. Wholesalers consolidate the demand of retailers in order to obtain better conditions. Travel agents are examples of intermediaries that aggregate products offered by hotels, airlines, and transportation companies into a

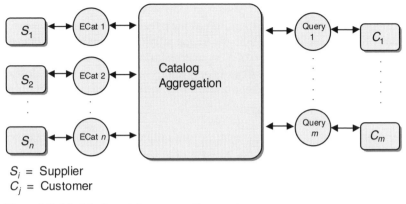

S_i = Supplier
C_j = Customer

Figure 2.8 Model of a catalog aggregation service.

package for the buyer. Many of these services can also be supported in electronic markets.

2.4.2.3 The Notification Service

One of the main purposes of a brokerage service is to allow users (information consumers and providers) to be more focused in dealing with information about commercial services in the global electronic marketplace. The notification service provides a means for market participants to target information towards interested parties in the market. The notification service pushes time-sensitive market information such as restricted offers or requests for bids to market participants. Suppliers can subscribe to certain classes of market information and get all of the customer requests forwarded. Customers can subscribe to a certain category of offers and get all of these forwarded. Thus, a notification service should provide the following capabilities:

■ A provider can supply a description of abilities to a broker for the purpose of forwarding them to registered consumers who have expressed an interest in the particular ability.
■ A consumer can supply the electronic broker with a specification of her interests, and the broker then forwards it to the providers who have expressed an interest in responding to such inquiries.
■ A brokerage policy can be established (indicating such things as identity propagation constraints, maximum number of responses and so on).

The notification service filters postings according to subscriber preferences. A recipient is not obliged to respond to any specification received. Usually, consumers prefer anonymity and privacy with regard to their buying habits whereas suppliers take advantage of such information. The general method for achieving anonymity and privacy in a market is the existence of trusted third parties who know the identities of the parties involved and guarantee anonymity inside and outside the scope of the transactions, and non-repudiation within the scope of a commercial transaction. Here, the broker can play the role of a trusted third party and protect against the disclosure of either the recipient's or the initiator's private information.

2.4.2.4 The Negotiation Service

Services such as "catalog aggregation" are rather simple mechanisms used to match buyers and suppliers based on the concept of fixed pricing (see section 3.2). Dynamically negotiating the price of a product relieves the seller from determining the value of the product *a priori*. As communication costs decrease in an electronic network, negotiations become more and more attractive to businesses. Therefore, a key question for the design of an electronic marketplace is choosing or developing an appropriate *negotiation protocol*. A "negotiation protocol" can be defined as the sequence of allowed messages which are exchanged between the negotiating parties. It can be seen as the actual implementation of a conceptual market mechanism, such as an English auction.

What makes the practical design of market mechanisms different from studying them conceptually is that the practical design carries with it a responsibility for detail (Roth, 1999). This complexity comes from the strategic environment itself and the participants' behavior. The design has to respond to a broad set of questions (Beam, Bichler, Krishnan and Segev, 1999) concerning

■ technologies
■ rules of the marketplace, and
■ strategies for the participants.

First, the negotiation protocol deployed is also determined by the *technologies* that are available for use in negotiations. Technology includes ontologies and message formats that provide the terminology and the associated semantics to facilitate communication. For example, for one-on-one negotiation using Internet support, the current architecture uses a technology composed of electronic mail and an ontology of the English language. In fully automated settings, participants with a heterogeneous set of information systems have to cooperate and exchange information. This requires well defined data structures as well as message formats and API definitions. Existing EDI protocols such as ANSI X.12 or UN/EDIFACT are extremely limited in their application to bargaining. In order to describe something such as a fuzzy green jacket, an ontology needs to be defined. Several research projects and industry initiatives are currently trying to solve this problem (see subsection 2.6.3).

Second, the *rules of the negotiation* have to be laid out in advance. For automated electronic transactions implicit rules are not sufficient and it requires explicit rules that govern behavior (Beam, 1999, p. 18):

- Which conceptual market mechanism is used in the marketplace?
- How does a participant join or leave a market?
- What constitutes an offer?
- Are offers binding?
- Does an offer have to be notarized?
- What attributes must an offer have?
- Does negotiation have to be sequential, or can a participant negotiate simultaneously with several parties at once?
- What constitutes a deal/contract?

There are several approaches to standardizing electronic negotiation protocols. The open trading protocol (OTP), an XML-based protocol for retail electronic commerce, introduces simple exchanges of offer requests and offer responses (OTP, 1999). A much more sophisticated example can be found in the submissions to the OMG Negotiation Request for Proposals. The submission of OSM, an industry consortium, defines process descriptions, state transition diagrams, and module specifications for three so-called "collaboration models," namely "bilateral negotiation," "multilateral negotiation," and "promissory encounter" (OSM, 1999). However, the negotiation processes are often oversimplified and do not cover the numerous strategic issues of commercial negotiations.

Finally, given a certain set of technologies and rules, the *strategy* issue has to be solved. How should a participant proceed to get the best deal and what are the consequences for buyers and sellers on the market? There are many problems involved with the issue and it is not an easy task to program an automated intelligent bargaining agent. How much information should be concealed by the agent, or is information revelation a good strategy? These questions depend heavily on the rules and the type of market mechanisms used. This is probably the reason why the CommerceNet Electronic Catalog Working Group designated "handling negotiation" as an activity with a "long" time horizon with the effort rated as "medium to hard" and the tools "to be defined" (CommerceNet, 1995).

Negotiation services of an electronic broker create value by bringing buyers and sellers together to negotiate prices on a dynamic and real-time basis. Current electronic brokerage services provide only minimal support for negotiations. Negotiations are complex social interactions and, therefore, there is not a single simple solution for all the different types of negotiation situations in electronic commerce. The greater part of this book is devoted to the analysis of automated negotiation and various negotiation protocols.

2.5   OFFER – A Sample Implementation

To illustrate the framework outlined in section 2.5, a prototype of an electronic brokerage service, called OFFER (*O*bject *F*ramework *f*or *E*lectronic *R*equisitioning) was tested (Bichler, Beam and Segev, 1998b, 1998c). OFFER is based on distributed object technology and utilizes the CORBA infrastructure specified by the OMG.

The OFFER framework defines a number of component interfaces in IDL which facilitate interoperability between the electronic broker and other software components in the electronic marketplace. A goal of the project was to provide knowledge about the functionality of the required software components, their granularity, and the interaction patterns between them. The environment consists of suppliers, customers, and electronic brokers. Suppliers and electronic brokers offer services which can be accessed over the Internet and which are accessed by customers. The OFFER electronic broker (e-broker) assists the user in three main ways. First, it provides a yellow pages service based on the CORBA Object Trader service. Second, it helps search in remote electronic supplier catalogs (e-catalogs), i.e. it implements a catalog aggregation service. Third, it provides auction mechanisms to support price negotiation between buyers and sellers.

The OFFER prototype is implemented entirely in Java and uses an Object Request Broker (ORB) as a distribution mechanism. It is comprised of several Java applets and applications which communicate with the e-broker and the remote e-catalogs implemented as CORBA servers. The products traded on the market are books since these are easy to describe and to categorize.

2.5.1   *The OFFER Yellow Pages and Catalog Aggregation Service*

Suppliers offer an e-catalog to the customer, and they can also register with the e-broker. Hence, a customer can search for a service either directly in the e-catalog of a supplier or she can use the e-broker to search the e-catalogs of all the suppliers which are registered with this broker. A standard IDL interface for the e-catalogs of a supplier and for the e-broker is standardized as part of the OFFER framework. Each supplier is responsible for implementing this interface; the implementations can be in any CORBA-compliant language such as C++, Java, or Smalltalk. The e-broker IDL provides two main operations, namely a `search()` operation which allows a customer to find a product on the marketplace and it supports an operation called `getSupplierProfiles()` which allows CORBA clients to receive information about the suppliers available

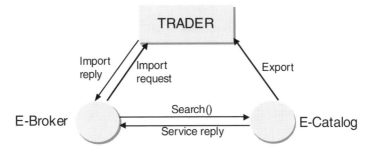

Figure 2.9 Catalog aggregation using an object trader.

through the e-broker. (Courier will be used throughout the book for code listings, function names, and anything that appears literally in a program.) Other CORBA components, in addition to those currently available, can easily create value-added services based on the services of the e-broker.

An important requirement is the ability for new e-catalogs to register with the e-broker. The electronic broker can either maintain its own database of registered e-catalogs or it can use the services of an Object Trader (see subsection 2.4.2.1). The Object Trader defines several functional interfaces (Lookup, Register, Link, Admin and Proxy). The Lookup interface, for example, lets the user discover objects based on the properties and services they provide. Via the Register interface new services can be registered (export) or unregistered (withdraw) with the trader. In this case, the e-catalogs act as exporters, advertising a service offer (consisting of name, location, and several other properties) with the trader. The e-broker acts as an importer, querying a list of references to actually available e-catalogs, according to certain constraints. The references can be used afterwards to send a search() message to these electronic catalogs and evaluate the results (see figure 2.9). Some Object Trader implementations provide the possibility of querying dynamic properties from an exporter at the time a query is made. The advantage of using an object trader is that the e-broker can rely on an already standardized and well understood service for the registration of new e-catalogs. Deployment of an Object Trader is especially useful in environments where it is already an established service.

There are several advantages to using the CORBA-based approach over CGI-based implementations (as described in subsection 2.3.1). CORBA version 2.0 provides the Internet Inter-ORB Protocol (IIOP), an efficient state-preserving protocol on the Internet which has several advantages over HTTP. As already mentioned, CORBA separates the interface from the implementation. Thus, a CORBA-based e-catalog can change its implementation without requiring the e-broker to rewrite the implementation.

This is an advantage over current client–server systems in which the application programming interface is often tightly bound to the implementation, and, therefore, very sensitive to changes (a more detailed discussion is given in Schwarzhoff, 1997). Nevertheless, a precondition for this infrastructure is that all suppliers of a certain market agree on a predefined interface standard for their e-catalogs. This is certainly a limitation for real-world applications.

2.5.2   The OFFER Negotiation Service

An e-broker provides a centralized marketplace where many buyers and suppliers meet. Hence, the e-broker is well situated to offer various kinds of negotiation mechanisms to buyers and suppliers. Unfortunately, no solid bargaining algorithms exist. Bargaining strategies between a buyer and seller are extremely complex. They frequently evolve over time, and often require shrewd judgments about how much information should be revealed, when not to be truthful, how many issues to involve, and which sequence of counter-proposals to use (see section 5.2 for details). In order to achieve efficient negotiation support within OFFER's e-broker, the buyer–seller negotiating session was replaced with a set of auction mechanisms. The strategy issue collapsed into the single dimension of bid formulation. The e-broker implements a range of different auction mechanisms, namely an English, Vickrey, and a first-price sealed-bid auction. In general, the question which negotiation protocol is best is non-trivial, and a detailed description of alternative negotiation protocols will be the focus of subsequent chapters.

This section will focus on the functionality of online auctions and in particular the negotiation service of the OFFER e-broker. Several authors provided a description of the functionality and the software architecture of online auctions. Wurman, Wellman and Walsh (2000) mention three core activities common to auctions:

- *Receive bids*: Bids are messages sent by a bidder to indicate their willingness to participate in exchanges
- *Clear*: The central purpose of an auction is to clear the market, determining resource exchanges and corresponding payments between buyers and sellers
- *Reveal intermediate information*: Auctions commonly supply agents with some form of intermediate status information, typically in the form of hypothetical results.

Kumar and Feldman (1998a) model auctions as finite state machines. They classify auctions according to the interaction format (open-cry or sealed-bid), who controls the bids, and whether it is an ascending-bid or descending-bid auction. They also mention additional policy variations such as:

- *Anonymity* (i.e. what information is revealed during the auction and after the auction closes). For instance, the identity of the bidders could be concealed.
- *Rules of closing the auction.* Open-cry auctions may end at a posted closing time or after a certain time has elapsed. This interval can be several minutes in an Internet auction and a few seconds for an auction being conducted in a meeting room. An auction can also be closed if either of the above two conditions is met or only when both conditions are met.
- *Setting the trading price.* Once the bidding phase is over, the bidders with the highest bids get the item being auctioned, and the price they pay could be the same as what they bid or lower. This is a particularly interesting question in cases where multiple identical items are auctioned off simultaneously. In a discriminative auction the winners pay what they bid. In a uniform-price auction people with winning bids pay the price paid by the winning bidder with the lowest bid.
- *Restrictions on the bid amount.* In all auctions the seller can specify the minimum starting bid. To speed up the bidding process, minimum bid increments are often enforced. The bid taker may also be allowed to specify a reserve price, which is a lower limit on price acceptable to the seller. The bidders may know that a reserve price exists but they may not know what the reserve price is.

An extensive discussion of the auction design space can be found in Wurman, Wellman and Walsh (2000). All these attributes have to be considered in an implementation. In follow-up paper Kumar and Feldman (1998b) describe an application of auctioning goods on the Internet. They present an object-oriented model for an auction application and describe the various processes that comprise the auction application.

OFFER also proposes an object-oriented design of auctions, since there is a natural correspondence between the decomposition of auctions into functional elements and an object-oriented design. Different auction mechanisms are best suited to different situations. For future uses of the framework, it is important to handle these mechanisms flexibly and provide easy extensibility. For the flexibility of object frameworks such as the OFFER brokerage framework it is crucial to identify so-called "hot spots." These are exchangeable components which should guarantee the extensibility of the framework in future applications (Pree, 1997). Well designed frameworks provide reusable architectures with flexibility in the right places. This

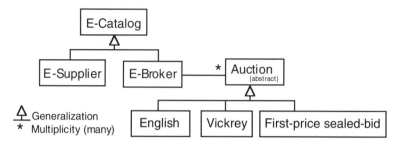

Figure 2.10 Abstract coupling of classes in a UML class diagram.

is achieved through abstract coupling of the EBroker class with the Auction class. Figure 2.10 shows a class diagram following the Unified Modeling Language (UML) (Fowler, 1997).

All auctions announce their starting times and the item(s) for sale as well as a possible minimum starting bid and minimum bid increment. A sealed auction has a publicly announced deadline, and will make no information about the current bids available to any future bidders until the auction is over, at which time the winner(s) is (are) announced. An open-cry auction will make information about current bids available to any future bidders until the auction is over, at which time the winner(s) is (are) announced. An auction can be opened with the e-broker operation startAuction(). As already mentioned above, this can be an English, a Vickrey, or a first-price sealed-bid auction. Through polymorphic messaging, the operations of the appropriate type of auction are triggered afterwards. For example, different auctions, closed via stopAuction() will compute the winners in different manners. Moreover, an English Auction has additional operations like getCurrentBids(), to get a market overview or getElapseTime(), to show how much time is left after the last bid until the auction closes. Figure 2.11 shows a screenshot of parts of the user interface.

Trust and security aspects have not been considered in the OFFER framework. For instant, Franklin and Reiter (1996) describe a secure protocol for eliminating fraudulent activity by the auctioneer. It employs multiple auction servers, at least some of which are trusted to stay honest. Harkavy, Kikuchi and Tygar (1998) used secure distributed computation to perform a sealed-bid electronic auction. Their protocol establishes privacy for all but the winning bid, even after the end of the bidding period. They also suggested a mechanism to establish non-repudiation of bids while preserving anonymity. Stubblebine and Syverson (1999) propose a high-level protocol for online auctions. The auction is fair in that the auctioneer commits to the submitted bids prior to their disclosure and cannot

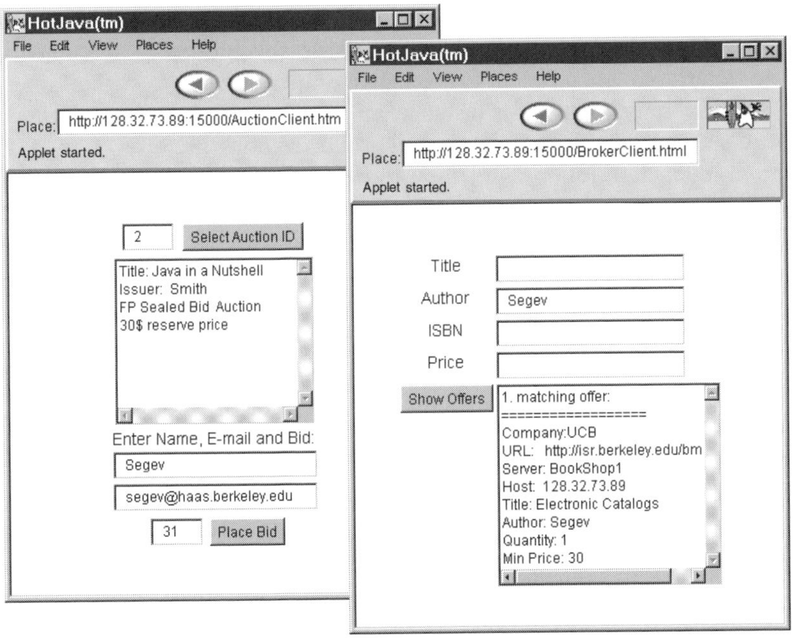

Figure 2.11 Screenshot of the E-Broker interface.

selectively close the auction after a particular bid is received. To achieve fairness, the protocol makes use of public notaries and certified delivery services. These approaches are helpful to achieve trust and security in online auctions.

2.6 Technical Challenges and Directions

The previous sections have outlined the services of electronic brokers and the difficulties of automating negotiations. However, before negotiation protocols in electronic markets are analyzed, this section discusses some of the technical challenges hindering the widespread establishment of an electronic brokerage infrastructure on the Internet.

2.6.1 The Interoperability Problem

The core competence of brokers is matchmaking between suppliers and potential customers. Matchmaking is to a large extent the mediation of market information. Application-level interoperability of electronic commerce systems across the Internet is a key issue for the implementation of electronic brokerage services. Standards for protocols, documents, and interfaces are crucial for achieving interoperability within inter-organizational systems. For instance, an Interoperable Catalog as defined by CommerceNet (1995) is an electronic catalog that uses standards for product descriptions and for protocols to communicate with other applications.

Unfortunately, current web-based technology makes it hard to gather information from underlying electronic catalogs dynamically. Web sites format their CGI requests and HTML outputs in vastly different and often changing ways, each of which must be processed differently. Writing and maintaining a program that keeps track of the various queries and parses the resulting HTML files individually is a cumbersome task (Schwarzhoff, 1997). The lack of interoperability standards between electronic commerce applications leads to high costs for the broker. Procuring from sixty hetero-geneous suppliers requires sixty different accommodations. Brokers face the challenge of combining all the information within a single coherent structure through which buyers can readily navigate.

New approaches that define high-level interoperability protocols for product listings, offers, or orders could make the automation of these tasks much easier. However, thus far, there are no widely adopted interoperabil-ity standards for Internet commerce (Segev and Bichler, 1999). The OFFER prototype uses high-level IDL interface standards to achieve interoperability between electronic commerce applications (e.g. between e-catalogs and e-broker). Many examples show that CORBA technology is very useful in combining heterogeneous information systems within an organization (Fayad and Schmid, 1997; Bichler, Beam and Segev, 1998b; Lewandowski, 1998). The OFFER prototype also works very efficiently as long as everyone in the marketplace adheres to the predefined IDL inter-faces and uses a CORBA-based system. In order to achieve interoperabil-ity in an electronic marketplace, these interfaces have to be standardized and adopted by all participants.

As already mentioned, OMG's Electronic Commerce Domain Task Force is trying to standardize interfaces for CORBA-based electronic com-merce components (see subsection 2.3.2.3). Unfortunately, standardization in OMG's Electronic Commerce Domain has been fairly slow. It is quite difficult to establish interface standards on which all participants of a certain market agree. Moreover, requirements for higher-level electronic commerce facilities such as brokers and catalogs can be very heterogeneous throughout different industries, which makes their standardization even more difficult (Thompson, Linden and Filman, 1997). So far, there have only been RFPs for low-level electronic commerce services in the OMG Electronic Commerce Domain.

Currently, there is a very large base of installed web-based electronic catalogs on the Internet that are not accessible via IIOP. It is not possible for a client to access the IDL interface of a CORBA server unless that client is written in a language for which there is CORBA mapping such as C++, C, Smalltalk, and Java, and it uses an ORB implementation. For widespread applicability of a brokerage service on the Internet, it is important to be accessible for a broader range of platforms (see also Werthner and Klein, 1999, p. 123, for an overview of integration issues).

2.6.2 Document-Centric Electronic Commerce Standards

During the past few years, there has been a strong movement towards document-centered protocols for interoperability between electronic commerce applications which can be handled by simple server scripts as well as distributed object technology-based applications (Bichler, Segev and Zhao, 1998). In the short term, these standards are more likely to be successful. Some of the first approaches in this direction have originated from the Internet Engineering Task Force (IETF) workgroup covering EDI (EDIINT), which has recommended standards for secure, interoperable electronic data interchange over the Internet. Member companies have demonstrated exchange of documents via Internet-based e-mail using the Secure MIME (S/MIME) protocol. Two draft standards have been proposed: MIME-based secure EDI, and EDIINT functional specifications. However, the problem with EDI standards such as ANSI X.12 or UN/EDIFACT is that start-up and support costs are very high owing to their inherent complexity (Segev and Bichler, 1999). In general, EDI standards facilitate large-scale, repetitive, pre-arranged transactions between businesses; and, thus, force business relationships to be established *a priori*.

CommerceNet's eCo framework <http://www.commerce.net>, OTP (1999), or ebXML <http://www.ebxml.org> are new approaches for specifying electronic commerce standards based on the XML (eXtensible Markup Language) standard. Created and developed by the W3C XML Working Group, the XML is derived from the widely used international text processing standard SGML (Standard Generalized Markup Language, ISO 8879:1986). Intended for efficient use on the World Wide Web. XML still retains ISO 8879's basic features – vendor independence, user extensibility, complex structures, validation, and human readability – in a form that is much easier to implement and understand. XML is primarily intended to meet the requirements of large-scale web content providers for industry-specific markup, vendor-neutral data exchange, media-independent publishing, workflow management in collaborative authoring environments, and the processing of web documents by intelligent clients. The language combines the simplicity of HTML with the computability of EDI standards. XML offers a way for making transaction sets easier to define and provides "self-describing" messages (Meltzer and Glushko, 1998).

However, XML alone does not solve the interoperability problem. Because XML is generic, it is necessary to define document type definitions (DTDs) for these services. DTDs are grammars that describe what the elements of document instances look like and how they are arranged. In other words, they are templates for specific instances of documents. The tags need to be semantically consistent across merchant boundaries at least for the value chain in a given industry. Initiatives are already underway to agree on standard XML DTDs within specific vertical industries or markets. Many industries (e.g. electronics, automotive, and aerospace) have already established sophisticated SGML DTDs. There will be considerable interest in converting these to XML for use in practical Internet commerce applications.

Interoperability standards for specific areas of electronic commerce are Information Content and Exchange (ICE) for the exchange of online assets among companies, Open Buying on the Internet (OBI) for high-volume indirect purchases, as well as niche protocols for special purposes such as Secure Electronic Transactions (SET) and Open Financial Exchange (OFX). A very broad initiative called eCo is currently organized by CommerceNet, an industry consortium of over 500 companies and organizations worldwide. The eCo specification is an architectural framework that enables businesses to identify each other, discover each others' product and service offerings, and quickly access a description of the electronic commerce standards and trading practices each potential partner has adopted (Chen *et al.*, 1999). The eCo initiative is also based on XML documents and registries that allows sellers to register their products/services, authenticate themselves and their service policies, and have their products accurately compared with those of other sellers. Software agents will then be able to utilize these registries to create secondary markets and interact on behalf of market participants. The United Nations body for Trade Facilitation and Electronic Business (UN/CEFACT) and the Organization for the Advancement of Structured Information Standards (OASIS) have now joined forces to initiate a worldwide project to standardize XML business specifications. It is still an open question which of these approaches will succeed, but probably future brokerage services will have to be able to handle several protocols (Segev and Bichler, 1999).

2.6.3   The Need for Shared Ontologies

Currently, the main technical barrier to electronic commerce lies in the need for applications for meaningfully sharing information. However, EDI is not ready to reap the full benefits of electronic commerce where agents act in an autonomous or semi-autonomous way, compare products or suppliers, or negotiate with other agents, etc. In order to enable consistent behaviors among the participants in an electronic market and to allow complex interactions such as negotiation and mediation, greater levels of semantic content need to be made explicit and be represented in a machine-readable way. EDI standards such as UN/EDIFACT define only messages, not a common vocabulary. "Ontology" is the term used to refer to the shared understanding of some area of interest. It is often used to refer to a certain vocabulary; yet, even the terms within a simple vocabulary may be prone to misinterpretation unless those terms have been chosen carefully. Electronic commerce applications must adopt common ontologies if they are to interact without misunderstanding each other. Content needs to be defined which enables both application interoperation and information synthesis (Poulter, 1998).

Several industrywide electronic commerce initiatives have already demonstrated by way of practical example that quite sophisticated representation issues can arise, even in what at first glance may seem straightforward commerce scenarios. RosettaNet <http://www.rosettanet.org> is such an approach targeted at the electronic components and information technology industry. Here, the need to represent the topology of the parts that make up complex electronics products is needed in the automation of the supply chain. As part of RosettaNet, two data dictionaries are being developed which provide a common terminology. The first is a technical properties dictionary (technical specifications for all product categories), and the second is a business properties dictionary which includes catalog properties, partner properties (attributes used to describe supply chain partner companies), and business transaction properties.

Realizing web automation in complex environments such as these reopens many of the debates and issues that the distributed systems and artificial intelligence communities have been wrestling with for the last two decades (Uschold and Gruninger, 1996). Technical research in ontologies includes Rosenschein and Zlotkin's (1994) *Rules of Encounter*, which was an attempt to put the soft terms of bargaining into hard, computer science-oriented terminology. Ontology work has continued with the development of the Knowledge Interchange Format (KIF) and the Knowledge Query and Manipulation Language (KQML), developed as part of the ARPA knowledge sharing effort to facilitate knowledge sharing and to represent ontologies (Singh, Genesereth and Syed, 1995). It is particularly successful in the field of multi-agent systems. These systems share the goals of distributed artificial intelligence, namely distributing problem solving tasks among different software modules, which may be executed in parallel on different machines or processors, where pre-defined ontologies are of particular importance (Nwana and Ndumu, 1997; Werthner and Klein, 1999). Based on KQML and KIF, the Foundation for Intelligent Physical Agents (FIPA) defined the Agent Communication Language (ACL) as a vendor independent language (FIPA, 1997).

Many newer approaches are based on XML (Poulter, 1998). However, XML in itself as a representation is too forgiving at the DTD definition stage (Smith and Poulter, 1999). Steps in the right direction are being taken, for example, with the definition of schema languages that enable the definition of objects in XML, or the Resource Description Framework (RDF) (Lassila and Swick, 1999). Schema languages can be used to define, describe, and catalog XML vocabularies (e.g. primitive data types) for classes of XML documents (Malhotra and Maloney, 1999). RDF provides mechanisms to describe the syntax as well as the semantics of web resources. It offers a model for representing named properties and property values for describing resources and the relationships between resources. For instance, Kaukal and Werthner (2000) have proposed RDF for describing tourism products and services. It still needs to be shown whether or not new approaches such as XML schema languages or the RDF will foster the development of shared ontologies for electronic commerce.

High-level interoperability standards and shared ontologies are some of the technical challenges for the development of an Internet brokerage infrastructure. The following chapters, however, will concentrate on the core competency of a broker – the matching between participants on a marketplace. In most of the examples described so far, this matching is done in a rather simple way. On the one hand, a number of suppliers can be found setting fixed prices for their offerings; on the other, there are buyers with more or less sophisticated search and retrieval tools trying to find offers that best fulfill their requirements. Setting optimal prices is crucial in this scenario and has been a research question in economics for a long time.

3 The Difficulty of Setting Prices

> As buyers and sellers do battle in the electronic world, the struggle should result in prices that more closely reflect their true market value.
>
> (*Business Week, May 4, 1998*)

Most companies are faced with the problem of pricing their products. This problem has been a focal research question of microeconomics and marketing. Microeconomists have developed a sound framework of markets which is a good starting point for an analysis of electronic markets. This section will provide a brief overview of microeconomic theory and the morphology used to describe different market structures. This framework provides a useful terminology for thinking and communicating about markets, and describes the basic ideas of price-setting.

Section 3.1 will focus on a number of market structures which are well analyzed in microeconomic theory. Of course, this can only be a rough description of the microeconomic theory, and by no means complete. (For a more rigorous discussion see Varian, 1992, 1996c; Mansfield, 1996; Browning and Zupan, 1999.) Section 3.2 will describe differential pricing, which is of particular importance to electronic commerce.

3.1 Market Structures

An *economic environment* consists of individual economic *agents*, together with an *institution* through which the agents interact (Browning and Zupan, 1999). The agents may be buyers and sellers, and the institution may be a particular type of market. The agents are defined by their economically relevant characteristics: preferences, technology, resource endowments, and information. An economic institution specifies the actions available to agents and the outcomes that result from each possible combination of agents' actions. Any environment where agents have limited resources and

Table 3.1. *Market structures*

Sellers/Buyers	One	Several	Many
One	Bilateral monopoly	Restricted monopoly	Monopoly
Several	Restricted monopsony	Bilateral oligopoly	Oligopoly
Many	Monopsony	Oligopsony	Polypoly

a preference over outcomes can be modeled as a *resource allocation problem*. Decentralized resource allocation is a central topic of economics.

A resource allocation mechanism is a protocol by which agents can realize a solution to the resource allocation problem. The mechanism maps messages or signals from the agents into a solution. In a market-based mechanism a price is assigned to each resource in the form of money. Prices are non-negative real numbers that determine the exchange value of resources in a market. They provide an aggregation of global information and enable agents to make rational decisions.

Economists have developed a large body of theory describing different market structures and the way prices are determined in these situations. A widespread microeconomic morphology of market structures is the classification along market participants on the buyer and seller side (see table 3.1).

A monopoly in this classification is a situation where one seller sells a product to many buyers and a polypoly is one where each participant in the market, whether buyer or seller, is so small in relation to the entire market that the product's price cannot be affected. A monopsony, on the other hand, is a situation in which there is a single buyer and multiple sellers. The situation is rather rare in business-to-consumer markets, but it is often the case in business-to-business markets (e.g. in the case of large food retailers, or car manufacturers, or labor markets with one big employer in a geographical region).

Another way of classifying markets is by type of products traded. Economists distinguish between a market with *homogeneous goods* and *heterogeneous goods*. Products traded on a market can be homogeneous, as is the case with stock exchanges where identical commodities are traded (e.g. stocks of ATandT), or they can also be heterogeneous, as is the case with journals or newspapers where some are close substitutes. In the case of homogeneous goods there are no differences whatsoever between the goods traded in a market. Consequently, buyers do not have any preferences over one product or another. Heterogeneous goods can be found in many real-world markets and describe situations where buyers have preferences for certain products.

3.1.1   The Ideal of a Perfectly Competitive Market

Many economics textbooks begin with an ideal model of a perfectly competitive market in order to illustrate the basic principles of a market economy. *Perfect competition* is defined by four conditions. First, perfect competition requires that the product of any one seller is exactly the same as the product of any other seller (i.e. products are *homogeneous*). Second, perfect competition requires each participant in the market, whether buyer or seller, to be so small in relation to the entire market that the product's price cannot be affected (i.e. a polypoly). Third, it requires that all resources are completely mobile and each resource is able to enter or leave the market. Finally, perfect competition requires that consumers, firms, and resource owners have perfect knowledge of the relevant economic and technological data.

A competitive company is one that operates under the conditions of perfect competition and takes the market price of output as being given and outside of its control (Varian, 1992). Of course, this company is free to set whatever price it wants and produce whatever quantity it is able to produce. However, if it sets the price above the prevailing market price, no one will purchase its product. If it sets its price below the market price, it will have as many customers as it wants, which is also true for the market price. Therefore, a competitive company ignores its influence on the market price, p, and it has to choose output, y, so as to solve

$$\max_{y} py - c(y). \tag{3.1}$$

By differentiating (3.1) the first-order condition for a solution is

$$p = MC(y^*) \tag{3.2}$$

where price equals marginal cost (MC). The company's supply function, $y(p)$, provides the profit-maximizing output at each price. Normally, this supply curve has a positive slope. The *industry supply function*, $s(p)$, measures the sum of the individual firm supply functions. Similarly, suppose that there are a number of consumers in a competitive market and their individual demand curves are given. Then these individual demand curves can also be added to an *industry demand curve*, $d(p)$. This function measures the total output demanded at any price.

An *equilibrium price* is a price where the amount demanded equals the amount supplied. Geometrically, this is the price, p^*, where the demand and the supply functions cross. For instance, if the industry demand curve is linear, $d(p) = a - bp$, and the industry supply curve is $s(p,m) = mp/2$ with p being the price and m the number of suppliers in the market, then the equilibrium price is the solution to

$$a - bp = mp/2, \tag{3.3}$$

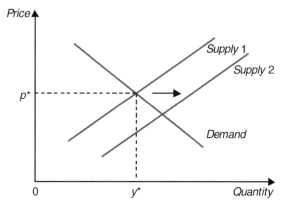

Figure 3.1 Entry of new firms on a competitive market.

which implies

$$p^* = \frac{a}{b + m/2}.$$ (3.4)

The equilibrium quantity, y^*, demanded and supplied is

$$d(p^*) = a - bp^* = a - \frac{ab}{b + m/2}.$$ (3.5)

Assuming that industry demand has a negative slope, the equilibrium price must decline as the number of firms increases (see figure 3.1).

It is not clear whether the equilibrium in a competitive market is a "good" solution. A general objective is the idea of *Pareto efficiency*. A solution to a resource allocation problem is Pareto efficient if there is no way to make any person better off without hurting anybody else (Varian, 1996c). For instance, at any amount of output less than the competitive amount, y^*, there is someone who is willing to supply an extra unit of the good at a price that is less than the price that someone is willing to pay for an extra unit of the good. If the good was produced and exchanged between these two people at any price between the demand price and the supply price, they would both be made better off. In contrast, the equilibrium output, y^*, is Pareto efficient because the price that someone is willing to pay to buy an extra unit of the good is equal to the price that someone must be paid to sell an extra unit of a good. Of course, efficiency is not the only goal of economic policy. For example, efficiency has almost nothing to say about income distribution or economic justice. However, efficiency is still an important goal.

A perfectly competitive market is hard to find; however, the model generates insights about real-world markets. Nearly perfect competition is given in many markets for wheat, corn, or shares of a company (stock exchanges). In these markets, many buyers ask for homogeneous goods provided by multiple sellers. As people do not have perfect knowledge about market conditions, they often use double auctions as a market mechanism (see section 5.3 for a detailed description). Auctions are a means for communicating the necessary information in an efficient way. The following sections provide a brief description of various market structures that can be observed in practice.

3.1.2 Monopolies, Bilateral Monopolies, and Monopsonies

Monopolies consist of a single seller on the one side and multiple buyers on the other side. For a monopolist there is no need to negotiate prices, she can simply set prices as she likes. There is a large amount of economic literature describing pricing strategies for monopolies. If the seller has complete information (e.g. about the market demand curve), a profit-maximizing price can be set by the seller. Since a monopolist charges a price in excess of marginal cost, she will produce an inefficient amount of output (see section 3.2). Price discrimination is a widespread method for maximizing prices in situations where market segmentation is feasible. In cases with incomplete information, the monopolist can use auctions as a market mechanism to determine prices. The theory of monopsonies is very similar to the theory of monopolies.

In a *bilateral monopoly,* bargaining – i.e. one-on-one negotiation – is used to determine the prices and conditions of the deal. The result of bargaining is hard to predict and depends on a number of parameters such as bargaining skills and the power of the negotiators. Game theory has explored these situations in the form of non-cooperative games and provided deeper insight into the dynamics of bilateral negotiations (see subsection 5.2.1 for details).

3.1.3 Oligopolies and Oligopsonies

The model of oligopoly is concerned with the strategic interactions that arise in an industry with a small number of suppliers (Varian, 1996c). Similarly, an oligopsony is a situation with many sellers and only a few buyers. There are several models that are relevant since there are several different ways for businesses to behave in an oligopolistic environment. The Stackelberg (quantity-leader) model is concerned with industries in which there is a dominant company, which sets quantities and other smaller firms following the decision of this supplier. Suppose that company 1 is the leader and that it chooses to produce a quantity y_1. Company 2 responds by choosing quantity y_2. Each company knows that the equilibrium price in the market depends on the total output produced and the leader has to take into account how its follower(s) will respond.

In the price-leader model, one company sets its price, and the other company chooses how much it wants to supply at that price. Again, the market leader has to take into account the behavior of the follower when it makes its decision. In the Cournot model, each company chooses its output so as to maximize its profits given its beliefs about the other firm's choice. In equilibrium, each company finds that its expectation about the other firm's choice is confirmed. A Cournot equilibrium in which each company has a small market share is very similar to a competitive industry, and the price will be close to marginal cost.

3.1.4   *Monopolistic Competition*

So far, only homogeneous goods have been considered. Markets with heterogeneous goods are also called markets with *imperfect competition*. A *monopolistic competition* describes a market structure in which product differentiation exists, i.e. there are a large number of companies producing and selling goods that are close substitutes, but which are not completely homogeneous from one seller to another. Retail trade is often cited as an industry with many of the characteristics of monopolistic competition. Monopolistic competition assumes that there is product differentiation and, consequently, that there is buyer preference for certain sellers. The market for automobiles, for example, is not purely competitive since there are not multiple producers of identical products.

As a result of consumer preferences, sellers are not price takers and can set prices considering the interdependencies with other sellers. Here, sellers have some market power as the product is different enough from other products so that the customers' willingness-to-pay (WTP) is a more important parameter for pricing than the competitors' behavior (Varian, 1996a). Practically, there is no clear border between monopolistic competition and a monopoly. One may say that all products are differentiated; it is just a question of "how much." Similarly, economists call a situation *monopsonistic competition* when there are many buyers but the inputs are not homogeneous and some buyers prefer some sellers' inputs to other sellers' inputs.

3.2   **Setting Optimal Prices**

The number of participants on each side in a marketplace can also be perceived as a substitute for bargaining power. In market structures such as a monopoly and under certain restrictions in a monopolistic competition, sellers are able to set prices autonomously. The same is true if there is only a single buyer (monopsony) or a monopsonistic competition. However, setting prices is not an easy task. This section will begin with the classic theory of pricing in a monopoly and will then describe the concepts of price differentiation. Differential pricing is becoming an increasingly popular means of selling goods online.

3.2.1 Maximizing Profits in a Monopoly

When there is only one company in a market that company will recognize its influence over the market price and choose the level of price and output that maximizes its overall profits (Varian, 1992, pp. 232 ff.). The monopolist can be viewed as choosing the price and letting the consumers choose how much they wish to buy at that price. Again, the participants are assumed to have full market knowledge, i.e. the monopolist knows the demand curve she is facing. Suppose that the monopolist faces a linear demand curve

$$p(y) = a - by. \tag{3.6}$$

Then the revenue function is

$$r(y) = p(y)y = ay - by^2. \tag{3.7}$$

The optimality condition for maximizing the revenue is straightforward: at the optimal choice of output, marginal revenue (MR) equals marginal cost ($MR = MC$). In the case of the competitive market discussed in subsection 3.1.1 marginal revenue is equal to the price and the condition reduces to price equals marginal cost. In a (Cournot) monopoly, the marginal revenue term is slightly more complicated (see also figure 3.2)

$$MR(y) = a - 2by = MC(y). \tag{3.8}$$

A competitive market operates at a point where price equals marginal cost. A monopolized industry operates where price is greater than marginal cost. Thus, in general, the price will be higher and the output lower if a company behaves monopolistically rather than competitively. Therefore, consumers will typically be worse off in an industry organized as a monopoly than in one organized competitively.

It can be shown that a monopoly is not efficient. If a monopolist could be forced to behave as a competitor and take the market price as being set exogenously, then the equilibrium price would be p^+ (see figure 3.2). As a monopolist, on the other hand, the company would choose its level of price (p^*) so as to maximize profits. Since the demand curve $p(y)$ is greater than $MC(y)$ for all the output levels between y^* and y^+, people are willing to pay more for a unit of output than it costs to produce it and there is a potential for Pareto improvement. For example, at the monopoly output level y^*, there might be someone who is willing to pay more for an extra unit of

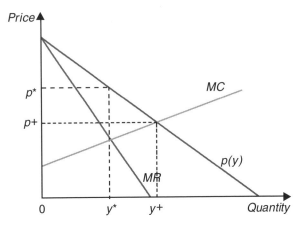

Figure 3.2 Monopoly with a linear demand curve.

output than it costs to produce an extra level. If the company produces this extra output and sells it at a price p where $MC(y^*)<p<p(y^*)$, the consumer is better off because she is willing to pay $p(y^*)$ and gets it for p. Similarly, it costs the monopolist $MC(y^*)$ to produce the extra unit and it is sold for $p>MC(y^*)$.

3.2.2   Price and Product Differentiation

It has been shown that a monopoly operates at an inefficient level of output since it restricts output to a point where people are willing to pay more for extra output than it costs to produce it (Bichler and Loebbecke, 2000). The monopolist does not want to produce extra output because it forces down the price that she is able to get for all of her output. If the monopolist could sell different units of this identical product at different prices, then the problem could be solved. This concept is called "differential pricing" (also known as "price discrimination") and can be deployed in monopolies as well as in monopolistic competition.

In most markets, the customers' willingness-to-pay is heterogeneous. Thus, it would be advantageous to charge different users different prices. The basic principle can be shown with a very simple example. Let's assume there are two consumers, X and Y. X is willing to pay US $5 and Y is willing to pay US $2. Further, the costs to produce the first item are assumed to be US $6 and the cost of every additional copy is assumed to be US $0 (think, for example, of an online journal). If every consumer paid a price according to her willingness-to-pay, the revenue would be US $7. If the seller charges a uniform price of US $2 which is accepted by both consumers, she will not be able to cover her costs. If she charged US $5, she would earn more but still not cover her costs. This is only one example where differential pricing is the only alternative to not producing the good and leads to prices that reflect more closely their true market value.

In the past, significant cost was associated with changing prices, known as the "menu cost." For a company with a large product line, it could take months for price adjustments to filter down to distributors, retailers, and salespeople. Networks such as the Internet reduce menu cost and time to nearly zero (Cortese and Stepanek, 1998). This concept is especially important in the case of digital goods where marginal costs are close to zero. However, there are two problems with differential pricing, if customers are generally assumed to be anonymous. First, a seller has to determine the willingness-to-pay of different groups of buyers. Second, the seller has to prevent customers with a high willingness-to-pay from purchasing the product intended for customers with a lower willingness-to-pay. This means that the market has to be separable – by artificial creation or naturally through some actual or imputed characteristics. Retrading or communication between market segments must also be limited.

One strategy is to base pricing on some customer characteristics (individual or group level), e.g. if the customer is a business or a private person or if the customer is a student or some kind of club member. Another strategy is to differentiate prices based on the characteristics of the product such as the quality or the time when it is shipped. A classic microeconomic taxonomy of price differentiation is the one by Pigou (1920) who uses the term price discrimination instead:

- "First-degree price differentiation" (or "perfect price discrimination") means a producer sells different units of output for different prices and the prices may differ from person to person.
- "Second-degree price differentiation" (or "non-linear pricing") means that the producer sells different units of output for different prices, but every individual who buys the same amount of the product pays the same price. This system implies quantity discounts and quantity premium.
- Finally, "third-degree price differentiation" occurs when each consumer faces a single price, but the price differs among categories of consumers. This is probably the most common type of price discrimination.

Differential pricing directs the consumer towards self-selection, as the consumer chooses the category in which she fits best. Shapiro and Varian (1999) use different and more descriptive terms, namely "personalized pricing," "group pricing," and "versioning." In the following sub-sections, these three forms of price differentiation will be covered in the context of electronic markets.

3.2.3   *Personalization*

Personalization (i.e. first-degree price differentiation) is an important concept in electronic markets. It aims at identifying potential customers and offering them the required products at the right time, price, and conditions. Theoretically, "personalization" assumes that suppliers know their customers' willingness-to-pay and extract from each consumer the full value of her consumer surplus. The ideal theoretical case of first-degree price discrimination sees a transformation of the entire area below the demand curve into producer surplus.

At present, perfect personalization has limited applications. It can occur only in the few cases where a company has a small number of buyers and is able to guess the maximum prices those buyers are willing to accept. However, the amount of information that can be gathered about customers by means of electronic catalogs enables more "personalized" offerings. The catalog owner can collect data about names, zip code, buying history, etc. and can target her offerings based on this information. For instance, Lexis-Nexis <http://www.lexisnexis.com>, an online database provider, sells to virtually every user at a different price, depending on the kind of industry and the size of the customer's organization, when and how often the database is accessed.

3.2.4   *Group Pricing*

Group pricing (i.e. third-degree price discrimination) occurs when each consumer is confronted with a single price and can purchase as much as desired at that price, but the price differs among categories or groups of consumers. People who have certain purchase histories, zip codes or behavior patterns are offered different prices (Shapiro and Varian, 1999). This is probably the most common practice of differential pricing. For example, it is often thought that business users have higher willingness-to-pay than educational users; hence, many suppliers of books and journals have educational discounts. Similarly, prices often depend on whether one is domestic or foreign, senior citizen, member of a club, etc. Essentially, what is required is knowledge of *group-specific demand functions*. It is essential to know the elasticity of demand with respect to price in order to differentiate prices.

Group pricing is already an accepted concept for selling goods on the web. Electronic catalogs, using rule-based techniques and active databases, allow merchants to differentiate their services depending on the characteristics and preferences of a specific customer (Mertens and Höhl, 1999). Suppliers use mechanisms such as targeted promotions and loyalty programs in order to distinguish their products from those of competitors and to establish customer relationships. A detailed knowledge about the customers' characteristics and needs is essential for group pricing. Unfortunately, in many cases it is rather difficult to learn about particularities of different customer groups. The difficulty with all these efforts is that online customers are mostly unknown, and therefore merchants are lacking customer-specific data. Moreover, often an individual's willingness-to-pay is not correlated with any of the characteristics mentioned.

On the Internet there are many new ways to learn about one's customers and consequently differentiate prices accordingly, some of which require the user's active involvement (typically through filling in a form) whereas others operate behind the scenes and track a user's behavior. Online registration is one way to gather customer data. The online version of the *New York Times* <http://www.nytimes.com> does not charge users for content, but requires them to register, providing information such as name, address, gender, and age. This information already gives a clear picture about demographics and reading habits. However, often users do not trust web sites and their privacy practices.

More elaborate approaches are based on customer-owned personal profiles which store information such as name, address, interests, etc. and give it away on a controlled basis to web site providers. The "Open Profiling Standard" of Netscape, Firefly and VeriSign, together with the "Web Privacy" submission of Microsoft evolved into a series of protocols known as the Platform for "Privacy Preferences Project" (P3P). P3P allows users to automatically tell trusted sites certain personal information (for instance, name, address, and phone number) without having to type it in for each site. The goal of P3P is to enable users to exercise preferences over web sites' privacy practices. P3P applications will allow users to be informed about web site practices, delegate decisions to their computer agent when they wish and tailor relationships with specific sites.

Another way to learn about one's customers is to track their online behavior and "click stream" by using cookies or by simply looking at an IP address in the web server's log file. Click stream analysis allows a merchant to instantaneously gauge a web user's interest in different products and product categories. There are several tools for analyzing web server log-file data. Once the data is processed, analyzers can create reports based on the results. However, from this data, it is still difficult to learn about a particular customer interaction. HTTP is a stateless protocol. Servers do not know if requests for any two pages or objects embedded were generated by the same person. If an application wants to have a "session" with a user (i.e. that state is retained as long as a user is browsing a web application) it needs to recognize this session through information stored on the server side or on the client side. Cookies are a widespread means of storing session data on the client side. They typically act as a customer's identifier for several HTTP requests. The classic example is an online shopping cart where the web site has to remember which products a customer already selected. The customer control of cookies is, however, less sophisticated than with P3P.

3.2.5   Versioning

The main conceptual difference between the previously mentioned "group pricing" and "versioning" is that "group pricing" focuses on customer characteristics, while "versioning" is based on product features (i.e. versions). With different versions of a product offered, customers sort themselves into different groups according to their willingness-to-pay for certain product features. Versioning is more than "second-degree" price differentiation and closer to product differentiation (Shapiro and Varian, 1999). Additionally, Pauwels (2000) describes versioning as third-degree price discrimination augmented with product differentiation. Offering different versions of the same product or service may surmount, by induction, the self-selection problem implied by third-degree price discrimination. Versioning appears to be the most popular approach for price discrimination on the Internet (figure 3.3).

In cases where observable exogenous customer characteristics have little to do with their willingness-to-pay, "quality discrimination" or "versioning" can be a good strategy. The seller in this situation provides at least two versions of a product and determines associated prices. A simple example is block pricing, where the price per unit declines with the quantity purchased by a particular customer (quantity discounts). Suppose an online database provider prices her information such that the first 10 MB of data downloaded sell for US $6 per MB, the second 10 MB for US $4, the third for US $2, and so on. An example of the demand curve in this scenario is depicted in figure 3.3 b) where the shaded area depicts the revenue of the database provider using block pricing. This tends to result in greater turnover because heavy users pay prices closer to marginal cost; however, it does not convert all consumer surplus into profit, as is the case with perfect personalization where the number of blocks would equal the number of customers.

Theoretically, the number of versions of a product offered should be equal to the number of different kinds of consumers in the market. Figure 3.3 a and 3.3 b demonstrate that the larger the number of versions is, the higher the overall turnover. However, in the business world, too many versions easily create confusion. Varian (1996b) suggests two versions of online academic journals, one for libraries and the other one for private

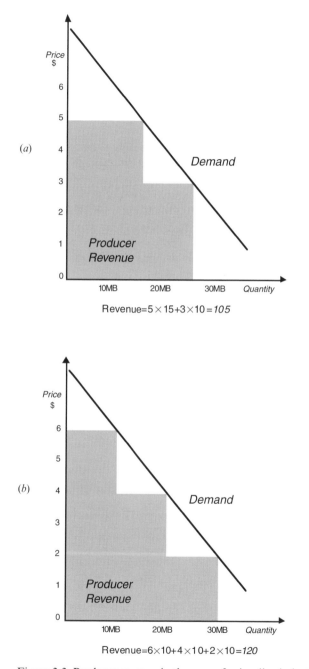

Figure 3.3 Producer revenue in the case of price discrimination.

individuals. The higher-priced version can be enhanced by hypertext links to cited articles, more powerful search engines, higher resolution images, etc. PAWWS Financial Network, another example, charges US \$8.95 per month for a portfolio accounting system that measures stock values using 20-minute delayed quotes and US \$50 per month for real-time quotes (Varian, 1997).

In the context of other products, various empirical investigations recommend offering three instead of two versions, as the "average customer" will most likely opt for the "middle version." Examples include airline cards with the versions "standard," "silver," and "gold," or software packages differentiated into "student," "professional," and "deluxe." In the case where three versions are offered, suppliers should be prepared to concentrate their production, distribution and service efforts on the middle version. Many sellers start out producing a high-end version and then downgrade it to obtain the versions for other segments of the market. Thus, sellers can increase their profits by reducing the quality of the product and then targeting it at consumers with a low willingness-to-pay at a reduced price.

3.2.6   *Product Bundling*

Another form of price discrimination results from "aggregation" or "product bundling," where products are sold together as a package. Many software packages (e.g. Microsoft Office) are bundles of individual components. Academic journals or newspapers are bundles of articles sold as a package and subscriptions of magazines can also be seen as product bundles of several issues (Shapiro and Varian, 1999). The pricing advantage of bundling goods can easily be demonstrated.

Let's assume that A has a maximum willingness-to-pay of US \$50 for product "abc" and US \$70 for good "xyz." B's willingness-to-pay is just the opposite: US \$70 for "abc" and US \$50 for "xyz" (see table 3.2). If the supplier for "abc" and "xyz" gives one price per product, she will charge US \$50 each and, thus, reach an overall turnover of US \$200. If she bundles "abc" and "xyz" together and then offers the package for US \$120, both customers stay in their willingness-to-pay limits, but the supplier achieves a turnover of US \$240. Obviously, in the case of perfect personalization, the overall turnover would also be US \$240; but in real-world settings on physical markets, bundling is rather common and easy to implement, while personalization assumes a detailed knowledge of customer WTPs and, thus, is barely feasible.

One of the most important effects of the Internet infrastructure has been to radically reduce the marginal costs of producing and distributing information products to consumers and businesses. Information products may,

Table 3.2. *Willingness-to-pay*

	Product "abc" US$	Product "xyz" US$
A	50	70
B	70	50

thus, enjoy economies of scale in production because of their low marginal costs, or demand-side economies of scale resulting from network externalities. This is a field where bundling is of great importance. Bakos and Brynjolfsson (1999) demonstrate how marketing strategies that exploit bundling can be used to gain an advantage when purchasing or developing new content. Firms can employ "economies of aggregation" to discourage or foreclose entry, even when competitors' products are technically superior. The same strategies can force a competitor with a higher quality product to leave the market. Finally, product aggregation can affect incentives for innovation, decreasing them for companies that may face competition from a bundler while increasing them for the bundler herself.

3.3 Towards Dynamic Pricing

According to an OECD survey on electronic commerce, "More and more products will be subject to differential pricing associated with customized products, fine market segmentation and auctions as it becomes easier to change prices," (OECD, 1998). Empirical data shows that differential pricing is already ubiquitous in industries that exhibit large fixed costs such as airlines, telecommunications, or publishing. Some market segments could not be served without differential pricing, and it can even be shown that differential pricing can be expected to contribute to economic efficiency (Varian, 1996a). With perfect price discrimination (personalized pricing), every unit has a marginal value to consumers greater than the marginal production cost. All net benefit from producing this product goes to the supplier as profit, but it is just a transfer of income from consumers to the supplier and not a net loss to society.

Unfortunately, setting prices is difficult. In many cases, sellers have very little information about customers' demand curves. It is particularly hard in the case of new products or in very dynamic markets such as financial markets, where prices and participants are quite often subject to change, to set the "right" price(s) or to differentiate the market appropriately. Price and product differentiation and bundling lead to rather sophisticated and complex product offerings and companies face the challenge of setting a new price for these offerings. That is, the perfect market knowledge and the given demand curve which can be found in economic models is an exception in reality.

List prices are a consequence of industrialization and for about two centuries most prices have been subject to negotiation. New information technologies have radically altered the economy. On the one hand, buyers can quickly and easily compare products and prices, putting them in a better bargaining position. At the same time, the technology allows sellers to collect detailed data about customers' buying habits and preferences. This leads to price uncertainty and high volatility of electronic markets. On the other hand, the global reach of Internet-based markets increases the number of participants. This makes it difficult to get a clear picture about competitors and customers, and consequently to set appropriate prices. Consequently, many experts and market research institutions expect more negotiations and new forms of dynamic pricing to take place in electronic markets (Stroebel, 2000) (see section 1.2). This book will focus on the design of electronic markets and the associated negotiation protocols. However, chapter 4 will first give an overview of the core disciplines needed for advanced market design.

4   Methods for the Analyses and Design of Electronic Markets

As the opportunities for humans and software agents to interact increase, the mediating role of negotiation systems is becoming more important.

(*Robinson and Volkov, 1998*)

Markets evolve, but they are also designed by entrepreneurs, economists, lawyers and engineers. *Market design* creates a meeting place for buyers and sellers and a format for transactions. Recently, economists and game theorists have begun to take a direct role and designed different kinds of market mechanisms.

An area in which market design is well developed is in the study of auction-based protocols. Although this is criticized by some authors (Kersten and Noronha, 1999a), auctions will be considered as a special type of negotiation. Leading economists such as Preston McAfee, John McMillan and Robert Wilson, among others, have successfully deployed game-theoretical analysis in order to design the bidding process in the case of the US Federal Communication Commission's (FCC) spectrum auctions as well as the design of energy markets. However, auction design is also an area in which there is a need to supplement the standard microeconomic theory.

Game theory is an important methodology, but it is not by any means the only technique necessary for successful market design. Market design practice is in its early stages and comprises methodologies such as equilibrium analysis, game theory, mechanism design theory, experimental economics, and computation. These techniques will be described in subsequent sections.

4.1   Equilibrium Theory

The basics of microeconomic theory were developed more than a century ago in Lausanne (Walras, Pareto), England (Jevons, Marshall), and Austria

(Menger, Böhm-Bawerk). Leon Walras' equilibrium theory has been the most influential school of thought. Some of the basics have been outlined in chapter 2. When a collection of interconnected markets achieves a perfect balance of supply and demand with respect to the maximizing behaviors of self-interested economic agents, then the economy is in *general equilibrium*.

In 1874, Leon Walras (1874) proposed a price-adjustment process he called *tâtonnement* in which agents respond to price signals for individual goods. In this system, the agents' interactions are coordinated by a central auctioneer who adjusts the general price levels towards a general balance, announcing a set of interim prices to elicit responses from the agents. Starting with the first market, the auctioneer incrementally adjusts the price to balance supply and demand in relationship to all other prices. A change in the first price will normally change excess demand in other markets. Next, the auctioneer considers the second market and adjusts its price to clear, and so on. At the end of each round, only the last market is guaranteed to be in equilibrium since a change of price in some markets normally destroys the equilibrium established in previous markets. However, Walras argued that the change in a product's price will have a more significant impact on its excess demand than it will on the change in other goods' prices, and, therefore, the prices will remain closer to general equilibrium than they were before and converge until all markets clear. Finally, the outcome rule is to carry out exchanges according to the equilibrium bids made by the agents. It appears that the only naturally occurring organized markets using a procedure similar to a Walrasian *tâtonnement* are the gold and silver bullion pricing markets (see Varian, 1992, pp. 387 ff., for a more elaborate discussion of *tâtonnement*).

Friedrich Hayek stressed the advantages of a "decentralized solution vs. a centralized solution." Initially each agent has information only about itself: consumers about their preferences, producers about their technologies, and resource holders about their resources. The difficulty of a centralized resource allocation is that all the relevant information has to be placed in the hands of a single agency. "The marvel of the price system is its efficiency in communicating information in a system in which the knowledge of the relevant facts is dispersed among many people" (Hayek, 1945).

Samuelson (1947) provided a comprehensive mathematical formulation of Walras' price-adjustment process and the associated notion of *equilibrium stability* – i.e. the fact that no group of agents can do better by not engaging in the market at all. In the 1950s and 1960s many economists studied and refined the process of decentralized resource allocation (see, for example, Arrow, Block, and Hurwicz, 1959), but it was also criticized as too far away from the actual price-formation process in real economies. For example, agents in a real economy are often faced with resources that are discrete in nature, and they are allowed to trade before demand equals supply. In an adapted model, the so-called *non-tâtonnement process*, agents are allowed to trade before the economy has reached an equilibrium. These refinements are usually more stable than *tâtonnement* processes (Fisher, 1983).

In general, situations in which either no equilibrium exists or the resource allocation process fails to converge are called *market failures* (Wurman, 1997). Failures of convergence are problems with the allocation process. Failures of existence are actually problems resulting from the formulation of the problem as a price system. For example, basic models of equilibrium theory assume continuous, convex, and strongly monotone demand functions. When these conditions are violated (e.g. discreteness or increasing marginal returns), the existence of competitive equilibrium is no longer guaranteed.

4.2   Game Theory

Classic equilibrium theory depicts the outcome of competition but not the activity of competing. Competition sets prices right, thereby allowing an efficient allocation of resources. Much of what is interesting and important about competition is hidden in the background. As pointed out in an article by Arrow (1959), the standard economic model of perfect competition is lacking in that it fails to explain where prices come from. "Once the *deus ex machina* of the Walrasian auctioneer is discarded who sets the prices?" A perfectly competitive company does not pay attention to what any of the other firms in the industry is doing. Instead, it passively accepts the market price. Game-theoretical models, in contrast, view competition as a process of strategic decision making under conditions of uncertainty.

It has only been relatively recently that the depth and breadth of robust game-theoretical knowledge has been sufficient for microeconomists and game theorists to offer practical advice on institutional design (Roth, 1999). The amount of literature in this field is vast, and this section can introduce only the basic concepts relevant for chapters 5 and 6 of this book. For a more rigorous discussion, see Fudenberg and Tirole (1991); Aumann and Hart (1992).

4.2.1   Static Games with Complete Information

Game theory is the study of the interaction of rational decision makers. The disciplines most involved in game theory are mathematics, economics, and the social and behavioral sciences. *Cooperative games* assume that a binding agreement can be imposed on the parties and poses the question of the division of the game's value. The efforts are concentrated on the search for efficient solutions and the rules for choosing from among different efficient solutions. The theory of non-cooperative or competitive games tries to find

Table 4.1. *A payoff matrix of a game*

		Player *B*	
		Left	Right
Player *A*	Top	1,2	0,1
	Bottom	2,1	1,0

rational strategies that parties choose in the conflict situation. The focus is on a solution which is "self-enforcing" in the sense that a party cannot obtain an advantage by unilaterally defecting from the solution.

Game theory was founded by the mathematician John von Neumann. His first important book was *The Theory of Games and Economic Behavior* which he wrote in collaboration with the mathematical economist, Oskar Morgenstern (von Neumann and Morgenstern, 1944). Von Neumann and Morgenstern restricted their attention to zero-sum games – that is, to games in which no player can gain except at another's expense. However, this restriction was overcome by the work of John Nash and Ariel Rubinstein during the 1950s. Games with complete information may be represented in *strategic* form:

$$\Gamma = (N, S, U(s)) \tag{4.1}$$

where

- N is the set of players, and the index i designates a particular agent $i \in N = \{0, 1, 2, 3 \ldots n\}$.
- S is the strategy space for the agents where $S = (s_1, \ldots, s_i, \ldots, s_n)$, the set of all possible strategies for i.
- $U(s)$ is a vector of utility or payoff functions, one for each agent. Each payoff function specifies the consequences for an agent, of the strategies defined for all agents.

The payoff functions provide, for each vector of strategies in S, a vector of n real numbers representing the consequences for all players.

In order to illustrate the ideas, the following game is borrowed from Varian (1996c, p. 481). Strategic interaction in games can involve many players and many strategies. This example is limited to two-person games with a finite number of strategies. Suppose that two people are playing a simple game. Player *A* will write one of two words on a piece of paper, "top" or "bottom". Simultaneously, person *B* will independently write "left" or "right" on a piece of paper. After they do this, the pieces of paper will be examined, and each player will get the payoff depicted in the *payoff matrix* shown in table 4.1. In this game, the payoffs and strategies are assumed to

Table 4.2. *A Nash equilibrium*

		Player *B*	
		Left	Right
Player *A*	Top	2,1	0,0
	Bottom	0,0	1,2

be common knowledge to the players and both players choose simultaneously (i.e. a *static game*).

If *A* says "top," and B says "left," then the payoff to *A* is the first entry in
the top left-hand corner of the matrix and the second entry is the payoff to
B. Player *A* has two *strategies*: to choose "top" or "bottom." These strategies could be a substitute for "raising price" and "lowering price" in an
economy. The depicted game has a simple solution. From the viewpoint of
person *A*, it is always better to say "bottom" since her payoffs from that
choice are always greater than the corresponding entries in "top." Similarly,
it is always better for *B* to say "left" since 2 and 1 dominate 1 and 0. This is
a *dominant strategy* – i.e. there is one strategy choice for each player, no
matter what the other player does, and there is an equilibrium
("bottom/left") in dominant strategies.

The game depicted in table 4.2 does not have a dominant strategy equilibrium. However, what can be formulated is: If *A* chooses "top," then the
best thing for *B* to do is to choose "left," since the payoff to *B* from choosing "left" is 1 and from choosing "right" is 0. If *B* chooses "left," then the
best thing for *A* to do is to choose "top" since then *A* will get a payoff of 2
rather than of 0. Such a pair of strategies (such as "top/left") is a *Nash equilibrium*, if *A*'s choice is optimal, given *B*'s choice and vice versa. In other
words, each player is making the optimal choice and has no incentive to
change her strategy, given the other person's choice. It is easy to see that
"right/bottom" also constitutes a Nash equilibrium. Unfortunately, there
are also games of this type that do not have a Nash equilibrium at all.

What has been considered so far is called a *pure strategy*, i.e. players make
one choice and stick to it. Another way of thinking about this is to allow
the agents to assign a probability to each choice. For example, *A* might
choose to play "top" 50 percent of the time and "bottom" 50 percent of the
time while *B* would play "left" 50 percent of the time and "right" 50 percent
of the time. This kind of strategy is called *mixed strategy*. If *A* and *B* follow
the mixed strategies given above, of playing each of their choices half the
time, then they will have a probability of ending up in each of the four com-
partments of the payoff matrix. A Nash equilibrium in mixed strategies
refers to an equilibrium in which each agent chooses the optimal frequency

Table 4.3. *The prisoner's dilemma*

		Player *B*	
		Confess	Deny
Player *A*	Confess	-3,-3	0,-6
	Deny	-6,0	-1,-1

with which to play her strategies, given the frequency choices of the other agent. Nash equilibria are stable, but not necessarily desirable. For example, in what is undoubtedly the best known and most-discussed instance of a game, the *prisoner's dilemma*, the unique Nash equilibrium is a state which is not Pareto efficient (see subsection 3.1.1). In this game, two prisoners who were partners in a crime are being questioned and have the choice of confessing the crime, and thereby implicating the other, or denying. Table 4.3 depicts the number of years in prison for each strategy.

If player *B* decides to deny committing the crime, then player *A* is certainly better off confessing. Similarly, if player *B* confesses, then player *A* is better off confessing. The same thing goes for player *B*. To be precise, both players confessing is not only a Nash equilibrium but also a dominant strategy equilibrium since each player has the same optimal choice independent of the other player.

4.2.2   Repeated and Sequential Games

At this point, the players have met only once and played the prisoner's dilemma game only once. The situation is different if the game is played repeatedly by the same players. In this case, there are new strategic possibilities open to each player, e.g. an opponent can be punished for bad behavior and players can establish a reputation. Since an opponent can modify her behavior based on the history of a player's choices, a player needs to take this influence into account.

However, it makes a difference whether the game is going to be played a fixed number of times or an indefinite number of times. It can be shown that if a game has a known, fixed number of rounds, then each player will defect (deny) in every round. If there is no way to enforce cooperation in the last round, there will be no way to enforce cooperation in the next-to-last round. In contrast, if there is an infinite number of games, the threat of non-cooperation in the future may be sufficient to convince people to play the Pareto efficient strategy. Axelrod (1984) showed that in the case of an infinite prisoner's dilemma, the strategy with the highest overall payoff is a

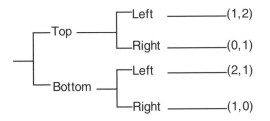

Figure 4.1 A game in extensive form.

simple "tit for tat," meaning that whatever your opponent did in the last round, you do in this round.

The above examples leave open entirely the dynamics of the game. That is, it abstracts from questions which are often of fundamental importance in applying game theory to actual situations. In many situations, one player gets to move first, and the other player responds. The most significant aspect of dynamics is information exchange: How much do particular players know about the strategies of other players? To incorporate this into a game, it can be represented in extensive form. An extensive-form game looks like a branching structure with sets of nodes which converge at an upper apex, representing the outcome (Holler and Illing, 1996, p. 14). Figure 4.1 shows the payoff matrix of table 4.1 in extensive form.

A game is not fully specified in extensive form until each player's path through the tree is completely identified, and indicates at which nodes subsets of players share information. Games in extensive form can easily be solved through backward induction, i.e. one solves the tree from right to left.

4.2.3   Games with Incomplete Information

Up until now, games of complete information have been considered where the payoff matrix is known to all players. Harsanyi and Selten (1972) describes games of incomplete information. It subsumes all of the uncertainty that one agent may have about another into a variable known as the agent's *type*. For example, one agent may be uncertain about another agent's valuation of some good, about her risk aversion and so on. Each type of player is regarded as a different player and a player has some prior probability distribution defined over the different types of agents. Each player knows that the other player is chosen from a set of possible types, but does not know exactly which one is played.

A *Bayes–Nash equilibrium* in a game is a set of strategies for each type of player that maximizes the expected value of each type of player, given the strategies pursued by the other players (Varian, 1992). This adds the notion of "uncertainty about the type of the other player" to the original definition of a Nash equilibrium. In order to have a complete description of an equilibrium there must be a list of strategies for all types of players. In a simultaneous game, this definition of equilibrium is adequate. In a sequential game, it is reasonable to allow the players to update their beliefs about the types of the other players based on the actions they have observed. Therefore, if one player observes the other choosing a certain strategy, she should revise her beliefs about what type the other player is by determining how likely it is that this strategy would be chosen by the various types. Games with incomplete information will be used to describe auction games in subsection 5.3.2.

The idea of the Bayes–Nash equilibrium is rather sophisticated. The problem is that the reasoning involved in computing Bayes–Nash equilibria is probably too difficult for real players. In addition, the choice that each player makes depends crucially on her beliefs about the distribution of various types in the population. Different beliefs about the frequency of different types lead to different optimal behavior. Ledyard (1986) has shown that essentially any pattern of play is a Bayes–Nash equilibrium for some pattern of beliefs.

4.3   Mechanism Design Theory

Hurwicz (1973) was one of the first to go beyond traditional equilibrium and game-theoretical analysis and to actively focus on the design of new mechanisms. *Mechanism design theory* differs from game theory in that game theory takes the rules of the game as given, while mechanism design theory asks about the *consequences* of different types of rules. It is a mathematical methodology concerned with the design of compensation and wage agreements, dispute resolution or resource allocation mechanisms that guide the economic actors in decisions that determine the flow of resources. "Just as chemical engineering is related to but different from chemistry, we can expect microeconomic engineering and economic design to be different from but related to microeconomics and game theory" (Roth, 1999).

4.3.1   Basic Thoughts

Formally, a mechanism M maps messages or signals from the agents, $S = \{s_1, ..., s_m\}$, into a solution as a function $M : S \to f$ of the information that is known by the individuals. This book is concerned with resource allocation mechanisms. A decentralized resource allocation problem can be described as a vector of resource types, R, and a set of agents, A. The n resource types are indexed by i, and the m agents by j. A subset, r, of the resources is specified as a vector, $\{x_1, ..., x_m\}$ where x_i is a quantity of resource i. An agent's preference relation over all possible combinations of resources is specified by its utility function, U_j. The utility that an agent j gets from r, is $U_j(r)$. Each agent is endowed with an initial allocation of resources, denoted e_j. A solution, $f = M(S)$, is an allocation of the resources to agents. The resources allocated to j in the solution f is denoted by r_j^f.

Virtually any environment where agents (human or computational) have limited resources and a preference for outcomes can be modeled as a resource allocation problem. As already mentioned in chapter 3, a *market-based mechanism* assigns a price to each resource in the form of money in order to allocate the resources. A mechanism is *iterative* if it reveals information about other agents, as individuals or together, and allows an agent to change its signal after receiving this feedback. An important type of mechanism in this context is a *direct revelation mechanism* in which agents are asked to report their true (i.e. honest) private information confidentially. Sealed-bid auctions are a direct mechanism whereas English and Dutch auctions are indirect (Wolfstetter, 1996).

Hurwicz (1973) proposes the concept of (*Pareto*) *satisfactoriness*, as a number of criteria for the evaluation of a new mechanism. First, the outcome of the mechanism should be *feasible*. In addition, the mechanism should *possess some equilibrium* for every type of environment that it is designed to cover and it ideally produces a *uniquely determined allocation*, i.e. only a single equilibrium price. Finally, a mechanism should be non-wasteful, i.e. (*Pareto*) *efficient*. Formally, a solution, f, is *Pareto efficient* if there is no other solution, g, such that there is some agent j for which $U_j(r_j^g) > U_j(r_j^f)$ and for all agents k, $U_k(r_k^g) \geq U_k(r_k^f)$. According to the *first welfare theorem* of classic welfare economics, a competitive mechanism is non-wasteful, i.e. (Pareto) optimal in environments that are free of externalities and public goods (Koopmans, 1957).

Even if the outcome of a mechanism is Pareto satisfactory, it can happen that it always favors one group of participants at the expense of another. Here again, welfare economics points the way. The *second welfare theorem* asserts that any Pareto optimum can be attained as a competitive equilibrium. That is, a mechanism does not necessarily accept a given distribution of resources. Rather it consists of two parts: reshuffling the initial endowment of agents followed by a *tâtonnement* procedure, in order to achieve the desired outcome. Several authors have criticized the basic assumptions of the first and second welfare theorem as too far away from real-world economies, in particular the assumptions of perfectly competitive markets.

4.3.2   *Considering Incentive Constraints*

Hurwicz (1973) has also stressed that incentive constraints should be considered coequally with resource (and budget) constraints which are the focus of classic microeconomic models. The need to give people an incentive to share private information and exert effort may impose constraints on economic systems just as much as the limited availability of resources. Mechanisms need to be designed in such a way that they give economic agents an incentive to share their private information in order to achieve an efficient allocation of resources. *Incentive compatibility* is the concept of characterizing those mechanisms for which participants in the process would not find it advantageous to violate the rules of the mechanism.

If a direct mechanism is incentive compatible, then each agent knows that her best strategy is to follow the rules according to her true characteristics, no matter what the other agents do. In other words, a direct mechanism is incentive compatible if one's reporting of valuations is a Nash equilibrium. A particularly strong and strategically simple case is a mechanism where truth-telling is a dominant strategy. In mechanisms which are not incentive compatible, each agent must predict what the others are going to do in order to decide what is best for her. In order to check for incentive compatibility of a mechanism, there must not be agents that could gain by disobeying the rules of the mechanism (e.g. revelation of one's true valuation for a good).

The concept can be illustrated by considering public goods. The existence of these collective consumption commodities creates a classic situation of market failure – the inability of markets to arrive at a Pareto efficient allocation. In these cases, agents have an incentive to "free ride" on others' provision of the goods in order to reduce the share that they themselves need to provide. Some economists have proposed creating a synthetic market for public goods where prices are based on an agent's demand signals. Allocating public goods efficiently would be feasible and successful if agents followed the rules; however, it is in the interest of each agent to give false signals, to pretend to have less interest in a given collective consumption activity than she really has. Consequently, efficient resource allocation cannot be achieved. Any institution or rule designed to accomplish group goals must be incentive compatible if it is to perform as desired.

One can now view incentive compatibility as a constraint and try to design mechanisms to attain the best level of efficiency. Vickrey (1961) showed that a second-price, sealed-bid auction (the so-called "Vickrey auction") is incentive compatible for the buyers because neither bidding higher nor bidding lower than the true valuation is beneficial (see subsection 5.3.2).

This property is of course meaningful only if agents have independent private values for the goods being traded.

In general, finding an *optimal mechanism* can be a difficult task, considering the large number of possibilities. Gibbard (1973) made a helpful observation that is now called the *revelation principle*. In order to find the maximally efficient mechanism, it is sufficient to consider only *direct revelation mechanisms*. In other words, for any equilibrium of any arbitrary mechanism, there is an incentive compatible direct-revelation mechanism that is essentially equivalent. Therefore, by analyzing incentive compatible direct-revelation mechanisms, what can be accomplished in all possible equilibria of all possible mechanisms can be characterized. The idea of restricting one's attention to direct-revelation mechanisms in which an agent reports all of her characteristics has also been criticized, because it provides little guidance for those interested in actual mechanism design. This might also be one reason why there has been limited success in using this theory to explain the existence of pervasive institutions such as the first-price sealed-bid auction.

Mechanism design theory now forms an integral part of modern economics. Its varied applications include the theory of choice, optimal tax theory, and the provision of public goods. Perhaps its most successful application has been with regard to auction theory. An early contribution of mechanism theory was the derivation of the *general revenue equivalence theorem* in auction theory (see subsection 5.3.2). Mechanism design and auction theory share commonality in the area of *optimal auction design*, where principles from mechanism design are combined with auction theory to design auctions that achieve the desired optimality, although different optimality measures exist (see subsection 5.3.4). Riley and Samuelson (1981) showed that all incentive compatible mechanisms would necessarily generate the same expected revenue. Varian (1995) used mechanism design theory to derive the so-called Generalized Vickrey Auction (see subsection 5.6.2.5)

4.3.3 Mechanism Design Guidelines

This book focuses on the design of new auction mechanisms. Equilibrium analysis and, in particular, mechanism design theory, define several desirable properties, which are helpful when designing an economic mechanism. Below, the most important properties introduced in the previous sections will be summarized:

■ The solution of a mechanism is in *equilibrium* if no agent wishes to change its signal, given the information it has about other agents. A dominant strategy equilibrium is one where the agents' strategy maximizes their utility regardless of the strategies played by other agents. In a *Nash equilibrium* each agent maximizes her expected utility, given the strategy of the other agents. A Bayes–Nash equilibrium is a set of strategies from which no agent would deviate given its beliefs about the distribution of other agent types. When designing a mechanism, it is important to know, if it *converges towards equilibrium* and if it produces a uniquely determined allocation.

■ A general criterion for evaluating a mechanism (assuming non-cooperative agents) is *efficiency*, meaning that the allocation resulting from the auction is Pareto optimal: No agent can improve its allocation without making another agent worse off. This means that an auction is efficient if there are no further possible gains from trade, and that the goods are allocated to the agents who value them most highly. On the whole, one can expect that an efficient auction also contributes to the maximization of the bid taker's revenue. In the prisoner's dilemma, the Nash equilibrium in which both players defect is not a Pareto efficient solution.

■ The solution of a mechanism is *stable*, or in the core (Varian, 1992, p. 388) if there is no subset of agents who could have done better by coming to an agreement outside the mechanism. If a mechanism is stable, then it is Pareto efficient, although the reverse is not true (Tesler, 1994).

■ A direct auction is *incentive compatible* if honest reporting of valuations is a Nash equilibrium. A particularly strong and strategically simple case is a mechanism where truth-telling is a *dominant strategy*. This is a desirable feature because an agent's decision depends only on its local information, and it gains no advantage by expending effort to model other agents (Milgrom and Weber, 1982; Ma, Moore and Turnbull, 1988; Wurman, Walsh and Wellman, 1998). Mechanisms that require agents to learn or estimate another's private information do not *respect privacy*.

■ *Speed of convergence* is an important issue in markets where transactions need to occur at a rapid rate. A good example is the Dutch flower auction. Since these auctions deal with very large volumes of perishable goods, each individual transaction needs to be completed quickly.

It is important to keep these guidelines in mind when designing a new mechanism. However, the designer of a resource allocation mechanism has to solve numerous other detail problems where these guidelines are of little help. Closing conditions such as the elapse time in an open-cry auction and the deadline for sealed-bid auctions need to be defined. In all types of auctions minimum starting bids and minimum bid increments can be defined. In addition, a designer of an auction has to decide about participation fees, the possibility of multiple rounds, etc.

4.4 Experimental Economics

Over the past forty years, experimental economics has become an important methodology for industrial organization, game theory, finance, public choice, and most other microeconomic fields. Laboratory experiments are an important complement to the methods which have been described so far since they allow us to test theoretical models. They help us to learn about how people behave, not only in environments too complex to analyze analytically but also in simple environments (in which economists' customary assumptions about behavior may not always be good approximations).

From a formal point of view, a theory consists of a set of axioms or assumptions and definitions, together with the conclusions that logically follow from them. A theory is formally valid if it is internally consistent. Theories organize our knowledge and help us to predict behavior in new situations. In particular, theories tell a researcher what data are worth gathering and suggest ways to analyze new data (Friedman and Sunder, 1994). Conversely, data collection and analysis often turn up regularities that are not explained by existing theory. The alternation of theory and empirical work, each refining the other, is the engine of progress in every scientific discipline.

A key distinction is between *experimental data*, which are deliberately created for scientific purposes under controlled conditions, and *happenstance data*, which are the by-product of ongoing uncontrolled processes. A less important but still useful distinction can be drawn between *laboratory data*, which are gathered in an artificial environment designed for scientific purposes, and *field data*, which are gathered in a naturally occurring environment. The main issues in comparing experimental and happenstance data are cost and validity. Laboratory environments are usually expensive to build, maintain, and operate, and each experiment requires additional costs such as payments to human subjects. Typically, the costs for field experiments are even higher.

There are many possible reasons for experiments. Some theorists see experimental economics primarily as a way to test theory. When analyzing institutions such as auctions or one-on-one bargaining, the experimental literature is particularly large (see section 5.5 for an overview of auction experiments). Many experimental observations about the outcomes of various types of auctions examine game-theoretical hypotheses such as the revenue equivalence theorem (Kagel, 1995).

Another scientific purpose of experiments is to discover empirical regularities in areas where existing theory has little to say. Laboratory experimentation can facilitate the interplay between the evolution and modification of proposed new exchange institutions. Experimenters can use repeat testing to better understand and improve the features of new market mechanisms. For instance, McCabe, Rassenti and Smith (1991) describe test-bed experiments of computer-aided markets for composite commodities such as computer resources and electrical power grids. They also compare the properties of several new market institutions whose theoretical properties are as yet poorly understood (McCabe, Rassenti and Smith, 1993). These experiments are sometimes called "heuristic." For the design of market mechanisms, it is useful to study new economic institutions in the laboratory before introducing them in the field. The scope for this type of institutional engineering is large and increasing all the time (Friedman and Sunder, 1994).

One fact that leaps out of both experimental and field data is that behavior in markets evolves, as people learn about the environment by interaction with it. In new markets, what people learn about initially is the behavior of other inexperienced players, so that an analysis that focuses only on equilibrium behavior may miss its importance, since markets which fail that early will not have the opportunity for players to learn about all their possible desirable outcomes.

Although the results of laboratory experiments are interesting, the question still remains, if the findings from experimental tests can be generalized. Experimental science uses "induction" as an underlying principle and assumes that regularities observed will persist as long as the relevant underlying conditions remain substantially unchanged. What makes experiments so different from the other methods microeconomists use is the presence of human subjects. Vernon Smith refers to this question as the "parallelism precept":

Propositions about the behavior of individuals and the performance of institutions that have been tested in laboratory microeconomies apply also to non-laboratory microeconomies where similar *ceteris paribus* conditions hold. (Smith, 1982)

Nowadays, experiments are commonplace in game theory, finance, electronic commerce, and many other fields (see Kagel and Roth, 1995, for a broad review). An experimental analysis of electronic markets is not possible without the implementation of an electronic market institution, though the construction of workable prototypes is yet another very helpful way of learning. Section 5.5 will review the results of laboratory experiments in testing the results of game-theoretical auction models. Finally, section 6.6 will provide a detailed description of a laboratory experiment designed to analyze the behavior of a proposed new market mechanism. Field studies have long been restricted to a few rare occasions, as it was generally too difficult to collect and compare data from field observations. With the advent of Internet markets, researchers have the ability to collect actual data from a large number of similar market transactions and perform statistical analyses. Section 5.7 will describe the results of field studies in online auction research.

4.5   Computational Economics and Simulation

Computational methods are a relatively new way of analyzing resource allocation mechanisms. Computational methods have spread across the broad front of economics to the point that there is now almost no area of economic research that is not deeply affected. This means that there is now a wide array of opportunities to push forward the understanding of economics using computational methods, including econometrics, macroeconomics, microeconomics, and qualitative economics. The Society of Computational Economics <http://wuecon.wustl.edu/sce/> has organized conferences in this field since 1995 and built up a growing community of economists interested in computational methods.

In a report of the NSF Workshop on Research Opportunities in Computational Economics (Kendrick, 1991), a group of scholars outlined opportunities in this very new field. The report mentioned microeconomics, game theory, and mechanism design as a few of the fields where computational methods might be a critical enabler:

Existing analytical approaches to mechanism design have yielded brilliant insights, but [they] have been limited to a small number of problems with very restrictive specifications of taste and technology in order to produce analytically tractable solutions.

In addition to methods such as mathematical programming and artificial intelligence, simulation methods are mentioned as a potential new methodology:

Simulation studies of the primary and secondary effects of complicated sets of rules such as tax codes and unemployment insurance [regulations] are proving to be extremely useful in microeconomic analysis. Simulation studies for devising institutions that improve markets such as varieties of electronic market making and looking at search techniques of market participants and their results are useful. (Kendrick, 1991)

4.5.1   *Economic Simulations*

Social scientists have always constructed models of social phenomena. A model is a simplification, less detailed and less complex of some other system (Gilbert and Troitzsch, 1999, p. 2). Simulation is a particular type of modeling. System simulation in economics has at least two origins. On the one hand, it continues mathematical modeling and is used wherever mathematics does not yield a closed analytical solution which is often the case in non-linear, and stochastic equations, or where a mathematical treatment of such equations would lead to a very complicated solution formula which would contribute less to understanding than a graphical representation of an equation system.

On the other hand, computer simulation is used in its own right, not as a substitution for more elegant mathematical solution algorithms, but "as a means of manipulating the symbols of the symbol system of programming languages" (Troitzsch, 1999). It enables a researcher to identify the structure of a system and understand its dynamics. Simulation has become a widespread method to help investigators check for inconsistencies, to test for empirical fits, and to derive new theoretical and practical results. Simulations may also be seen as a thought experiment which is carried out with the help of a computer. Ostrom (1988) points out that there are three different symbol systems used in social sciences – verbal argumentation, mathematics, and computer simulation. He also mentions that "simulation is neither good nor bad mathematics, but no mathematics at all."

Computer simulation has become an important new method for modeling social and economic processes (Gilbert and Troitzsch, 1999). In particular, it provides a "middle way" between the richness of discursive theorizing and rigorous but restrictive mathematical models. Simulations cannot provide a comprehensive system description but are an appropriate tool for analyzing dependencies between entities in a complex system. They have at least two purposes. One might be called explanatory, while the other comprises different types of prediction and prescription, including parameter estimation and decision making. The first question analyzes which kinds of behavior can be expected under arbitrarily given parameter combinations and initial conditions. The second question tries to find which kind of behavior a given target system will display in the future.

Acquiring sufficient understanding of a system to develop an appropriate conceptual, logical, and, finally, simulation model is one of the most difficult tasks in simulation analysis. After model validation and the calibration of parameters, the performance of a system can be evaluated in the form of a "what if" analysis, the heart of every simulation analysis. Simulation in natural sciences and engineering is used to distinguish between three different kinds of validity (see also Troitzsch, 1999):

- *Replicative validity*: The model matches data already acquired from the real system.
- *Predictive validity*: The model matches data before data are acquired from the real system.
- *Structural validity*: The model reproduces the observed real system, and reflects the way in which the real system operates to produce this behavior.

Since empirical data are often very poor in economics, simulation models try to be structurally valid and do not bother much about replicative or predictive validity. In designing, analyzing, and operating such complex systems, researchers are interested not only in performance evaluation but also in sensitivity analysis and optimization. A typical stochastic system has a large number of control parameters that can have a significant impact on the performance of the system. To establish a basic knowledge of the behavior of a system under variation of input parameter values and to estimate the relative importance of the input parameters, sensitivity analysis applies small changes to the nominal values of input parameters.

Monte Carlo, discrete event, and continuous simulations are the most widely used types of simulation methods. Monte Carlo simulations are appropriate for the analysis of static problems with known probability distributions. Discrete event simulations are simulations of dynamic systems which evolve in time by the occurrence of events at possibly irregular time intervals. Examples include queuing systems such as traffic systems, flexible manufacturing systems, computer-communications systems, production lines, and flow networks (Banks, Carson and Nelson, 1999). Most of these systems can be modeled in terms of discrete events whose occurrence causes the system to change from one state to another. In some systems, the state changes continuously, not just at the time of certain discrete events. For example, the water level in a reservoir with given inflow and outflow may change all the time. In such cases, continuous simulation is more appropriate, although discrete event simulation can serve as an approximation. Continuous simulation models typically contain a number of differential equations to model the time and state changes of the variables (Domschke and Drexl, 1998).

4.5.2   Agent-Based Computational Economics

Traditional economic models are based on a "top-down" view of markets or transactions. In general equilibrium theory, for example, solutions depend on an omnipotent auctioneer who brings all production and consumption plans throughout the economy into agreement. The mathematical modeling of dynamic systems such as artificial societies and markets often needs too many simplifications, and the emerging models may not therefore be valid. Operations research and system sciences often use simulation methods for analyzing stochastic problems which would otherwise require very complex mathematical models. Advances in information technology have made it possible to study representations of complex dynamic systems that are far too complex for analytical methods. Weather simulations are a good example of the potential for these methods.

A number of economists have started to explore different approaches to economic modeling. Here, the model maker has to specify in detail how agents evaluate information, form expectations, develop strategies, and execute their plans. Simulation is an appropriate methodology in all of these cases. This newly developing field, also called *agent-based computational economics* (ACE), is roughly defined as the computational study of economies, modeled as evolving decentralized systems of autonomous interacting agents (Tesfatsion, 1998). The models address questions which are often ignored in analytical theory such as the role of learning, institutions, and organization. ACE is a specialization of the basic *artificial life paradigm* to economics (Tesfatsion, 1997a). "Artificial life" is the name given to the discipline that studies "natural" life by attempting to recreate biological phenomena from scratch within computers.

Agents in ACE models are typically modeled as heterogeneous entities that determine their interactions with other agents and with their environment on the basis of internalized data and behavioral rules. These agents can be characterized by autonomous and intelligent behavior, an individual world view, as well as communicative and cooperative capacity – i.e. the agents can exchange information with their environment and with other agents. Consequently, they tend to have a great deal more internal cognitive structure and autonomy than can be represented by mathematical models. Most analytical models are restricted to the analysis of purely rational agents. In ACE models, evolution and a broader range of agent interactions are typically permitted.

A central problem for ACE is understanding the apparently spontaneous appearance of regularity in economic processes such as the unplanned coordination of trading activities in decentralized market economies which economists associate with Adam Smith's "invisible hand." Another objective is to develop individual strategies that individual agents can pursue and which ensure that a common goal can even be achieved without central regulation.

An example of this is the Trade Network Game (TNG) developed by Tesfatsion (1997b) for studying the formation and evolution of trade networks. TNG consists of successive generations of resource-constrained traders who choose and refuse trade partners on the basis of continually updated expected payoffs and evolve their trade strategies over time. Each agent is instantiated as an autonomous, endogenously interacting software agent with internally stored state information and with internal behavioral rules. The agents can, therefore, engage in anticipatory moments. Moreover, they can communicate with each other at event-triggered times. Experimentation with alternative specifications for market structure, search and matching among traders, expectation formation, and the evolution of trade site strategies can easily be undertaken.

Another recent example is IBM Research's "Information Economies" project. The project simulates price wars and dynamics in agent-based economies. Kephart, Hanson and Sairamesh (1998) consider the cases in which a broker sets its price and product parameters based solely on the system's current state, without explicit prediction of future events. The results show that the system's dynamic behavior in such shortsighted cases is generically an unending cycle of disastrous competitive "wars" in price/product space. In their 1998 paper, Tesauro and Kephart (1998) propose several heuristic approaches to the development of pricing algorithms for software agents that incorporate foresight, i.e. an ability to model and predict competitors' responses. They show how the introduction of even the smallest amount of prediction in the agents' pricing algorithms can significantly reduce or eliminate the occurrence of price wars.

However, simulations can not only be used as a tool to describe economic processes, but also to constructively design economic institutions. Roth (1999) used computational experiments and simulations in order to test the design of new labor markets:

Computational methods will help us analyze games that may be too complex to solve analytically. When game theory is used primarily as a conceptual tool, it is a great virtue to concentrate on very simple games. When game theory is used to study empirical environments, simplicity of the models is a more nuanced virtue. But when game theory is used for designing working markets, there is no choice but to deal with the complexities that the market requires.

Simulation of new market designs can play different roles, from explorations of alternative design choices, to data exploration, and theoretical computation. Section 7.2 will give a more detailed explanation of how simulation can be used for market design.

In this chapter we have concentrated on methods for the design of new mechanisms. Compared to physical markets it is rather easy to collect and evaluate transaction data in electronic markets. Many econometric methods such as regression models or time-series analysis have been developed to evaluate empirical data of this sort. These methods are crucial for the fine-tuning of parameters such as the optimal length of an auction period. Although important, these methods are not described, since this is beyond the scope of the book. The interested reader is referred to textbooks such as Johnston (1991) or Berthold and Hand (1999).

5   Automated Negotiations – A Survey of State-of-the-Art Practices

> Over forty years of intense theoretical research have failed to produce an adequate general, computational theory of bargaining and negotiation.
>
> *(Gresik and Satterthwaite, 1989)*

Negotiation is a crucial part of commercial activities in physical as well as in electronic markets (see section 1.3). Current human-based negotiation is relatively slow, does not always uncover the best solution, and is, furthermore, constrained by issues of culture, ego, and pride (Beam and Segev, 1997). Experiments and field studies demonstrate that even in simple negotiations people often reach suboptimal agreements, thereby "leaving money on the table" (Camerer, 1990). The end result is that the negotiators are often not able to reach agreements that would make each party better off.

The fact that negotiators fail to find better agreements highlights that negotiation is a *search process*. What makes negotiation different from the usual optimization search is that each side has private information, but neither typically knows the other's utility function. Furthermore, both sides often have an incentive to misrepresent their preferences (Oliver, 1997). Finding an optimal agreement in this environment is extremely challenging. Both sides are in competition but must jointly search for possible agreements. Although researchers in economics, game theory and behavioral sciences have investigated negotiation processes for a long time, a solid and comprehensive theoretical framework is still lacking. A basic principle of microeconomics and negotiation sciences is that there is not a single, "best" negotiation protocol for all possible negotiation situations. Different negotiation protocols are appropriate in different situations, and, thus, any generic mediation service should support a range of options (Wurman, Wellman and Walsh, 1998).

Recent developments in electronic markets' research offer the promise that new negotiation protocols will not only leave less money on the table but also will enable new types of transactions to be negotiated more cost effectively. There have been many approaches for supporting or automating commercial negotiations, and this section will provide an overview of the most recent.

5.1 A Roadmap to Negotiation Situations in Electronic Commerce

Chapter 4 shows how negotiations can be studied from multiple perspectives. Many analytical methods have their roots in economics where the first formal models of bargaining and negotiations were developed. Microeconomic theory is an excellent starting point for thinking about negotiation situations in electronic commerce. However, in order to cover the broad range of possible negotiation protocols, the framework needs to be extended. In the following section, a roadmap for negotiation situations in electronic commerce will be developed and approaches for supporting these different situations will be described.

As in microeconomic theory, an important characteristic of negotiations in electronic commerce is the number of participants on each side, ranging from one-on-one bargaining situations (1:1) to multiple participant negotiations ($m:n$). The *number of participants* on each side clearly affects the outcome of a negotiation. A monopolist can get a different deal from a vendor who is one of a hundred possible sellers. One-on-one negotiations are again quite different.

Economists also distinguish between *homogeneous and heterogeneous products* traded on a market (see section 3.1). For example, a standardized item (e.g. a stock) does not require a complex ontology. The items are easy to describe and negotiations focus mainly on the price. Complex goods such as cars, however, require a much more sophisticated IT infrastructure. Therefore, a more elaborate set of taxonomies and standards is needed to describe all attributes of a product, and there are more attributes to negotiate about than simply the price. Besides, time-sensitive information or perishable goods may impose tight constraints on the duration of the negotiation.

There should also be a distinction between situations where only a *single unit of a product* is traded at a point in time and *multi-unit* negotiations. The simultaneous assignment of multiple goods may improve the quality of an allocation and reduce the time required for the negotiation. In the multi-unit case, there is again a distinction between identical, homogeneous goods and heterogeneous goods. Multi-unit negotiations on homogeneous goods cover bids which contain price–quantity pairs. In the case of heterogeneous goods bidders can express preferences for certain combinations of products or product attributes.

Table 5.1. *Different types of negotiation situations*

Number of participants	Single-unit		Multi-unit	
	Homogeneous goods	Heterogeneous goods	Homogeneous goods	Heterogeneous goods
1:1	Negotiation support systems, Agent-based negotiations			
1:n	Single-sided auctions	Multi-attribute auctions	Multi-unit auctions	Combinatorial auctions
m:n	Double auctions	—	–discriminatory –uniform-price	Multi-attribute auctions

Single-unit negotiations also cover situations (e.g. in corporate procurement) where people bargain about identical goods and situations with heterogeneous goods where complex product descriptions need to be compared. A participant has to negotiate on the basis of the multiple attributes of the product. Negotiations on multiple issues are much more complex, for a number of reasons. Taking different combinations of these characteristics yields different negotiation situations (Bichler, 2000b). Table 5.1 provides a classification framework and a number of negotiation protocols which can be used in various situations. The mechanisms mentioned in table 5.1 will be covered in subsequent sections.

Of course, there are several other factors influencing the type of negotiation protocol required which are not covered in table 5.1. These factors have to be considered in all of the various negotiation situations. For example, a market designer has to determine whether she is concerned with a *cooperative or a competitive negotiation situation*. Game theory assumes that in a competitive situation there is at least some conflict of interest (e.g. bilateral price negotiations). Cooperative situations are described as non-zero-sum games where parties resolve a conflict over multiple interdependent but non-mutually exclusive goals. The degree of goal incongruency and the methods for managing the conflict which arises determine the best strategies for agents to adopt under different circumstances. Companies trying to define a contract about a joint venture might well discover cooperative aspects during the contract negotiations. This book is mainly concerned with competitive situations.

The *type of participants* can also play a role. Professionals such as market makers on a stock exchange or purchasing managers in business-to-business electronic commerce have a better knowledge about market conditions and products traded on a market than customers in a retail market and, thus, need a very different form of IT support (Guttman and Maes, 1998). Moreover, it makes a difference whether a market designer is concerned with a product such as insurance where participants require a high level of trust and where partners are reluctant to reveal too much information up front or she is concerned with a low-cost, low-volume retail transaction such as the purchase of groceries where trust and information revelation are not an issue. The interactions can be *mediated* by an outside third party to help in locating one another, negotiating and settling a deal, or they can be conducted directly between the negotiating parties. Moreover, there is a distinction between *one-time matching mechanisms* such as a first-price sealed-bid auction and *iterated* (*or multi-stage*) *negotiation* where some kind of back-and-forth negotiation takes place.

The following sections will describe negotiation protocols and how they can be deployed for use in the various types of negotiation situations. The section will begin with an overview of one-on-one bargaining and then introduce single-unit and multi-unit auction mechanisms. This book will focus on auction mechanisms since these are the most widespread form of negotiation protocols currently in use.

5.2 One-on-One Bargaining

Bargaining situations can concern as few as two individuals who may try to reach an agreement on any of a range of transactions. Over the past decade, there have been several approaches to supporting or describing one-on-one negotiations, ranging from game theory and negotiation support systems to intelligent agents who bargain the details and finally close the deal without any further user interaction.

5.2.1 Game-Theoretical Models of Bargaining

Many theories of negotiation and group decision have a common heritage in game theory (see section 4.2 for an introduction). Edgeworth (1881) noted that modeling traders only by their initial endowments and indifference curves, while often adequate for determining a unique competitive equilibrium in a market, would leave the outcome of bargaining indeterminate. With the advent of game theory, attempts were made to develop theories of bargaining which would predict particular outcomes of bargaining. John Nash (1950, 1953) initiated two related and influential approaches. In his 1950 paper, he proposed a model which predicted the outcome of bargaining based only on information about each bargainer's preferences, as modeled by an expected utility function over a set of feasible agreements and the outcome which would result in the case of a disagreement. Nash described a two-person multi-item bargaining problem with complete information and used the utility theory of von Neumann and Morgenstern (1944). In his 1953 paper, entitled "Two-Person Cooperative Games," Nash considered a simple model of the strategic choices facing bargainers and argued that one of the strategic equilibria of this game which corresponded to the outcome identified in his 1950 paper was particularly robust. Nash's approach for analyzing bargaining, using abstract models which focus on outcomes, in the spirit of "cooperative" game theory, and more detailed strategic models, in the spirit of "non-cooperative" game theory, has influenced many researchers.

Harsanyi and Selten (1972) extended Nash's theory of two-person bargaining games with complete information to bargaining situations with incomplete information and found several equilibria. Chatterjee and Samuelson (1983) studied a problem with two-sided incomplete information in which a single buyer and a single seller attempted to agree on the price of a single item. Each bargainer knew the potential value she placed on a transaction but had only probabilistic information concerning the value that the other player had placed on the transaction. Buyers and sellers submitted a single sealed bid and if the buyer's bid was greater than or equal to the seller's bid, the item was sold, at a price halfway between the two bids. Buyer and seller shaded their bids from their true valuations. Consequently, even when the buyer valued the good more than the seller, the optimal strategies often made a successful sale impossible because of imperfect information.

In dynamic (i.e. sequential) games, the players do not bid at the same time, but one player moves and then the other player responds. These dynamic games are more difficult to solve than static ones. Rubinstein (1982) calculated perfect equilibrium in a bargaining model which involved a pie, two players, and sequential alternating offers of how to split the pie. An accepted offer ends the game, a rejected one incurs a cost for each player and allows the other player to make an offer. Each player has her own different cost per time period. Rubinstein showed that if player 1 has a lower time cost than player 2, the entire pie will go to player 1. This work initiated a decade of intense interest in a variety of bargaining models, particularly models with incomplete information in which delay and inefficiency may arise. Most models with incomplete information exhibit a multitude of equilibria which are viewed in a negative light, owing to the fact that these models have little predictive power. In response, theorists have applied additional assumptions that guarantee unique equilibria. Watson (1998) gives an overview of outcomes in dynamic bargaining games. Rosenthal (1993) argues that in real-world situations players behave by rules of thumb instead of using optimal strategies for games. He presents a model in which individuals from two large populations expect to be randomly matched with a member of the other population on an ongoing basis to play a randomly selected game from some predetermined set each time. Before a game, each player must choose the rule of thumb by which she will play each type of game.

Game theory is the most rigorous approach towards conflict resolution and allows for formal problem analysis and the specification of well defined solutions. Many laboratory experiments have been designed to test the predictions of bargaining theories. Although some of their qualitative predictions have received some support, the existing models have performed poorly as point predictors (Kagel and Roth, 1995). Balakrishnan Sundar and Eliashberg (1995) point to several empirical studies, some of which suggest that fundamental concepts in game theory fail. Neslin and Greenhalgh (1986) present empirical evidence which shows that the outcomes of buyer–seller negotiations, for the most part, do not correspond to the settlement prescribed by Nash's theory of cooperative games.

Real-world negotiations are much more complex than has been described in formal models. Often formal models suffer from false assumptions or from assumptions that seem unreasonable and the results have very limited impact both on research in other areas and on real-life problem solving. Game-theoretical bargaining models assume perfect knowledge and rationality of participants and do not model factors such as the history of transactions and the negotiation process between two parties, or the quality and complexity of goods. Moreover, real-life agents are often constrained by the bounds of rationality, and the negotiations do not concentrate on price alone. Linhart and Radner (1992) summarize several restrictions regarding game-theoretical models of bargaining:

- Most models assume a common prior knowledge for the valuation of the negotiated object to the buyer and seller, yet "ordinary experience seems to indicate that what makes horse races is variation among priors."
- "In sealed-bid bargaining under uncertainty, there is a continuum of equilibria; even if only pure strategies are considered, empirical evidence suggests that regularities do exist. Even in the simple case of complete information, two famous axiomatic solutions (the Nash and the Kalai–Smorodinsky) predict different outcomes."
- "One frequently bargains over not just price but also quantity, various parameters of quality, delivery data, penalties for late delivery, and so on indefinitely" (Linhart and Radner, 1992).

In an oft-cited article, Myerson and Satterthwaite (1983) proved that given private information and individual incentives of two traders, no trading mechanism can be *ex post* efficient, i.e. can guarantee that a deal occurs given that the buyer's valuation is greater than the seller's. Myerson and Satterthwaite considered the case of a seller and a buyer, who are both risk-neutral and have independent private values for the object in question (see also subsection 5.3.6). This model concludes that the attainment of full *ex post* efficiency of resource allocation in bilateral bargaining problems cannot be guaranteed. The only exception would be if outside subsidies were paid into the system. In other words, optimal strategies for trade involving two-sided incomplete information are not only difficult to formulate and solve but also impossible in this model. Linhart, Radner and Satterthwaite add that "adequate theories of bargaining exist only for the degenerate, polar cases of perfect competition and monopoly" (Linhart, Radner and Satterthwaite, 1992). Although game theory has failed to describe human bargaining thus far, it is seen as a potential candidate for implementing negotiation strategies in agent-based environments (see subsection 5.2.3). The following subsection will focus more on human-factor approaches for supporting the negotiation process.

5.2.2   *Negotiation Analysis and Negotiation Support Systems*

Humans have been bargaining for thousands of years and many studies of the process focus on culture, politics, and tactics. There are several *qualitative theories* from the social sciences which analyze bargaining situations. Fisher and Ertel (1995) and Raiffa (1982), for example, focus on interpersonal bargaining and how to deal constructively with conflict. These theories stress behavioral and cultural issues and describe techniques such as looking for joint gains and separating the people from the issues. In contrast to game theory, negotiators and decision makers are assumed to be intelligent and goal-oriented individuals, rather than exhibiting full game-theoretical rationality. Parties can assess the attractiveness of the no-agreement situation and select possible agreements which yield higher utility without restricting its efficiency. This is, among other things, achieved with the specification of the *best alternative to negotiated agreement* (BATNA), which serves as a benchmark for compromise decisions.

Walton and McKersie (1965) proposed the classification of negotiations into *integrative* and *distributive* types. In distributive negotiations, one issue is subject to negotiation and the parties involved have opposing interests. Distributive negotiations are also characterized as win–lose negotiations. The more one party gets, the less the other party gets. Their interest in the other party goes only as far as the other party affects the achievement of their own objectives. Bargaining on price alone is an example for distributive negotiations. In integrative negotiations, multiple issues are negotiated and the parties involved have different preferences towards these issues. These variant valuations can be exploited to find an agreement with joint gains for both parties (so called "win–win negotiations"). In other words, integrative negotiations are based on the premise that solutions can be found during the process which reconcile the parties' interests. The two types of negotiations represent two extremes on a spectrum of mixed negotiations that involve a significant element of conflict and a considerable potential for cooperation (Walton and McKersie, 1965).

The distributive view of negotiations is typical for traditional economics but not for negotiation theory and practice, yet it underlies many of the approaches taken in the decision and computer sciences (Kersten and Noronha, 1999b). The negotiation literature which focuses on real-life negotiations states that parties should attempt to conduct integrative negotiations (Fisher and Ertel, 1995). Discussions and analysis of real-life negotiations in business and trade show the importance and benefits of integrative negotiations.

Negotiation analysis attempts to take the evolving nature of the process into account (Kersten, 1997). It is more of a framework of thought in which some analytical methods are used than a unified formal approach towards negotiations. The contribution lies in the consideration of new aspects disregarded in game-theoretical analysis. Most of the existing analytical approaches focusing on human factors assume a well defined and fixed situation (e.g. issues, parties, alternatives) that is being modeled and analyzed. This allows for the construction of mappings between the structure of the problem, preferences, and criteria, and the ultimate outcome which is a compromise or a set of efficient solutions. However, the negotiation behavior of the parties can change the problem structure and the outcomes. Thus, the negotiation analytic approach tends to downplay the application of game-theoretical solution concepts or efforts to find unique equilibrium outcomes. Instead, negotiation analysts generally focus on changes in perceptions of the zone of possible agreement and the distribution of possible negotiated outcomes, conditional on various actions (Sebenius, 1992). More quantitative approaches to negotiation analysis study the outcomes of bargaining situations in laboratory experiments. For example, Dwyer and Walker (1981) found in an experiment conducted with MBA students that a symmetric power distribution with a single buyer and a single seller led to fair outcomes and asymmetric power distribution (e.g. two buyers and a seller) created a powerful bargainer who achieved a very favorable agreement.

The results of qualitative and quantitative analysis cannot be directly applied to the automation of negotiations but they influence the design of so-called *negotiation support systems* (NSS). NSS are a special form of decision support systems which assist human negotiators in making a deal. The literature places a relatively heavy emphasis on human factors such as behavioral characteristics, cognitive differences, and negotiation theories, and most of these approaches focus on one-on-one negotiations about

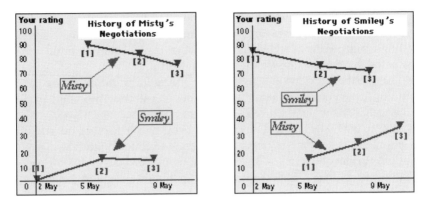

Figure 5.1 Graphical representation of negotiation dynamics for each of the two users in the INSPIRE system.

single as well as multiple attributes. NSS have seen commercial use in purchasing (Foroughi, 1995; Perkins, Hershauer, Foroughi and Delaney, 1996) and in operations management (Alty *et al.*, 1994). Kersten (1997) presents a survey on NSS for group decisions and bargaining and provides an overview of utility theory and artificial intelligence approaches. Recently, NSS have also been used over the Internet, with notable success in international applications where cultural barriers play a crucial role (Kersten and Noronha, 1998).

A good example of an Internet-based NSS is INSPIRE which is part of the InterNeg project of Carleton University (Kersten, 1998). INSPIRE is a web-based NSS for conducting bilateral business negotiations. Between July 1996 and August 1999, over 2,000 users from 80 countries have used the system. INSPIRE structures a negotiation and progresses through three distinct stages: negotiation analysis, bargaining, and post-settlement, i.e.:

■ Negotiation analysis involves understanding the negotiation problem, issues and options, and preference elicitation via hybrid conjoint analysis leading to the construction of a utility function (see the description of "conjoint analysis" in the appendix, p. 223).

■ The conduct of negotiation involves support for offer construction and counter-offer evaluation by means of ratings based on the utility function, and graphical representation of the negotiation's dynamics (see figure 5.1).

■ INSPIRE has also a post-settlement stage, during which it uses the preference information provided by each user to determine whether it is possible to construct packages that are better for the two parties.

In addition to the above three major functions there is a number of smaller auxiliary tools. The communication support functions include the exchange of structured offers with accompanying arguments, free-text messages, and an automatic e-mail notification of the opponent's activity (Kersten, 1997). Typically INSPIRE negotiations take up to three weeks. The process may result in a compromise, or one party may terminate the negotiation at any time. Upon completion of INSPIRE negotiations, users are requested to fill in a post-negotiation questionnaire.

The system uses the client–server model of distributed systems to partition the main components. The client comprises dozens of HTML pages as well as Java applets. They reside on the INSPIRE site but are displayed or executed on demand on the user's computer. The engine is a collection of programs in C++. These programs are executed on the INSPIRE host itself and invoked via the web server and the CGI protocol. A follow up system called InterNeg Support System (INSS) <http://interneg.org/tools/inss> is more flexible and allows, for example, the addition of new issues during the negotiation process.

While NSS often make negotiations more productive than would be possible without them, they require constant human input, and both the initial problem setup and all final decisions are left to the human negotiators.

5.2.3   Automated Agent-Based Bargaining

Several approaches from the distributed artificial intelligence (DAI) field attempted to achieve automated bargaining. They typically require programming autonomous software agents to negotiate with each other:

Autonomous agents are systems that inhabit a dynamic, unpredictable environment in which they try to satisfy a set of time dependent goals or motivations. Agents are said to be adaptive if they improve their competence at dealing with their goals based on experience. (Maes, 1997)

These software agents should be smart enough to bargain a favorable deal for the user. In order to be called an "intelligent agent" the software must satisfy several criteria which have been summarized in Weld (1995) and Werthner and Klein (1999):

- *Autonomy*: An agent can take initiative and control its own actions.
- *Temporal continuity*: The software is continuously executing.
- *Communication and cooperation*: The agent has the ability to be engaged in complex communication with the user or other agents.
- *Integration*: The agent must support an understandable and consistent interface.

- *Adaptability*: An agent should possess the ability to adapt itself automatically to the preferences of its user based on previous experience.
- *Mobility*: An agent can travel from one machine to another to achieve its goal.

Currently, no single implementation satisfies all of the criteria (Werthner and Klein, 1999, p. 117), but there are several promising results for bargaining, "intelligent" agents. The ContractNet Protocol proposed by Smith (1980) was an early architecture which enabled distributed problem solving. Different nodes in a network communicated to negotiate task allocation in a context of distributed sensing. Sandholm (1993) extended the ContractNet Protocol for decentralized task allocation in a vehicle routing context in a network of distributed agents called TRACONET. The architecture allowed multiple agents to pass private messages to each other in an asynchronous fashion, and it allowed the agents to enter and leave the system at any time. The ontology was restricted to a relatively simple messaging protocol which specified the load to be delivered, the bid price, and the acceptance or rejection of an offer. Despite several shortcomings, this was among the first automated multi-agent negotiation environments.

Another example of agent-based bilateral bargaining is Kasbah (Chavez and Maes, 1996). Kasbah is a marketplace for negotiating the purchase and sale of goods using one-on-one negotiation between multiple software agents. Software agents in Kasbah receive their complete strategies through a web form from the users who specify the way in which the acceptable price is allowed to change over time. The products are described using six characteristics, including the desired price, the transaction deadline, the reservation price, the price decay function, whether to obtain human user approval before finalizing the deal, and whether to send e-mail to the human user when the deal is closed. A description of what exactly the item comprised was left blank, and the attribute for negotiation was price alone. After buying and selling agents are matched, the only valid action in Kasbah's negotiation protocol is for buying agents to offer a bid to selling agents with no restrictions on time or price. Selling agents then have to accept or reject. The agents were created and piloted by human users in an experiment. An extension and redesign of MIT's Kasbah project is called Marketmaker <http://ecommerce.media.mit.edu/maker/maker.htm>.

ADEPT (Advance Decision Environment for Process Tasks) (Alty *et al.*, 1994) is a rather sophisticated approach where automated bargaining agents are programmed with formalized rules of thumb distilled from intuitions about good behavioral practice in human negotiations. Sierra, Faratin and Jennings (1997) formalizes a negotiating agent's reasoning component; in particular, they concentrate on the process of generating an initial offer, of evaluating incoming proposals, and of generating counter-proposals.

Offers and counter-offers are generated by combinations of simple functions, called tactics, which use a single criterion. Different weights in the combination allow the varying importance of the criteria to be modeled. A strategy denotes the way in which an agent changes the weights of the different tactics over time. Sycra (1991) introduces case-based reasoning to plan and support labor negotiations. Through the manipulation and merger of case elements, representation of a given negotiation problem is achieved. The construction of a new case which represents the negotiation which the user faces is guided by predefined utility values assigned to elements of past cases. The cases are also used to obtain argumentation for particular proposals.

There are also several approaches which use adaptive behavior and learn to solve the problem. Dworman, Kimbrough and Laing (1993) describes the idea that autonomous learning agents can discover a particular and attractive equilibrium in a certain class of games. Marimon, McGrattan and Sargent (1990) study a simple exchange economy in which agents must use a commodity or money as a medium of exchange in order to trade. The agents were artificially intelligent and modeled using classifier systems to make decisions. For most of the simulated economies, trading converged to a stationary Nash equilibrium even when agents started with random rules. Oliver (1996) provides a good overview of autonomous, intelligent agents and investigates two-person multi-issue negotiations. He uses genetic algorithms and genetic programming as a machine-learning technique for discovering effective negotiation strategies. Oliver found that agents can learn general negotiation strategies and also develop new strategies. Zeng and Sycara (1998) proposed a similar multi-agent system called Bazaar, where the agents learn based on genetic algorithms and they are capable of updating a negotiation's tactics using Bayesian probability. The major apparent disadvantage of genetic programming is that it requires many trials against opponents which need to be as realistic as possible in order to achieve the good strategies in the end. This may be unrealistic in real-world environments.

An interesting finding in this context is that, in many situations, simple, unintelligent agents achieve better results than sophisticated and complex, intelligent agents. Vidal and Durfee (1997) show in a model that dumb agents may be better in dynamic environments than smart ones and give mathematical proofs to explain this behavior. A similar result can be found in the Santa Fe Double Auction programming contest in the context of multilateral negotiations. Here, a simple "rule of thumb" agent was able to outperform more complex algorithms that used statistically based predictions of future transaction prices, explicit optimizing principles, and sophisticated learning algorithms (Rust, Miller and Palmer, 1993).

The danger is that these artificial agents will be badly exploited by new agents which have been programmed to take advantage of their weaknesses. Binmore and Vulkan (1999) emphasize the advantages of using game theory to predict the outcome of agent-based negotiations. Game theory has been criticized for its "hyper-rational" view of human behavior, but in the context of agent negotiations such hyper-rationality may be an appropriate model (Varian, 1995). Game theorists have been interested in the definition of protocols that limit the possible tactics that can be used by players (see section 4.2). Rosenschein and Zlotkin (1994) provide several bargaining protocols for autonomous agents, but they are relatively simple. An example is the *monotonic concession protocol* for two conflicting agents in which each agent must make a concession toward agreement or end the negotiation. If the negotiation ends without an agreement, each agent receives a payoff which is worse than the agreed payoff. Vulkan and Jennings extend this line of work and propose an auction-based negotiation protocol in which agents can follow a dominant strategy (Vulkan and Jennings, 2000). They argue that the high costs of counter-speculation can be reduced to a minimum in such an environment.

Much promising research is being conducted in the field of agent-based one-on-one negotiations, but the applicability of these models has not yet been demonstrated in commercial applications. If a greater market results in a higher number of agreement candidates, bargaining is more complex because it requires comparing multiple preference profiles and managing multiple simultaneous bilateral negotiation sessions. With regard to costs, the fact that transaction costs are low is not critical for bargaining because integrative negotiations do not rely on high quantities of standardized, simple interactions such as auctions. Interactions in integrative negotiations are much more unstructured and costs are generally associated with the decision process. To summarize the previous few sections: Although much research has been accomplished automated bargaining is currently restricted to a small number of applications in commercial environments.

5.3   Multilateral Negotiations

An auction is an effective way of resolving the one to many bargaining problem. (Binmore and Vulkan, 1999)

On the Internet, participants have access to a global market and there are multiple buyers and sellers even for very exotic kinds of products. Therefore, multilateral negotiation situations are ubiquitous. This section will concentrate on classic auction mechanisms and omit other multilateral negotiation protocols such as unstructured bidding, following the standard view among economists that an auction is an effective way of resolving the one-to-many or many-to-many negotiation problem.[1] Milgrom (1987) considers a seller in a weak bargaining position. Out of a wide variety of feasible selling mechanisms, he finds that conducting an auction without a reserve price is an expected-revenue-maximizing mechanism. Binmore (1985) even shows that the problem of multi-person bargaining becomes an auction in the case of perfect information. Their simple procedural rules for resolving multilateral bargaining over the terms of trade enjoys enduring popularity.

According to the experiments described in Roth (1995), the outcome of market competition is more likely to conform to game-theoretical rationality than the outcome of a bilateral negotiation. Bidding competition is also a good substitute for bargaining skills. Economists view competition as a means of setting prices right, thereby generating an efficient allocation of resources. Being a bid taker puts much less of a burden on the seller's knowledge and abilities than being a negotiator in a bargaining process, simply because she does not need to know the range of possible buyer valuations. The winning bid is on average below the item's true but unknown value, but with the introduction of more and more bidders, the price approaches its true value.

Auction theory has been among the most successful branches of economics in recent years. The theory has developed rapidly, and is increasingly being consulted for developing practical applications. A recent example of successful market design was the case of radio spectrum auctions by the US Federal Communications Commission (FCC) (see subsection 5.6.2). The US market for electric power is another good example. The problems here were the physics of power transmission and the line congestion that each transaction brought to other users of the network. Therefore, electricity markets not only have to match buyers and sellers but they also have to ensure the provision of adequate reserve capacity to increment and decrement the flows in response to network requirements. Economists designed auction markets, permitting decentralized decision making in situations where, before, decisions were necessarily made centrally, and often inefficiently (Wilson, 1999).

One reason for the great success of auctions on the Internet is simply their feasibility. The technical infrastructure required to support auctions in an online environment is currently available and well accepted. Internet auctions are similar to traditional auctions, but bids are placed by filling in

---

[1] Of course, it is clear that an auction is not always the appropriate matching mechanism. Field and Hoffner (1998) give an example of an electronic insurance marketplace where a multi-stage unstructured bidding process is used because of the special requirements for information revelation in this market.

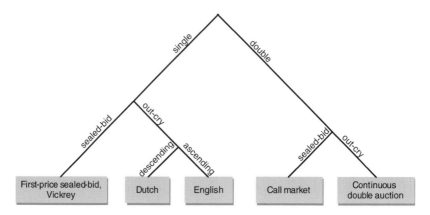

Figure 5.2 A classification of classic auction types.
Source: Wurman, Wellman and Walsh (2000).

an online form, possibly with room for a bidder's credit card number. After
the form is submitted, the web server processes the bid (see section 5.7).
The following subsection will provide an overview of basic auction formats
which can be used in one-to-many and many-to-many negotiation situations.

5.3.1 Basic Auction Formats

As already introduced in section 1.3, McAfee and McMillan have defined
auctions as "a market institution with an explicit set of rules determining
resource allocation and prices on the basis of bids from the market participants" (McAfee and McMillan, 1987). The competitive process serves to
aggregate the scattered information about bidders' valuations and to
dynamically set a price. In an auction, a bid taker offers an object to two or
more potential bidders who send bids indicating their willingness-to-pay
for the object (Milgrom and Weber, 1982). Four basic types of auctions are
widely used and analyzed: the ascending-bid auction (also called the open,
oral, or English auction), the descending-bid auction (or Dutch auction),
the first-price sealed-bid auction, and the second-price sealed-bid auction
(also called the Vickrey auction).

   Oral or open-cry auctions reveal price quotes and require public and
adjustable bids. After a certain elapsed time, the auction clears, meaning
that it matches buyers and sellers and determines the price. In the case of
an *English auction* the auctioneer begins at the seller's reservation price, and
solicits progressively higher oral bids from the audience until only one
bidder is left, thus making the reservation prices of all unsuccessful bidders

known. The winner claims the item at the price of the last bid. In a model often used by auction theorists (also called the Japanese auction), the price rises continuously while bidders gradually quit the auction. There is no possibility for one bidder to pre-empt the process by making a large "jump bid."

The descending auction works in exactly the opposite way: the auctioneer starts at a very high price, and then lowers the price continuously. In a *Dutch auction* the auctioneer begins with a price too high for anyone in the audience to pay, and regressively lowers the price until one bidder calls out that she will accept the current price. The winner claims the item, and pays the price she bid. This auction is often used in the Netherlands for the sale of flowers.

Sealed-bid auctions do not reveal price quotes and require private, committed bids which are opened simultaneously. The highest bidder acquires the object and pays the seller her own bid price in a *first-price sealed-bid auction*, and pays the second-highest bid price in a *second-price* or *Vickrey auction*. A little reflection shows that, in a second-price sealed-bid private values auction, it is optimal for a bidder to bid her true value, whatever other players do, i.e. truth-telling is a dominant strategy equilibrium (see section 5.3.2 for a detailed discussion). Of course, these single-sided auctions can also be reversed and used in the context of procurement.

Double auctions admit multiple buyers and multiple sellers at once. The continuous double auction (CDA) matches bids in the order received. When a new buy bid is processed, the auction checks whether the offered price matches the lowest (i.e. best) existing sell bid, and vice versa. On detection of a match, the auction clears at the price of the existing bid, and generates a new price quote. A transaction is completed when an outstanding bid or ask is accepted by another trader. The CDA is a common mechanism for organized exchanges such as stock and commodity markets. A periodic version of the double auction, termed a *call market* or *clearing house*, instead collects bids over a specified interval of time, then *clears* the market at expiration of the bidding interval at a price that maximizes the turnover. A Double Dutch auction is a laboratory generalization of a Dutch auction in which two price clocks are used alternately until they converge to a single price. In general, double auctions are not nearly as well understood theoretically as single-sided auctions.

These standard auction types are in common use. Wurman, Wellman and Walsh (2000) provide a description of the parameter space for designing auction mechanisms. The English auction is often used to sell art and other collectibles, for example. The Dutch auction is commonly used to sell perishables, such as flowers. First-price sealed-bid and second-price sealed-bid auctions are most often used in procurement situations. Double auctions are favored institutions for trading securities and financial instruments. The following subsection will summarize the most important game-theoretical models describing auction games.

5.3.2   The Independent Private Values (IPV) Model

Auctions have been used for ages, but they entered the literature on economics only relatively recently. A very early contribution was made by Vickrey. His auction papers were decidedly a major factor in his 1996 Nobel Prize, and his 1961 paper is still essential reading (Vickrey, 1961). In 1969, Wilson introduced the pure common value model (see subsection 5.3.5) and developed the first closed-form equilibrium analysis of the winner's curse. The full flowering of auction theory came at the end of the 1970s with contributions from Milgrom, Riley, Samuelson, and others. A very readable introduction to the state of the field up to the late 1980s is in McAfee and McMillan (1987). A newer survey can be found in Wolfstetter (1996).

Auctions are appropriate subjects for applications of game theory because they present explicit trading rules that largely fix the "rules of the game." Moreover, they present problems of practical importance for strategic behavior. Auctions are modeled as dynamic games under incomplete information (see subsection 4.2.3). The most thoroughly researched auction model is the symmetric *independent private values (IPV)* model. In this model:

- A single indivisible object is put up for sale to one of several bidders.
- Each bidder knows her valuation, $v \in \Re$ (which no one else does), and can revise her valuation when that of rival bidders is disclosed. If v is higher than the bid, $b \in \Re$, then the bidder makes a profit of $v - b$.
- All bidders are symmetric/indistinguishable (i.e. the values are drawn from a common distribution).
- Unknown valuations are independent, identically distributed, and continuous random variables.
- The bidders are *risk-neutral* concerning their chance of winning the auction, and so is the seller.
- The seller's own valuation or reservation price, r, is normalized to $r = 0$.

An example of an object which would fall under IPV would be a work of art purchased purely for enjoyment. It is interesting to learn if the auctions achieve the same equilibrium price, or if the different auction formats can be ranked in any order. IPV assumes strategic equivalence between the Dutch auction and the first-price sealed-bid auction as well as the English auction and the Vickrey auction (see table 5.2). That is, the best strategy for bidders is the same in both auction formats. Strategic equivalence between the Dutch auction and the first-price sealed-bid auction is intuitive to many

Table 5.2. *Strategic equivalence of single-sided auction formats*

First-price sealed-bid auction	⇔ Dutch auction
Second-price sealed-bid auction	⇔ English auction

people. In either case, a bidder has to decide how much she should bid or at what price she should shout "Mine" to claim the item. Therefore, the strategy space is the same, and so are the payoff functions and hence equilibrium outcomes. Putting it somewhat differently, when the Dutch and first-price sealed-bid auctions are modeled as strategic games, the games are identical.

Similarly, the English auction and the Vickrey auction are strategically equivalent, but for different reasons and only under the assumptions of the private values framework. In an English auction the bidders have a dominant strategy for bidding up to their private valuation, v. In the Vickrey auction, the dominant strategy is to bid the true valuation, v. To confirm this, consider bidding $v - x$ when your true value is v. If the highest bid other than yours is w, then if $v - x > w$ you win the auction and pay w, just as if you bid v. If $w > v$ you lose the auction and get nothing, just as if you bid v. But if $v > w > v - x$, bidding $v - x$ causes you to lose the auction and get nothing, whereas if you had bid v, you would have won the auction and paid w for a net surplus of $v - w$. So a bidder never gains, and might even lose if she bids $v - x$. Now consider bidding $v + x$ when your true value is v. If the highest bid other than yours is w, then if $v > w$ you win and pay w, just as if you bid v. If $w > v + x$ you lose and pay nothing, just as if you bid v. But if $v + x > w > v$, having bid $v + x$ causes you to win an auction you otherwise would have lost, and you have to pay $w > v$ so you get negative surplus.

The dominant bidding strategy in an English and a Vickrey auction does not depend on the number of bidders, risk attitudes, or the distribution from which private values are drawn; and, therefore, English and Vickrey auctions converge to a dominant equilibrium. The outcome of both auctions is also Pareto optimal. That is, the winner is the bidder who values the object most highly. The essential property of the English auction and the Vickrey auction is that the price paid by the winner is exclusively determined by rivals' bids. This is an interesting result for automated negotiation because bidding strategies in software agents can be very simple.

The outcomes of the English and second-price auctions satisfy a strong criterion of equilibrium: They are dominant equilibria – that is, each bidder has a well defined best bid, regardless of how high she believes her rivals will bid. In contrast, a first-price sealed-bid auction does not have a dominant equilibrium. Instead, the equilibrium satisfies the weaker criterion of

Nash equilibrium – Each bidder chooses her best bid given her guess at the decision rules being followed by the other bidders.

For further analysis, only the outcomes of two auctions have to be compared, e.g. the Vickrey and the first-price sealed-bid auction. In a first-price sealed-bid auction with incomplete information, the type of the player is simply her valuation. Therefore, a Bayes–Nash equilibrium for this game will be a function, $b(v)$ that indicates the optimal bid, b, for a player of type v. The standard procedure for solving a particular auction, like any other game, is to first solve equilibrium strategies and then compute equilibrium payoffs. This procedure can be applied to arbitrary probability distribution functions, not just to uniform distributions.

The Bayes–Nash equilibrium can easily be shown in a two-player first-price sealed-bid auction (Varian, 1992, pp. 280 ff.). Each player is assumed to follow an identical strategy. The function $b(v)$ is strictly increasing, i.e. higher valuations lead to higher bids. The inverse function $V(b)$ then gives the valuation of someone who bids b. The probability of winning for a bidder with valuation v is the probability that the other player's valuation is less than $V(b)$. Since v is uniformly distributed between 0 and 1, the probability that the other player's valuation is less than $V(b)$ is $V(b)$. In a two-player sealed-bid auction the expected payoff for a bidder is

$$(v-b)V(b) + 0[1 - V(b)]. \tag{5.1}$$

The first term is the expected consumer's surplus if she has the highest bid. The second term is the zero surplus she receives if she is outbid. The optimal bid must then maximize

$$(v-b)V'(b) - V(b) = 0. \tag{5.2}$$

Since $V(b)$ is the function that describes the relationship between the optimal bid and the valuation, this leads to

$$(V(b) - b)V'(b) \equiv V(b). \tag{5.3}$$

The solution to this differential equation is

$$V(b) = b + \sqrt{b^2 + 2C} \tag{5.4}$$

where C is a constant of integration. This leads to $V(b) = 2b$ or $b^*(v) = v/2$ which is the optimal bid in a Bayes–Nash equilibrium. That is, it is a Bayes–Nash equilibrium for each player in this two-player sealed-bid auction to bid half of her valuation. To generalize this, let n be the number of bidders participating in an auction. What is bidder i's best bid? If she bids an amount b_i and wins, she earns a surplus of $v_i - b_i$. The probability of winning with a bid b_i is the probability that all $n-1$ other bidders have valuations v_j such that $b(v_j) < b_i$. This probability is $[F(V(b_i))]^{n-1}$ where F

represents the distribution of valuations. Bidder i then chooses her bid b_i to maximize her expected surplus:

$$\pi_i = (v_i - b_i) \, [F(V(b_i))]^{n-1}. \tag{5.5}$$

By differentiating π_i, an optimally chosen bid b_i must satisfy

$$\frac{d\pi_i}{dv_i} = [F(V(b_i))]^{n-1}. \tag{5.6}$$

This is bidder i's best response to an arbitrary decision rule being used by his rivals. In a Bayes–Nash equilibrium, b_i corresponds to $b(v_i)$. When this is substituted into the optimality equation (knowing that $b^{-1}(b_i)$ is $V(b_i)$), an equation defining bidder i's expected surplus in a Nash equilibrium is obtained:

$$\frac{d\pi_i}{dv_i} = [F(v_i)]^{n-1}. \tag{5.7}$$

In a Nash equilibrium, all n bidders must maximize simultaneously, so that this condition must hold true for all n bidders. McAfee and McMillan (1987) solve this equation and show that for the case where the distribution of valuations F is uniform and the lowest possible valuation is zero, the bidder's optimal bid, $b^*(v)$, in a first-price sealed-bid auction is

$$b^*(v) = (n-1)v/n. \tag{5.8}$$

In other words, the bidder bids a fraction $n-1/n$ of her valuation, v. This result corresponds to the two-player game where $b^*(v) = v/2$. The bidder estimates how far below his own valuation the next highest valuation is on average, and then submits a bid that is this amount below his own valuation. Remember, the optimal bid in a Vickrey auction is $b^*(v) = v$. It can be shown that $b^*(v)$ is equal to the expected second-highest valuation condition on the bidder's valuation. From the point of view of the seller who does not know the winner's valuation, v_1, in a first-price sealed-bid auction the expected price is the expected value of $b(v_1)$, which in turn can be shown to be equal to the payment expected by the seller in a Vickrey auction (Milgrom, 1989).

Hence, on average, the price in a first-price sealed-bid auction is the same as in an English or second-price auction. Thus, the surprising outcome of the IPV model is that, with risk-neutral bidders, all four auction formats are payoff equivalent (Vickrey, 1961). This is also known as the *revenue equivalence theorem*. The revenue equivalence theorem does not imply that the outcomes of the four auction forms are always exactly the same. In an English or second-price auction, the price exactly equals the valuation of the bidder with the second highest valuation. In a first-price sealed-bid or

Dutch auction, the price is the expectation of the second-highest valuation. Note that the result applies both to the IPV and to the common value models (described in subsection 5.3.5), provided bidders' signals are independent. A detailed mathematical description of the proof is given in Klemperer (1999).

This result is in striking contrast to the apparent popularity of the English auction as an open-cry auction and the first-price sealed-bid auction. A strong argument for the English auction is its strategic simplicity. In this auction bidders need not engage in complicated strategic considerations. Even an unsophisticated bidder should be able to work out that setting a limit equal to one's true valuation is the best one can do. This is not the case in the first-price sealed-bid auction. This auction game has no dominant strategy equilibrium. As a result, understanding the game is more complex. There is also a simple reason why many people favor a first-price sealed-bid auction over a Vickrey auction, even though it is strategically more complicated than a Vickrey auction. Second-price auctions can easily be manipulated by soliciting phantom bids, which are very close to the highest submitted bid. The following subsection will analyze a few examples of auctions that violate the prerequisites of the IPV model and the resulting consequences.

5.3.3   Robustness of the IPV Results

Assuming the IPV model with risk-neutral agents, the amazing result is that all auctions share the same equilibrium payoffs. However, there are several deviations from the original model that violate the prerequisites of revenue equivalence, and, thus, fail to result in payoff equivalence. Under different modeling assumptions, auction theorists have shown that Vickrey's revenue equivalence theorem does not always hold true. A few of these cases will be discussed below.

5.3.3.1   Removing Bidder's Risk Neutrality

In the IPV context, the only risk bidders are assumed to have is the risk of losing the auction. Therefore, risk-averse bidders are not cautious, but anxious to win. If bidders are risk-averse, the extent of their aversion to risk will influence their bidding behavior. With *risk aversion*, the revenue equivalence theorem breaks down as first-price and Dutch auctions generate higher expected revenues than English or second-price auctions. The intuition behind this result can be seen by examining the problem facing an agent in a first-price sealed-bid auction. If she loses, she gets nothing, while if she wins, she obtains a positive profit which means she is facing risk. By marginally increasing her bid, she lowers her profit if she wins, but increases the probability of this event. The increment in wealth associated with winning the auction at a reduced bid counts less than the possible loss of not winning owing to such a bid. This risk aversion works to the seller's advantage (McAfee and McMillan, 1987, p. 719). If bidders are risk-averse, this does not affect the equilibrium strategy under the English auction. A seller should still optimally set a reserve price and possibly add an entry fee as well. In a Vickrey auction, risk aversion has no effect on a bidder's optimal strategy. Therefore, since standard auctions are revenue equivalent with risk-neutral bidders, a risk-neutral seller faced by risk-averse bidders *prefers the first-price or Dutch auction over the Vickrey or English auction.* Maskin and Riley (1984) develop and generalize these results. Page (1993) extends this work and develops a general auction model in which buyers and seller are risk-averse and private information is correlated.

5.3.3.2 Removing Independence of Private Values
Another crucial assumption of the IPV model is the independence of bidders' valuations. If the *independence assumption* from the IPV model is removed, then there is *correlation* among the bidders' valuations. The main consequence is that it makes bidders bid lower in a Dutch auction, but again it does not affect bidding in an English auction. Correlation in a first-price sealed-bid auction means that those with low valuations also think that it is more likely that rivals have a low valuation and, thus, shade their bids more. Consequently, high-valuation bidders do not have to bid so aggressively.

Milgrom and Weber (1982) introduced the similar concept of *affiliation* in bidders' valuations: "Bidders' valuations of an object are affiliated if they are not negatively correlated." In practice, affiliation means that given that one bidder believes an object is worth a large amount, the other bidders will not think the object is worth less. Again, when bidders with affiliated values participate in English auctions, the information disclosed during the bidding can cause the remaining bidders to privately revise their valuations and possibly raise them. This could be one reason why English auctions tend to yield higher average selling prices (McAfee and McMillan, 1987). Therefore, in the case of affiliated values, sellers should use the English auction because it yields the highest expected revenue, followed by the Vickrey auction. The first-price auction should yield lower revenues than the second-price auction. Moreover, a seller should still set reserve prices and entry fees.

5.3.3.3 Removing Symmetry
If the *symmetry assumption* from the IPV model is removed bidders fall into recognizably different classes, i.e. the private values are not drawn from a

common distribution. This again has no effect on the English auction. However, the revenue equivalence breaks down in the case of a first-price sealed-bid or Dutch auction. The first-price sealed-bid or Dutch auction can even lead to inefficient outcomes (McAfee and McMillan, 1987). Suppose, for example, there are two bidders, A and B, characterized by their random valuations between [0,5] and [3,7]. Consider the Dutch auction. Obviously, B could always win and pocket a gain by bidding the amount 5. But B can do even better by shading her bid further. But then the low-valuation bidder A can win with positive probability, violating Pareto optimality.

This is an important result for reverse auctions in the public sector where efficiency is crucial. If a public authority uses auctions as an allocation mechanism, this suggests that a Vickrey auction should be employed. Maskin and Riley (1993) suggest that the first-price sealed-bid auction tends to generate higher expected revenue when the seller has less information about bidders' preferences than bidders do about each others' preferences. If the seller is equally well informed and sets appropriate minimum prices, the ranking might be reversed.

5.3.3.4 *Introducing Uncertainty about the Number of Bidders*

Of course, the *number of bidders* also has an effect on the outcome of an auction. The more bidders (i.e. competition) there are, the higher the valuation of the second-highest-valuation bidder is on average. Thus, *on average the number of bidders increases the revenue of the seller*. In many auctions, bidders are *uncertain about the number of participants*. McAfee and McMillan (1987) explored this issue. They showed that if bidders were risk-averse and had constant or decreasing absolute risk aversion, numbers uncertainty led to more aggressive bidding in a first-price sealed-bid auction. However, numbers uncertainty has no effect on bidding strategies under the three other auction rules. Consequently, numbers uncertainty favors the first-price sealed-bid auction.

5.3.3.5 *Repeated Auctions*

In cases where a seller has several units of a good, she may also sell them sequentially, one unit after another. This is often done in the auctioning of wine, race horses, and used cars. In some of these markets, it was observed that prices tend to follow a declining pattern. Several explanations have been proposed to explain this phenomenon. Declining prices follow easily if each bidder's valuations for the different objects are independently drawn from an identical distribution, and each bidder wants to buy only one unit (Bernhardt and Scoones, 1994). In a study of sequential second-price auctions of identical objects, Weber (1983) pointed out that bidders should bid less than their valuation in the first round to account for the option value of participating in subsequent rounds. Since Weber assumed identical objects, bidders with a higher valuation also had a higher option value; and, therefore, they were advised to shade their bids in the first round by a greater amount than bidders with a lower valuation. This way, all gains from waiting are removed, and, as Weber showed, the expected prices in all rounds are the same.

5.3.3.6 Bidder Collusion

A crucial concern about auctions in practice is the ability of bidders to *collude* (also called bidder rings), but the theoretical work on this issue is rather limited. To rank different auctions in the face of collusion, suppose that all potential bidders have come to a collusive agreement. They have selected their designated winner who is assumed to be the one with the highest valuation, advising her to follow a particular strategy, and committing others to abstain from bidding.

Robinson (1985) makes the point that a collusive agreement may be easier to sustain in a second-price auction than in a first-price auction. In a Dutch or first-price sealed-bid auction the designated winner will be advised to place a bid slightly higher than the seller's reservation price, whereas all other ring members are asked to abstain from bidding. However, each bidder can gain by placing a slightly higher bid, in violation of the ring agreement. Not so under the English or Vickrey auction. Here, the designated bidder is advised to bid up to his own valuation and everybody else is advised to abstain from bidding. No one can gain by breaking the agreement because no one will ever exceed the designated bidder's limit. That is, the English auction is particularly susceptible to auction rings, and the bid taker should opt for a Dutch instead of an English auction if she is dealing with an auction ring.

Even if auction rings can write enforceable agreements, the ring faces the problem of how to select the designated winner and avoid strategic behavior by ring members. This can be done by running a pre-auction. In a pre-auction, every ring member is asked to place a bid, and the highest bidder is chosen as the ring's sole bidder at the subsequent auction. However, if the bid at the pre-auction affects only the chance of becoming designated winner at no cost, each ring member has a reason to exaggerate her valuation. This problem can be solved only if the designated winner shares her alleged gain from trade. Graham and Marshall (1987) proposed a simple scheme for the pre-auction. Essentially, the scheme uses an English auction to select the designated winner. If the winner of the pre-auction also wins the main auction, she is required to pay the other ring members the difference between the price paid at the main auction and the second-highest bid from the pre-auction.

In summary, the common auction institutions are all simple and robust, they work well in a variety of environments, and usually lead to a tolerably efficient allocation of the items being sold. For fixed quantity environments, the English auction possesses a variety of characteristics that help explain its popularity. It leads to efficient outcomes in a wide range of environments and it economizes on information gathering and bid preparation costs.

5.3.4   *Optimal Auction Design*

An important branch of traditional mechanism design theory is concerned with the design of *optimal mechanisms and auctions*. One direction in optimal auction theory is concerned with the design of efficient mechanisms (Vickrey, 1961). Here, the primary objective of the planner is to maximize social efficiency. Another branch of theory concentrates on auctions which *maximize the expected revenue of the seller*. This theory uses mechanism design techniques to characterize, in general terms, the auction that maximizes the seller's expected revenues. One of the main conclusions of optimal auction theory is that for many distributions of private information (normal, exponential, and uniform distribution) *the four standard auction forms with suitably chosen reserve prices or entry fees are optimal* from the perspective of the seller.

Myerson (1981) proposes a general approach towards optimal auction design based on mechanism design theory, in particular on the revelation principle. That is to say, in the context of auctions a designer may restrict attention, without loss of generality, to incentive compatible, direct auctions (see section 4.3). Therefore, the auction that is optimal among the incentive compatible direct auctions is also optimal for all types of auctions. An auction is called "direct" if each bidder is asked only to report her valuation to the seller, and the auction rules select the winner and the bidders' payments. Sealed-bid auctions are direct, English and Dutch are not. A direct auction is incentive compatible if honest reporting of valuations is a Nash equilibrium. A simple case is an auction where truth-telling is a dominant strategy. Vickrey showed that a second-price sealed-bid auction is incentive compatible in the sense of a dominant strategy mechanism. Since optimality is considered from the point of view of the seller, incentive compatibility requires only that buyers reveal their valuations, but not that sellers report their own valuations.

The significance of the revelation principle is that it shows how the modeler can limit his search for the optimal mechanism to the class of direct, incentive compatible mechanisms. This is helpful as the number of possible auction formats is huge, and attention can be restricted to one relatively simple class of mechanisms. The optimal direct mechanism can be found as the solution to a mathematical programming problem involving two kinds of constraints: individual rationality and incentive compatibility. Individual rationality means that the bidders would not be better off if they refused to participate.

Riley and Samuelson (1981) begin with a simple characterization of revenue equivalence relationships and then reduce the optimal auction problem to the *optimal choice of the reservation price*. That is, an optimal auction requires the seller to set a reserve price, r, below which she will not sell the item and make it public (i.e. a minimum bid). This price is set to mimic the expected bid of the second-highest bidder and is greater than the seller's reserve valuation, v_0. The optimal level of the reserve price is determined by a trade-off. The disadvantage of setting a reserve price is that it is possible for the remaining bidder to have a valuation that lies between the seller's valuation and the reserve price, $v_0 < v < r$. In this case, the seller loses the sale even though the bidder would have been willing to pay the seller more than the product is worth. On the other hand, if the reserve price is above the second-highest bidder's valuation, the bidder pays more than she would have in the absence of the reserve price. In summary, the seller imposes the reserve price in order to capture some of the informational profits that would otherwise have gone to the winner.

Riley and Samuelson derive the reservation price for the seller optimal auction. Remarkably, this optimal reserve price is independent of the number of bidders n. This is a powerful result, as no restrictions have been placed on the types of policies the seller can use. For instance, the seller can have several rounds of bidding, or charge entry fees, or allow only a limited time for the submission of bids. None of these procedures would increase the expected price for the seller.

Bulow and Roberts (1989) showed the relationship of optimal auction theory to the theory of price differentiation in monopolies. In an optimal auction, the objects are allocated to the bidders with the highest marginal revenues, just as a price-discriminating monopolist sells to buyers with the highest marginal revenues. Moreover, just as a monopolist should not sell below the price where marginal revenue equals marginal cost, an auctioneer should not sell below a reserve price set equal to the value of the bidder whose marginal revenue equals the value of the auctioneer retention of the unit.

The results of optimal auction theory have also been criticized because the results so far seem to be of theoretical rather than practical significance. For most practical purposes, the cited models do not seem to be realistic enough. "The 'optimal' auctions are usually quite complex, and there is no evidence for their use in practice" (Rothkopf and Harstad, 1994).

5.3.5   *The Common Value Model*

Another approach for analyzing auctions is the *common value model* which assumes that the valuation of an object by a bidder is determined both by the private signal mentioned above and also by one or more external factors, such as the object's resale value or the opinions of other bidders. In this case, expert opinions or information about competing bidders' valuations of the object may change the bidder's perceived valuation. In a famous experiment, Bazerman and Samuelson (1983) filled jars with coins and auctioned them off to MBA students. Each jar had a value of US $8 which was not made known to bidders. A large number of identical runs were performed. The average winning bid was US $10.01; and, therefore, the average winner suffered a loss. That is, the winners were the ones who lost wealth (the so-called "winner's curse").

Many auctions involve some common value element where the value of the product is not known or is unsure during the auction. As an illustration you may think of oil companies interested in the drilling rights to a particular site that is worth the same to all bidders. Even if bidders at an art auction purchase primarily for their own pleasure, they are usually also concerned about the eventual resale value of the artwork. This suggests that a comprehensive theory of auctions should cover private as well as common value components.

In a pure common value auction, a theoretical simplification, the item for sale has the same value for each bidder. At the time of bidding, this common value is unknown. Bidders may have some imperfect estimate, but the item's true value is known only after the auction has taken place. Suppose all bidders obtain an unbiased estimate of the item's value, then the auction will select the one bidder who made the most optimistic estimate as the winner. Failure to take into account the bad news about others' signals that comes with any victory can lead to the winner paying more than the item is worth. Increasing the number of bidders has two conflicting effects on equilibrium bids. On the one hand, competitive considerations require more aggressive bidding. On the other, accounting for the adverse selection bias requires greater discounts.

Wilson (1977) defined a symmetric Nash equilibrium of the common value auction game which was generalized by Milgrom and Weber (1982). The main lesson learned from the analysis of the common value model is that bidders should adjust their bids downwards accordingly since auctions always select the bidder who received the most optimistic estimate of the item's value as the winner, and, thus, induce an adverse selection bias. Consequently, if the agents have uncertain correlated values, then, even in an incentive compatible auction, an agent should generally bid below the estimated valuation in order to avoid the "winner's curse." Altogether, common value auctions are more difficult to play, and unsophisticated bidders may be susceptible to the winner's curse. Of course, the winner's curse cannot occur if bidders are rational and properly account for the adverse selection bias. However, experimental evidence demonstrates that it is often difficult to bid rationally in a common value auction.

5.3.6 Double Auctions

Until recently, there have been no adequate theories of double auction markets in terms of games with incomplete information because of the difficulties in modeling strategic behavior on both sides of the market. In a double auction, buyers and sellers are treated equally with buyers submitting bids and sellers submitting asks. Thus, the double auction literature provides a link to the bargaining models discussed in section 5.2. The seminal model is the k-double auction of Chatterjee and Samuelson (1983) in which a single buyer and a single seller submit a bid b and an ask s. If the bid exceeds the ask a trade is consummated at the price $kb + (1 - k)s$ where $0 <= k <= 1$. For instance, if $b = 30$, $s = 20$, and $k = 1/2$, this results in a price of 25. Of course, both buyer and seller have an incentive to misrepresent their true values, so deals that are efficient will not necessarily be made.

Related work includes Myerson and Satterthwaite's (1983) analysis of mechanism design for bilateral trading. They show that the symmetric version ($k = 1/2$) of Chatterjee and Samuelson's two-player double auction is in fact an optimal mechanism in that it maximizes the expected gains from trade, especially if the agents' valuations are independently drawn from identical uniform distributions. This result also demonstrates that *ex post* efficiency cannot be achieved in bargaining between a seller who initially owns the asset and a buyer when there is private information about valuations (see also subsection 5.2.1).

Wilson (1985) and Satterthwaite and Williams (1989) studied the generalization of this to the multi-buyer/multi-seller case in which each agent can trade at most one indivisible unit for money. Each seller offers one indivisible unit and each buyer demands one unit; their valuations are independent and identically distributed on the same interval, the traders are risk-neutral, and the numbers of sellers and buyers are common knowledge. If the clearing price is p, then a trader's payoff is $p - v$ or $v - p$ for a seller or buyer with the valuation v who trades, and zero otherwise. A symmetrical equilibrium comprises a strategy σ for each seller and a strategy ρ for each buyer where each strategy specifies an offered ask or bid price, depending on the trader's privately known valuation. The key result is that a double auction is efficient, in the sense that with sufficient buyers and sellers there is no other trading rule for which, dependent on agents' values, it is common knowledge that all agents would be better off in expectation. Several other approaches have followed (see Wilson, 1992, for a review of research along these lines). Gode and Sunder's budget-constrained zero intelligence trading model describes buyers who bid randomly between their valuation and zero, and sellers who offer randomly between their cost and the upper boundary of cost distribution (Gode and Sunder, 1993).

Wurman, Walsh and Wellman (1998) have taken a constructive approach and developed and analyzed a number of new double auction formats. They introduce the so-called Mth-price auction and the $(M+1)$st-price auction. In a market with a set of L single-unit bids, M bids are sell offers and the remaining $N = L - M$ bids are purchase offers. The Mth-price auction clearing rule sets the price as the Mth highest among all L bids. Similarly, the $(M+1)$st-price rule chooses the price of the $(M+1)$st bid. The Mth and $(M+1)$st prices determine the price range that balances supply and demand. Consider a simple case where there is one buyer willing to pay no more than US $\$x$, and one seller willing to accept no less than US $\$y$, with $x > y$. The Mth price is US $\$x$, and the $(M+1)$st price is US $\$y$. If the price is above US $\$x$, then no agent would be willing to buy. Only if the price is between US $\$x$ and US $\$y$, is the excess demand zero.

In fact, the Mth and $(M+1)$st-price rules belong to the class of k-double auctions already mentioned. In a k-double auction the parameter $k \in [0,1]$ specifies the fraction between the $(M+1)$st and the Mth prices at which the clearing price is set. Wurman's analysis concentrates on the two extreme points 0 and 1 of the equilibrium price range. When $M = 1$, the Mth price is simply the highest bid and the $(M+1)$st price corresponds to the second highest which is equal to a Vickrey auction. Wurman, Walsh and Wellman (1998) show that the $(M+1)$st-price sealed-bid auction is incentive compatible for single-unit buyers and that the Mth-price sealed-bid auction is incentive compatible for single-unit sellers under the IPV model. This incentive compatibility result cannot be extended to multi-unit bids, or simultaneously to both, buyers and sellers.

5.4   A Critical Review of Game-Theoretical Auction Models

The volume of transactions conducted through the use of auctions gives meaning to their theoretical study. Many scholars criticize the limited usefulness of much theory to those who decide how much to bid and those who design auctions. Of course, many issues of game-theoretical models such as the revenue equivalence or the winner's curse have also been discussed by practitioners. However, Rothkopf and Harstad (1994) state that "we are not aware of any bidders using game-theoretical models directly to decide how much to bid in particular auctions. Nor are we aware of bidders in oral auctions directly using formal bidding models." This should not discourage the use of formal models, but encourage researchers to enrich current models through additional aspects, and to analyze auction institutions from different perspectives and with a variety of different methodologies. Some of the main reasons why game-theoretical models are poor point predictors in real-world auctions will now be summarized.

5.4.1 Behavioral Aspects

Behavioral research has shown that many social factors influence a bidder's behavior. For example, in a sociological treatment, Smith (1989) claims that the mechanical law of supply and demand rarely governs the auction process. Rather, value is determined by a complex social process combining both the beliefs and actions of the auction participants and the assumptions and practices on the auction floor. In summary, the bidders' rationality assumed in game-theoretical models is hardly given in real-world auctions, which is also a main reason for the poor predictive quality of game-theoretical models.

Many behavioral assumptions in standard auction models are described as naive by commercial auctioneers. For example, a behavioral assumption that underlying probability distributions which generate bidders' information are commonly known is prevalent in the literature, but often untenable in practice. Commercial auctioneers have also described as unrealistic the common assumption that the auction form is chosen to maximize expected revenue. Auctioneers strive for a balance in prices high enough to keep sellers consigning assets to them for sale, yet low enough to keep bidders attracted in sufficient numbers.

Modelers need to be aware of the fact that the outcome of auction models is very sensitive to the assumptions which are made about the economic agents. In many auction models, a bid taker is better off with a greater number of competing bidders. Suppose, however, the model is enriched to let bidders participate only when a rational calculation shows that the prospect of winning is worth the cost of participating. Thus, in a wide variety of circumstances, the bid taker prefers policies yielding less bidder participation (Rothkopf and Harstad, 1994, p. 365).

5.4.2 Information Feedback in Open-Cry Auctions

Game-theoretical research often limits the analysis on direct revelation mechanisms, which is a consequence of the revelation principle (see section

4.3). The idea of restricting one's attention to direct revelation mechanisms in which an agent reports all of her characteristics has also been criticized because it provides little guidance for those interested in actual mechanism design.

One of the disadvantages of a direct revelation auction is that there is no opportunity for the bidders to react to other bids, but instead estimates of other bidders' strategies need to be used. Speaking from a purely theoretical point of view, this should yield the same results; but, in practice, things often work out differently. For instance, FreeMarkets Online claims on their web site <http://www.freemarkets.com> that they achieve savings of up to 25 percent when using an English auction instead of a sealed-bid auction. One hypothesis is that information feedback conveys a higher sense of competition among bidders, and will have a positive impact on the efficiency of the auction. This might be a reason why there has been limited success in using game theory to explain the existence of pervasive institutions such as the English auction.

5.4.3   *Auctions in an Economic Context*

Up until now, game-theoretical auction models have considered single, isolated markets, whereas in real-world environments there are often a number of competing markets and there is a possibility of arbitrage. Auctions are embedded in a set of economic and social relationships that may be affected by the outcome of the auction, and these relationships can have a huge effect on the performance of future auctions. Just as general equilibrium theory has highlighted inter-relations across markets in an economy, behavior in auctions tends to be altered by the context in which the auctions arise.

This also implies that the information revealed in one auction will influence future ones. A seller will adjust his reserve price based upon the information garnered from previous sales of related assets. Similarly, a bidder will adjust his willingness-to-pay for an asset and perhaps even his decision to participate in a sale based upon his interpretation of prices fetched in previous sales. Standard game-theoretical models of auctions make no mention of the effects of price information following bid submission since most theory relates to single-period auctions in which such feedback is considered irrelevant.

In the USA, government agencies typically report back the full set of bids, along with bidders' names, since they are required to do so by law, but the private sector typically does not report any prices to losing bidders, telling them only that they were not successful. Isaak and Walker (1985) have studied the effects of price information feedback in IPV auctions. They found that in first-price auctions with four bidders, prices under the condition of limited information were consistently higher than under the condition of full information, but there were no significant differences in efficiency between the two information conditions. Subsequent laboratory experiments analyzed the effects of price information in the multiple rounds of sealed-bid auctions, but did not find a significant effect on bidding (Battalio, Kogut and Meyer, 1990; Cox, Smith and Walker, 1994). However, this issue needs to be examined more thoroughly.

5.4.4   Basic Assumptions of Game-Theoretical Models

Among the common assumptions of game-theoretical models is symmetry of bidders, common knowledge, a fixed number of bidders, and unbending rules. Many of these basic assumptions are not given in practice. In particular when online auctions are considered, bidders cannot be assumed to have a common knowledge and the number of bidders varies. Of course, in reality bidders often look for ways to bend, change, or get around the auction rules.

Game-theoretical auction theory tends to take mathematical formalism seriously and in doing so may lose insights from less rigorous analyses. While all models necessarily abstract from some aspects of reality, auction models have shown a tendency for the answers to change as enrichments to their realism are introduced (e.g. the introduction of risk-averse bidders in subsection 5.3.3.1). Whether game-theoretical models of competitive bidding can be made realistic enough so that bidders will have reason to use them remains to be seen.

Nevertheless, game-theoretical models are helpful to the extent that their answers approximate observations in real-world environments. The theory provides useful metaphors for thinking and communicating about auctions, and the modeling presents a variety of useful, but sometimes misunderstood, examples of causal relationships. In order to get a more complete picture of real-world auction processes, research needs to analyze auctions from different perspectives.

Although auction theory falls short in explaining human behavior in real-world auctions, most of the assumptions of the game-theoretical models are reasonable in an agent-based economy (e.g. perfect rationality). So far, many of the approaches for designing multi-agent systems have focused on the intelligence of agents and concentrated on teaching them effective strategies for negotiation and coordination. The need for broad adaptability of agents, however, suggests that as little as possible should be encoded directly into automated agents, simply because an artificial agent must guard against dynamic strategies that could extract private information like reservation prices or bid strategies (Oliver, 1996). Therefore, many new projects focus more on the environmental rules, requiring relatively little processing from the software agents.

A goal is to design the protocols of the interaction so that desirable social outcomes follow even though each agent acts based on self-interest (Sandholm, 1993). Incentive compatible auction mechanisms such as the Vickrey auction can avoid strategic behavior of agents by making truth-telling a dominant strategy. If agents use an incentive compatible auction mechanism, then there is no need for the agents to worry about keeping their valuation private (Varian, 1995; Zelewski, 1998). In particular, dominant strategies have several desirable properties when applied to automated agents. First, they permit a much weaker form of rationality. If agents can reach the equilibrium by elimination of dominated strategies, then this can be done with relatively little counter-speculation about what the other players will do. Given the complexity of counter-speculations, mechanisms that rely on dominant strategies are clearly desirable. Second, a mechanism that relies on dominant strategies will be robust even if the computational economy is invaded by one or more irrational agents (Vulkan and Jennings, 2000).

5.5   Experimental Analysis of Standard Auction Mechanisms

Because auctions are such simple and well defined economic environments, they provide a very valuable testing-ground for economic theory. Experimental economists have conducted a considerable number of auction experiments testing the results of auction theory described in the last section. Another scientific purpose of experiments is to discover empirical regularities in areas for which existing theory has little to say. Kagel and Roth (1995) give a comprehensive overview of experimental auction analysis.

Many experiments are conducted in order to test game-theoretical results and, therefore, deploy similar experimental procedures. An experimental session typically consists of several auction periods in each of which a number of subjects bid for a single unit of a commodity under a given pricing rule. The item is often referred to as a "fictitious commodity," in order to keep the terminology as neutral as possible. Subjects' valuations are determined randomly prior to each auction and are private information. Valuations are typically independent and identical draws from a uniform distribution where the lower and the upper boundary are common knowledge. In each period, the highest bidder earns a profit equal to the value of the item minus the price; other bidders earn zero profit for that auction period.

In sealed-bid auctions, after all bids have been collected, the winning bid is announced. English auctions have been implemented using an open-outcry procedure where bidding stops when no one indicates a willingness to increase the price any further, and an English clock procedure (Japanese auction) where prices begin at some minimal value and increase automatically, with bidders indicating the point at which they choose to drop out of the auction. Subjects are sometimes provided with examples of valuations and bids along with profit calculations to illustrate how the auction works. Sometimes experimenters perform only dry runs with no money at stake to familiarize subjects with the auction procedures.

5.5.1   Tests of the Revenue Equivalence Theorem

Tests of the revenue equivalence theorem involve two basic issues. Some test the strategic equivalence of first-price and Dutch auctions and of second-price and English auctions. Others test revenue equivalence between first-price/Dutch auctions and second-price/English auctions. Given the strategic equivalence of these different auctions, average prices are predicted to be the same, independent of bidders' attitudes towards risk.

The experimental data show that subjects do not behave in strategically equivalent ways in first-price and Dutch auctions or in English and second price auctions (Cox, Roberson and Smith, 1982). Bids in single unit first-price and Dutch auctions are commonly above the risk-neutral Nash equilibrium bidding strategy consistent with risk aversion. Prices are also above the equilibrium dominant bidding strategy in second-price sealed-bid auctions, although here bidding is independent of risk attitudes. In English auctions, bidding generally converges to the dominant strategy prediction. There are several explanations for the lower bidding in Dutch versus first-price auctions. In one model, Dutch auction bidders update their estimates of their rivals' valuations, assuming them to be lower than they initially anticipated as a consequence of no one having taken the item as the clock ticks down.

Kagel, Marstad and Levin (1987) also report failures of strategic equivalence in second-price and English auctions. In Vickrey auctions, prices average 11 percent above the dominant strategy price. Bidding above the dominant strategy in second-price auctions has been found in a number of other experimental settings. Kagel and Levin (1985) report that in an experiment 30 percent of all bids were at the dominant strategy price, 62 percent of all bids were above the dominant strategy price, and only 8 percent of all bids were below. In contrast, in English auctions market prices rapidly converged to the dominant strategy price. Bidding above the dominant strategy price in a Vickrey auction is mostly based on the illusion that it improves the probability of winning with little cost as the second-highest bid price is paid. Further, the idea that bidding modestly above the dominant strategy bid increases the chances of winning only in cases where you do not want to win is far from obvious.

There has been considerable debate among experimenters regarding the role of risk aversion in bidding above the risk-neutral Nash equilibrium strategy. The work of Cox, Smith and Walker (1983) demonstrates that a model of heterogeneous risk-averse bidders provides a better fit to the experimental data than homogeneous risk-neutral, or risk-averse, bidding models. The model argues that deviations from risk neutrality observed in first-price sealed-bid auctions may be a consequence of low expected costs of deviation from the risk-neutral Nash equilibrium strategy.

A recent field experiment of revenue equivalence in online auctions (see section 5.7) was conducted by Lucking-Reiley (2000). Vickrey's predicted equivalences between first-price sealed-bid and Dutch auctions, and between second-price sealed-bid and English auctions (Vickrey, 1961), were tested using field experiments that auctioned off collectible trading cards over the Internet. The results indicate that the Dutch auction produces 30 percent higher revenues than the first-price auction format, a violation of the theoretical prediction and a reversal of previous laboratory results, and that the English and second-price formats produce roughly equivalent revenues, consistent with Vickrey's theoretical IPV model, although bid-level data indicate some tendency for bidders to bid higher in the English than the second-price auction format. Of course, the particularities of the auction software in use can influence the result of various auction formats which might also be a reason for the higher revenues of the Dutch auction in these field experiments.

In summary, in private value auctions the revenue equivalence theorem fails in most experimental tests. In many auction experiments, subjects do not behave in strategically equivalent ways in first-price and Dutch auctions or in English and second-price auctions. Bidding above the dominant strategy in second-price auctions is relatively widespread, whereas, in English auctions, market prices rapidly converge to the dominant strategy price. The behavioral breakdown of the strategic equivalence of first-price and Dutch auctions and of second-price and English auctions is analogous to the preference reversal phenomenon where theoretically equivalent ways of eliciting individual preferences do not produce the same preference ordering. There is even a small amount of literature by psychologists showing that dominance is often violated in individual choice settings when it is not transparent which would explain bidder behavior in Vickrey auctions.

5.5.2   *Analysis of Efficiency, Varying Numbers of Bidders, etc.*

(Pareto) efficiency in private value auctions is measured in terms of the percentage of auctions where the high-value holder wins the item. Cox, Roberson and Smith (1982) observed different efficiency in first-price and Dutch auctions. They found that 88 percent of the first-price auctions and 80 percent of the Dutch auctions were efficient. The frequency of Pareto efficient outcomes in Vickrey auctions is quite comparable to first-price sealed-bid auctions. For example, 82 percent of the first-price auctions and 79 percent of the Vickrey auctions reported in Kagel and Levin (1993) were Pareto efficient.

Theory also predicts that if bidders have constant or decreasing absolute risk aversion and there is uncertainty about the number of bidders this uncertainty raises revenue on average, compared to revealing information about the number of bidders. Behavior changed in most experiments from the way theory predicts. Moreover, experiments showed that an increased number of bidders almost always results in higher bidding in first-price auctions. For example, Battalio, Kogut and Meyer (1990) report a series of first-price sealed-bid auctions in which they exogenously varied the number of bidders while holding the distribution of private valuations constant. The large majority of individuals increased their bids, on average, when the market size increased from five to ten bidders.

As already mentioned, information revelation can be an important factor in auctions. There is considerable diversity in price information feedback following the submission of sealed bids. Government agencies typically report back the full set of bids, along with bidders' names. Standard non-cooperative game-theoretical models of auctions do not consider the effects of price information revelation. It is interesting to speculate about how price feedback impacts on bidding. Several laboratory experiments analyzed the effects of price information in multiple rounds of sealed-bid auctions (Battalio, Kogut and Meyer, 1990; Cox, Smith and Walker, 1994), but did not find a significant effect on bidding. There has been little study of learning and adjustment processes in private value auctions. There is, however, increasing evidence of systematic adjustments in bidding over time in first-price auctions. Smith and Walker (1993) report that more experienced bidders bid significantly higher, as if they are more risk-averse, than inexperienced bidders in auctions with four bidders.

5.5.3 Tests of Common Value Auctions

In pure common value auctions the value of the auctioned item is the same for all bidders. What makes the auction interesting is that bidders do not know the value at the time they bid. Instead, they receive signal values that are related to the value of the item. Although all bidders obtain unbiased estimates of the item's value, assuming homogeneous bid functions, they win only in cases where they have the highest bid. Unless this adverse selection problem is accounted for in the bidding, it will result in winning bids that produce below-normal or even negative profits. This failure is the "winner's curse."

Common value auctions are substantially more complicated than private value auctions as they incorporate a difficult item estimation problem in addition to the strategic problems involved in competitive bidding. A strong winner's curse is reported for inexperienced bidders in sealed-bid common value auctions as high bidders earn negative average profits and consistently bid above the expected value of the item, conditional upon a high signal value. Arguments that these results can be accounted for on the basis of bidders' limited liability for losses have been shown to be incorrect (Kagel and Levin, 1991).

5.6   Towards New Frontiers – Multi-Unit Auctions

Low transaction costs on the Internet have led to an interest in the design of new auction mechanisms and people build exchanges for many goods and services which were previously the domain of fixed pricing rules. There are a myriad of possible auction rules and the design space for creating new auction formats is huge. So far, auction theory has explained only a small proportion of the variety of possible auction schemes. Over the past few years a lot of research has been done to extend the framework of auctions in order to enable more powerful exchanges.

Most classic auction theory restricts attention to the sale of a single indivisible unit. Auctions which allocate multiple units of a good have received increasing attention in the theoretical literature. Many articles analyze multi-unit auctions in which bidders submit both the number of units of a homogeneous good they wish to buy and how much they are willing to bid per unit. Combinatorial auctions are an approach for achieving efficient allocations in cases where bidders place bids on combinations of possibly heterogeneous goods. These bids allow them to express dependencies and complementarities between goods (Sandholm, 1999a). The following subsection will provide an overview of multi-unit auction schemes.

5.6.1   *Multi-Unit Auctions of Homogeneous Goods*

With the assistance of a computerized system it is possible today to run multi-unit auctions. In a traditional setting, it was virtually impossible to keep track of the complicated mechanics of a multi-unit auction with bids on both price and quantity. The auctioneer had to continuously keep an updated, sorted list of high bidders according to various sorting rules. In online auctions this has become very popular (see section 5.7).

For single-unit auctions, a bid simply indicates whether it is to buy or sell, and at what price. A *multi-unit* bid generalizes this by specifying a set of price–quantity pairs for multiple identical goods. The first-price auction has two multi-unit generalizations which are used in practice – *discriminatory auctions* in which the bidders who bid the highest prices pay their bid, and *uniform-price auctions* in which all k-successful bidders pay the $(k+1)$st bid price. The uniform price is set by the bid on the $(k+1)$st unit, which is not a winning bid as there are only k-units on sale.

A substantial part of the literature focuses on comparing those two auction formats, owing to the controversy about how government debts should be auctioned off. Uniform-price auctions correspond to second-price auctions in the sense that each bidder has a dominant strategy of bidding her private valuation. The k-highest bidders receive one unit and pay that price. If a bidder bids higher than her true value, under certain market structures she may end up with a negative surplus. If she bids lower, she merely reduces the chance of winning the auction without changing the price she pays. In a generalized first-price or discriminatory auction, the k-highest bidders are awarded the k-items and each pays her own bid. Discriminatory auctions correspond to single-unit first-price auctions in the sense that with risk-neutrality, expected revenue is the same as the uniform-price auction, and with risk aversion bids will be above the past highest, yielding greater expected revenue for the seller.

The literature on the sale of multiple units is much less developed, except in the case where *bidders demand only a single unit each*. Maskin and Riley (1989) extend Myerson's (1981) analysis of optimal auctions to the case in which buyers have downward-sloping demand curves, independently drawn from a one-parameter distribution, for quantities of a homogeneous good. Properties of single unit first-price and English auctions extend to multi-unit auctions in these cases. However, revenue equivalence generally fails if buyers are interested in buying several units, and their demand is a function of price.

Wilson (1979) first analyzed so-called "share auctions" in which each bidder offers a schedule specifying a price for each possible fraction of the item (e.g. a certain volume of treasury notes). He showed that a uniform-price auction might foster collusive agreements. Discriminatory auctions are, therefore, likely to be more profitable for a seller. As already mentioned, revenue equivalence fails in the case of multi-unit auctions where bidders are allowed to buy several units, depending on the price. An analysis of price dependent demand can be found in Hansen (1988) who showed that first-price auctions led to a higher expected price than the second-price auction and revenue equivalence is no longer valid. An important application concerns procurement contracts in private industry and government. Hansen's results explain why procurement is usually in the form of a first-price sealed-bid auction.

One recent topic in auction theory is that of demand reduction in multi-unit auctions. When bidders have multi-unit demand for a good with multi-unit supply, there will be an incentive for bidders to pretend their demand is low, potentially causing allocative inefficiency (Engelbrecht-Wiggans, 1989). This problem can be solved with the Vickrey multi-unit sealed-bid auction format, which is a relatively complicated mechanism in that, if bidders understand it, they have incentive to reveal their full demand and restore efficiency of the auction.

The main message of much of the current research on multi-unit auctions is that it is hard to achieve efficient outcomes. Combinatorial auctions described in the following subsection are a promising new approach. These mechanisms are especially useful in situations where multiple heterogeneous goods have to be assigned simultaneously and bidders have preferences over different combinations of goods.

5.6.2   Multi-Unit Auctions with Preferences Over Bundles

Goods are said to be combinatorial when the value of a bundle of goods is not equal to the sum of the values of the same goods unbundled, i.e. the bidders' valuations are not additive. In layman's terms, the "whole" can be worth more or less than the sum of its parts. Examples of goods which are thought to exhibit such a property include airport landing slots, electromagnetic spectrum licenses, land parcels, oil leases, and shipping space. A slot at a certain airport, for example, is more or less valuable to an airline depending upon whether the airline has obtained an appropriate time slot at an appropriate paired city (Rothkopf and Pekec, 1998). However, economists also noticed that the simple versions of the auction processes they were testing could not directly incorporate the expression of such combinatorial values. Several solutions to this problem have been proposed.

5.6.2.1   Sequential Auctions

One possible allocation mechanism is a sequential auction, where the items are auctioned one at a time. Determining the winners in such a protocol is easy because this can be done by picking the highest bidder for each item separately. However, if a bidder has preferences over bundles, then bidding in such auctions is difficult. To determine the valuation for an item, the bidder needs to guess what items she will receive in consecutive auctions. This requires speculation on what the others will bid in the future because that affects what items the bidder will receive. This counter-speculation introduces computational cost and can lead to inefficient allocations when bidders do not get the combinations that they want. Moreover, in auctions with a large number of items such prediction is intractable and there is no way to bid rationally.

5.6.2.2 Parallel Auctions

Another approach is a parallel auction in which the items are opened for auction at parallel times. This has the advantage that the others' bids partially signal the bidder about what the others' bids will end up being for the different items, so the uncertainty and the need for prediction is not as drastic as in sequential auctions. However, the same problems arise in the case of a large number of goods. Moreover, there is an additional difficulty in that each bidder would like to wait until the end to see what the going price will be, and to optimize her bids so as to maximize payoff given the final price. Because it would be best for every bidder to wait, no bidding would commence. Of course, this can be enhanced by certain activity rules (e.g. each bidder has to bid at least a certain volume by a defined point in time, otherwise the bidder's future rights are reduced). Unfortunately, the equilibrium bidding strategies in such auctions are not game-theoretically known.

5.6.2.3 The Federal Communication Commission's Spectrum Auctions

It has already been shown that in sequential and parallel auctions, the cost of prediction and counter-speculation is high. After the early recognition of the combinatorial features of the airport slot problem (Rassenti, Smith and Bulfin, 1982), the combinatorial allocation problem received significant attention during the design process for the Federal Communication Commission's auction of spectrum rights for Personal Communication System services. Between 1994 and early 1997, the Federal Communication Commission raised a striking US $23 billion from 13 auctions. Most of this revenue came from auctions of licenses for wireless cable television, digital audio radio, and specialized mobile radio used by taxi dispatchers. Each of the licenses covers a certain bandwidth of the electromagnetic spectrum over a particular geographic area. The licenses permit the company holding them to use the spectrum for specified mobile telecommunications applications. The design of the spectrum auctions resulted from a complicated debate. The Federal Communication Commission's original notice of proposed rule making, proposing an auction design, received many responses from telecommunications companies, a number of them with papers by leading economists appended. There were also sophisticated rounds of replies to the responses, three conferences to discuss issues in the auction design, and pilot experiments conducted at the California Institute of Technology.

The Federal Communication Commission introduced the so-called *simultaneous ascending auction*. It expected that a telecommunications company would value a license more highly if it also owned a geographically contiguous license. These licenses complement one another to a certain extent (McMillan, 1994). The simultaneous ascending auction was designed to permit bidders to assemble efficient bundles of licenses. The auction has two main features. It is ascending, so that there are multiple rounds of bidding and bids keep increasing until no one wants to bid more. And it is simultaneous, so that many licenses are open for bidding at the same time, and all remain open for bidding as long as there is bidding activity on any one of them. The Federal Communication Commission also allowed bidders to retract their bids. Retracted items were opened for re-auction and if the new winning price was lower than the old one, the bidder that retracted the bid had to pay the difference (Sandholm, 1999a). This guarantees that retractions do not decrease the auctioneer's payoff. However, it exposes the retracting bidder to considerable risk. Another approach would be to set penalties for backing out up front or to sell options for backing out where the price of the option would be paid in advance. Each of these methods can be used to implement bid retraction before or after the winning bids have been determined. This novel auction form was chosen because it helped mitigate the winner's curse and it took into account the complementarities and synergies among the licenses.

5.6.2.4 Combinatorial Auctions

The Federal Communication Commission's auction design tried to fix inefficient allocations achieved in purely sequential or parallel auctions, adapting a basically non-combinatorial process in some manner to take account of combinatorial values. *Combinatorial auctions* (also called *combinational*) are an approach for achieving efficient allocations in the first step. Here we will consider single-sided combinatorial auctions with a single seller and multiple buyers. The reverse situation, with a single buyer and multiple sellers, is symmetric. A situation with multiple buyers and sellers will not be considered. The concept of combinatorial auctions has already been implemented by a number of logistics and consulting companies,[2] and is similar to what is sometimes described as *bundle auction* or *matrix auction* (Gomber, Schmidt and Weinhardt, 1998a), which can be used for the assignment of multiple goods or services to multiple bidders.

The potential advantage of allowing combinatorial bids in a simultaneous auction is that it allows bidders to express their synergistic values. When such synergies are present, this should result in both greater revenue for the bid taker and economically more efficient allocation of assets to

---

[2] SAITECH-INC offers a software product called SBIDS that allows trucking companies to bid on bundles of lanes. <Logistics.com> have a system called OptiBid™. In May 2000, the company announced that 35 major North American shippers had employed OptiBid™ to award over $5 billion in annual transportation service provider contracts.

bidders (Rothkopf and Pekec, 1998). In a combinatorial auction bidders can place bids on combinations of different goods which permits expressing *complementarities* between goods, i.e. the bidder is willing to pay more for the whole than the sum of what she is willing to pay for the parts. *Substitutability* describes cases when the goods are homogeneous, and the bidder is willing to pay for the whole only less than the sum of what he is willing to pay for the parts.

McMillan (1994) reports that, at the time, the mechanism designers employed by the Federal Communication Commission did not feel that combinatorial auctions were well developed enough to be used in practice. Considerable effort has been focused on the problem in the last few years. However, so far, only a few scholarly papers have considered the auction design problems introduced by value interdependencies among different items for sale. Rothkopf (1977) considered the bidder's problem in a simultaneous auction without combinatorial bids when there is an interdependency introduced by a constraint on the total of the bidder's bids. Smith and Rothkopf (1985) consider the bidder's problem in a simultaneous auction without combinatorial bids when there is a fixed charge incurred if any bid succeeds. Rassenti, Smith and Bulfin (1982) describe laboratory experiments with simultaneous auctions and interdependent values.

Banks, Ledyard and Porter introduced a single-sided, iterative mechanism, called the *adaptive user selection mechanism* (AUSM) (Banks, Ledyard and Porter, 1989). AUSM posts the current best allocation on a bulletin board visible to all of the participants, and lets the bidders figure out how to improve it. To become part of the current best allocation, a new bid has to offer more than the sum of all of the bids it displaces. Bids that are not part of the best allocation are posted in a standby queue designed to facilitate the coordination of two or more smaller bidders combining on a new bid large enough to displace a larger bidder. In 1982, Forsythe and Isaak (Forsythe and Isaak, 1982) reported the extension of the Vickrey auction into a demand-revealing, multi-unit, private goods auction that could incorporate combinatorial values. Recently, a number of computer scientists have approached this topic (Parameswaran, Stallaert and Whinston, 1999; Sandholm, 1999a).

While combinatorial auctions have the desirable feature that they can avoid the need for prediction by the bidders, they impose significant complexity on the auctioneer who needs to determine the winners. In the following, an example of the assignment of multiple heterogeneous goods to bidders in a procurement scenario is provided (see also Gomber, Schmidt and Weinhardt, 1998, for a detailed example). Bidders in this scenario calculate a bid for each combination of n goods ($2^n - 1$ combinations). Of course, the valuation of a combination of goods may differ significantly

Table 5.3. *Matrix for the allocation of goods*

Goods	(1)	(2)	(3)	(1,2)	(2,3)	(1,3)	(1,2,3)
Bidder *A*	5	32	40	65	10	−20	−60
Bidder *B*	5	−10	30	−30	40	80	90
Bidder *C*	−10	80	50	35	−20	5	15
Bidder *D*	5	40	35	40	60	−30	50

from the sum of the individual valuations and may even be negative, depending on the bidders' preferences for certain combinations of goods. Bidders transmit their bids to the auctioneer who determines an efficient allocation by setting up a matrix (see table 5.3) with all combinations in the columns and the bidders in the rows. The cells of the matrix contain bidders' bids for each combination. The algorithm for this assignment problem has to take into account that a bidder cannot receive more than one bid assigned. Beyond this, columns/combinations of goods that have any item in common must not be selected jointly. The shaded cells of table 5.3 show the optimum allocation for an example with three goods and four bidders. The optimum overall allocation is 160. Bidder *B* gets the goods 1 and 3 assigned and bidder *C* gets good 2.

5.6.2.5 The Generalized Vickrey Auction

There are a number of pricing mechanisms that can be deployed in this situation. However, the capability to determine an efficient allocation depends crucially on whether bidders report their contribution margins correctly. One mechanism for determining the prices in this resource allocation problem is the *generalized Vickrey auction* (GVA), described in Varian (1995). The GVA is an incentive compatible direct mechanism in which true revelation is the dominant strategy for a bidder. Initial ideas have already been described in Clarke (1971) and Groves (1973), and, therefore, the mechanism is also called a Vickrey–Clarke–Groves auction. Therefore, the bidder has to report its entire utility function. As already mentioned, this is particularly useful in the field of agent-based electronic commerce infrastructures. Moreover, transaction costs are reduced in a direct mechanism compared to open-cry auction schemes.

Suppose there are $i = 1,...,I$ bidders and n goods, i.e. $j = 1,...,2^n - 1$ combinations. b_{kj} represents the bid of a bidder k for the combination of goods j and v_{kj} is her true valuation for a combination of goods j. x_{ij}^* are the variables of the optimal assignment (with $x_{ij}^* = 1$ if bidder i receives the combination j and $x_{ij}^* = 0$ otherwise) and $x_{ij}^{*|k}$ are the variables of the optimum assignment with the row of bidder k skipped. The price for a bidder k in the

Table 5.4. *Matrix for the allocation of goods with bidder C skipped*

Goods	(1)	(2)	(3)	(1,2)	(2,3)	(1,3)	(1,2,3)
Bidder A	5	32	40	65	10	-20	-60
Bidder B	5	-10	30	-30	40	80	90
Bidder C	5	40	35	40	60	-30	50

efficient allocation is computed by deducting the sum of the bids of all other bidders in x_{ij}^* from the sum of the bids in $x_{ij}^{*\rceil k}$, i.e. the price paid by the bidders is

$$p_k = \sum_{\substack{i=1 \\ i \neq k}}^{I} \sum_{j=1}^{2^n-1} b_{ij} x_{ij}^{*\rceil k} - \sum_{\substack{i=1 \\ i \neq k}}^{I} \sum_{j=1}^{2^n-1} b_{ij} x_{ij}^*. \tag{5.9}$$

In the example of table 5.3 with an efficient allocation of 160 the price of bidder C results from deducting the sum of the bids of all other bidders in the efficient allocation (here, 80) from the sum of the bids in the optimum assignment with bidder C skipped (this would add up to 120 in the example). Therefore, C has to pay $p_C = 120 - 80 = 40$ for good (2). Bidder B also has to pay $p_B = 120 - 80 = 40$ for the combination of goods (1,3) (table 5.4).

Gomber, Schmidt and Weinhardt (1998b) show that in fact the dominant strategy for a bidder k in this case is to make bid $b_{kj} = v_{kj}$, i.e. to reveal her true valuation. The payoff g_k of a bidder k results from the difference between her individual valuation and the price she has to pay, i.e.

$$g_k = v_{kj} - \left(\sum_{\substack{i=1 \\ i \neq k}}^{I} \sum_{j=1}^{2^n-1} b_{ij} x_{ij}^{*\rceil k} - \sum_{\substack{i=1 \\ i \neq k}}^{I} \sum_{j=1}^{2^n-1} b_{ij} x_{ij}^* \right). \tag{5.10}$$

Each bidder aims to maximize his payoff, g_k. The sum of the bids in the optimum solution with the row of bidder k skipped (*ii*) cannot be influenced by bidder k, i.e. bidder k's objective is the maximization of

$$g_k = v_{kj} + \sum_{\substack{i=1 \\ i \neq k}}^{I} \sum_{j=1}^{2^n-1} b_{ij} x_{ij}^*. \tag{5.11}$$

The auctioneer in this example will choose x_{ij}^* so as to maximize

$$b_{kj} + \sum_{\substack{i=1 \\ i \neq k}}^{I} \sum_{j=1}^{2^n-1} b_{ij} x_{ij}^*. \tag{5.12}$$

Obviously, the objective functions of each bidder and the auctioneer are equivalent and bidder k makes a bid $b_{kj} = v_{kj}$ (Varian, 1995). Therefore, each bidder reports its true valuation and receives a payoff which corresponds to its contribution to efficiency (Gomber, Schmidt and Weinhardt, 1998a).

In this example, bidder C receives a payoff $g_C = 80 - 40 = 40$ which corresponds to the difference between the optimum allocation and the optimum allocation without the participation of C ($160 - 120 = 40$). The same holds true for B. The results discussed above also apply to negative valuations. In summary, the pricing mechanism of the GVA ensures efficiency by establishing compatibility of local and global goals. However, as can be seen, it suffers from its computational complexity.

5.6.2.6 Determination of Winners in Combinatorial Auctions

While bidding in combinatorial auctions is easier, as bidders do not have to speculate on other bidders' behavior in other auctions, it requires much more effort to determine the winner, i.e. the revenue-maximizing bids in these auctions. This issue was raised in the Federal Communication Commission's auction design debate. In the worst-case scenario, the bid taker offering n assets could receive offers on $2^n - 1$ different combinations of assets. Clearly, bid evaluation will present a computational problem when n is large. In a non-combinatorial multi-unit auction determining the winner can be done in $O(am)$ time,[3] where a represents the number of bidders, and m the number of items. In contrast, Sandholm (1999a) proved that the number of allocations in a combinatorial auction is $O(m^m)$ and that determining the winner so as to maximize revenue is NP-complete.[4]

The winner determination problem is the same problem as the abstract problem called weighted set packing. Set packing problems are well investigated in combinatorial optimization. In general, they can be formulated as follows. Given a finite set V and a system of subsets $U_1, ..., U_k \subseteq V$ with values b_i, $i = 1, ..., k$ find a subsystem $U_{i1}, ..., U_{il}$ of paired disjoint subsets such that $b_{i1} + ... + b_{il}$ is maximized. The fact that weighted set packing is NP-complete means that no algorithm can find a revenue-maximizing allocation in combinatorial auctions in polynomial time (see also Sedgewick, 1992, p. 673). This does not scale beyond auctions with a small number of items.

Several researchers address this problem. Rothkopf and Pekec (1998) investigate a set of restrictions that could be imposed upon allowed combinations, and which can make the computation of the best set of bundles tractable. They use dynamic programming which takes $O(3^m)$ steps to solve this problem. The dynamic programming algorithm determines the highest possible revenue that can be acquired for each set U of items using only the items in U. The algorithm proceeds systematically from the smallest sets to

---

[3] The O-notation describes the worst-case performance of an algorithm, ignoring constant factors, in order to determine the dependence of the running time on the number of inputs (Sedgewick, 1992).

[4] NP-completeness means that no known polynomial time algorithm exists for these problems.

the largest. Consequently, for each U, all possible subsets (together with that subset's complement in U) are tried. Sandholm (1999a) optimizes this procedure and proposes a search algorithm for winner determination in polynomial time by capitalizing on the fact that the space of bids is necessarily sparsely populated in practice. Sandholm (1999b) also describes an Internet-based implementation of this algorithm called eMediator.

5.6.3 Multi-Stage Extended Vickrey Auctions

Nowadays, many production companies integrate their procurement processes using online marketplaces and network-based supply chain management systems. However, this is not the case for the service industry. The auctioning of service contracts poses several additional problems. A particularly interesting problem is how to achieve an efficient allocation in negotiation situations where multiple services need to be assigned to a number of bidders, but it is not clear at the beginning how the services should be decomposed. This situation is not unusual in transportation and logistics.

The Multistage Extended Vickrey Auction (MEVA) (Gomber, Schmidt and Weinhardt, 1996) is based on the concept of dividing the auction process into several stages instead of just one stage, as conventional auction theory assumes. Game theory states that multi-stage auctions can be modeled as an extensive game, and, thus, should be equivalent to a single-stage auction. Engelbrecht-Wiggans (1989) was one of the first to investigate multi-stage single-unit auctions and showed that a multi-stage process can sometimes yield increased revenues. In MEVA, goods are auctioned off in an iterative bidding procedure whose number of iterations i equals the number of participating bidders. In each iteration a Vickrey auction is carried out and coalitions with i participants make a bid. In the first iteration, each single agent makes a bid for the good. The auctioneer stores all bids and the name of their respective bidders, but does not announce them. In the second iteration the auctioneer calls on coalitions with two participants to make their bids, and so on. Bilateral negotiations lead to coalition formation. Finally, the bidder or the coalition of bidders with the highest bid of all iterations is awarded the good. The price corresponds to the second-highest bid of all iterations. The step of coalition formation in each stage should lead to an efficient allocation, i.e. the good should be awarded to the "best" coalition from among all candidates.

5.6.4 The OptiMark Case

An interesting real-world example of a multi-unit double auction can be found in financial markets. OptiMark® is a system which is particularly suitable for block trading at the Pacific Exchange (San Francisco, Los

Angeles) and also at New York's NASDAQ. Block trading, by definition, includes trades over 10,000 shares, but such trades can be several million shares or more. Block trading volumes are growing rapidly, and block sizes are increasing, and are now commonly between 50,000 and 100,000 shares. In 1994, institutional trading accounted for 75–80 percent of NYSE volume (Clemons and Weber, 1998). However, today's market conditions impose costs and constraints on institutional investors. Some large institutional customers believe that they are poorly served by the existing exchanges, and many industry participants believe that better alternatives for handling large institutional-size trading orders are needed. A fundamental problem of block trading is that large blocks often lead to adverse price movements.

The OptiMark (OPTImal MARKet) system provides an anonymous, exchange-linked, order matching system that enables customers to describe their trading strategies and their pricing preferences in considerable detail. Traders access the system on existing financial networks such as the NASDAQ network or via the Internet, and submitted orders must designate one or more of the customer's broker–dealer member firms to provide credit and clearing. The OptiMark system provides three special features:

■ In OptiMark, a trader works from a graphical user interface (see figure 5.3) to develop a trading "profile" – a three-dimensional rendering of price, quantity, and satisfaction weight that is submitted to OptiMark and indicates trading preferences. Therefore, an OptiMark user may indicate her willingness to buy, for instance, up to 10,000 at US $30 or less, and up to 50,000 if the price is US $29.50 or less. By keeping submissions confidential and avoiding the potential conflicts of interest between investors and block trading desks, OptiMark expects traders to reveal large orders to the system that will provide liquidity and attract additional large submissions to their system. The OptiMark user's profile is not disclosed to others until matched with a counter-party and a trade occurs.

■ The system can capture odd supply and demand curves that can in some cases closely resemble investors' true trading intentions. For example, a buyer may be willing to pay no more than US $50 for 50,000 shares, but may also have an order to purchase 250,000 for US $52 as a whole. This feature of OptiMark can lead to trades that would otherwise be unlikely, given the hazards of disclosing large trading interests.

■ The system permits making bids on price–quantity pairs and adds a third dimension called the "willingness-to-trade" which is expressed as a number between zero and one. The varying degrees of willingness-to-trade encompass the diminishing surplus a seller receives by selling at lower prices, and a buyer receives by buying at higher trade prices. OptiMark's pricing and matching algorithm seeks to improve upon

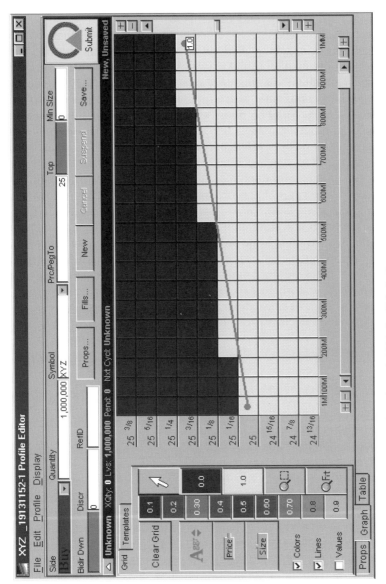

Figure 5.3 The OptiMark user interface. © 2000 OptiMark, Inc.

traders' submitted reservation prices, and will match at a price only if nothing better is available. The algorithm has to find an allocation of price–quantity combinations maximizing the overall utility given a set of restrictions (Clemons and Weber, 1998).

OptiMark plans to match buyers and sellers every 15 minutes. When OptiMark runs its matching, it processes all submitted order profiles and computes an optimal pricing and matching result for users based on their willingness-to-trade across the range of prices and sizes. Buying coordinates and selling coordinates with a full satisfaction value of 1 will first be converted to trades, based on priority rankings of price, standing, time of entry, and size. Next, any remaining coordinates including coordinates with a partial satisfaction (i.e. willingness-to-trade) value of less than 1 but greater than 0, will be matched, based on the joint mutual satisfaction value (That is, the product of the specific satisfaction values associated with the buying coordinate and selling coordinate). The algorithm has two parts:

- During the *aggregation phase* OptiMark processes potential trades where the buyer and seller both have full satisfaction (i.e. a satisfaction value of 1) even though the orders may not overlap in size. OptiMark selects prices that maximize the volume of mutually agreeable trades. In the case of ties, OptiMark ranks by order potential matches using time of entry, size, and whether the trading is conducted for public customers. At this stage of calculation, smaller-size coordinates may be aggregated to build sufficient size to be matched with larger-size orders.

- During the *accumulation phase*, OptiMark attempts to arrange beneficial trades with less than full satisfaction. A match with a higher mutual satisfaction value takes precedence over other potential matches with lower satisfaction values. The accumulation stage is used to find additional matches of profiles that did not match in the aggregation stage. Revelation of trading preferences should occur, since failing to indicate partial satisfaction may limit beneficial trade opportunities.

Subscribers will log in from their own computer terminals and communicate over commercial information services and market data networks of their choice. They can revise or cancel their own profiles at any time prior to commencement of the next scheduled processing cycle. OptiMark users are responsible for any expressions of trading interest and any other message submitted to the system under their password and access code.

The OptiMark algorithm has been criticized for its preference elicitation scale between 0 and 1. Teich, Wallenius, Wallenius and Zaitsev (1999) question why anyone would be willing to furnish preference scores between 0 and 1 and not specify a unique single best 1 cell. Even if traders share the same preference scale and accurately portray it, ranking the cells based on the product of preference scores is arbitrary. For example, the product of

0.6 and 0.6 is the same as 0.4 and 0.9. One could be argue that 0.6 times 0.6 would be a better match. Since the OptiMark system is a black box, the traders also do not know that if they were to trade off a different price/quantity combination, they would both benefit. OptiMark justifies this seemingly irrational trait by saying that traders actually prefer higher quantities of shares traded (Kersten and Noronha, 1999a).

5.7   Analysis of Online Auctions

During the past few years there have been a tremendous number of auctions conducted over the Internet. This form of electronic commerce is projected to account for 30 percent of all electronic commerce by 2002 (Hof, Green and Judge, 1999). Online auctions provide several benefits relative to traditional auctions (see also sections 1.2 and 1.3). They give bidders increased convenience, both geographical and temporal, relative to traditional auctions. These increased conveniences can also benefit the seller, by creating a larger market for the auctioned good. On the Internet, a relatively large group of bidders can easily be obtained at short notice, rather than scheduling an auction a month in advance and being restricted to local bidders who could travel to the auction at the scheduled time. Participants in an online auction benefit directly from low transaction costs. Whereas providers generally have to pay setup costs and a proportional sales fee, the participation of consumers is free, which again amplifies the size factor. Searching for the right auction item is also inexpensive and already supported by various search engines and agents (e.g. AuctionWatch <http://www.auctionwatch.com>). From the point of view of the researcher, it has become much easier to collect field data as compared to traditional auctions. This enables the validation of basic behavioral assumptions in theoretical auction models.

Online auctions also have their disadvantages relative to physical auctions. First, it is hard for bidders to inspect the goods before bidding in an Internet auction. Another difficulty is the potential problem of fraud. A winning Internet bidder must trust that the seller will actually send the good in return for the payment of the bid amount. In fact, there have been a number of cases of fraud reported in online auctions. However, the amount of fraud is tiny compared with the number of transactions which takes place.

5.7.1   Empirical Data

Despite the obvious practical relevance, specific research regarding online auctions is not very extensive. Turban (1997) gave an overview of some of the products that are being auctioned electronically and outlined some potential benefits, such as cost reduction and inventory clearance. Wrigley (1997) suggested that electronic markets in general and auctions in particular will occur when one of the following characterizes the goods to be sold: perishability, scarcity, possibility to deliver electronically or to a geographically constrained market (such as second-hand goods, for instance). Nowadays, online auctions such as Onsale offer a wide variety of goods, and these three characteristics seem to be too narrow. Van Heck, Koppius and Vervest (1998) compared four electronic auctions on the Internet and identified some common success factors, the most important ones being increased scale of the market for the seller and greater market visibility for the buyer.

The following subsections will outline the state-of-the-practice of online auctions. It will draw on articles by Beam and Segev (1998) as well as by Lucking-Reiley (1999). Of course, field studies like this are only a snapshot at a given point in time and both articles describe the market as it existed in 1998. Nevertheless, both studies should provide a first overview of this dynamic field. Both articles try to answer how many goods are being auctioned online, what types of goods are being sold, what auction formats are being used, and what business models are utilitzed by the auction sites.

5.7.2   *Types of Goods Sold*

In a field study, Lucking-Reiley (1999) analyzed 142 web sites in the autumn of 1998. Fifty-eight percent of the auction sites were relatively small, serving small niche markets. Fifteen percent of sites in the survey had sales of more than US $100,000 per month, and 5 percent had sales larger than a million dollars per month. The variety of goods sold at auction on the Internet is much wider than has ever been auctioned before. The following list of categories in table 5.5 gives an overview of the variety of goods sold in online auctions.

The survey concentrated on business-to-consumer and consumer-to-consumer auctions, and, therefore, the largest category by far was that of collectibles. As can be seen in table 5.5, a large number of 86 sites specialized in a single category of goods, whereas the other sites followed a broad strategy, featuring goods in multiple categories.

5.7.3   *Closing Rules and Auction Formats*

A field study of Beam and Segev (1998) analyzed 100 online auctions between September 1997 and February 1998. Ninety-four percent of the auction sites surveyed were from the USA. The sample contained a large

Table 5.5. *Types of items sold at 142 online auction sites (Lucking-Reiley, 1999)*

Category	Sites featuring that category	Sites specializing in that category
Collectibles	90	56
Antiques	40	10
Celebrity memorabilia	16	7
Stamps	11	5
Coins	17	2
Toys	17	0
Trading cards	14	0
Electronics and computers	48	9
Jewelry	17	1
Computer software	16	0
Used equipment	15	7
Sporting goods	13	4
Travel services	7	5
Real estate	4	2
Wine	3	2

number of business-to-consumer and consumer-to-consumer auctions and only a small number of business-to-business ones (6 percent).

The online auctions do not always exactly match the traditional types, often owing to newly enabled experimentation with auction rules. By far the most popular auction in the data sample of Beam and Segev was the English auction (85 percent). Seven auction sites featured first-price sealed-bid auctions, four sites a Dutch auction, and only one a continuous double auction. In Lucking-Reiley's sample 121 out of the 142 online auction sites used the English auction, three used Dutch descending-price rules, five a Vickrey auction, and four were continuous double auctions. Six of the sites had more than one auction format available.

The English auction is a popular Internet auction because it is relatively easy to understand, allows bidder interaction and competition, and is particularly well suited to periods longer than a few minutes. A surprising number of English auctions went against traditional English auction theory by providing the bidders with each other's contact information, making it possible for rings of colluding bidders to form. An interesting question is why the Vickrey auction was not more popular with the online auctioneers. Beam and Segev's sample did not contain a single Vickrey auction, and Lucking-Reiley's sample contained only five Vickrey auctions. Theoretically, the Vickrey auction is an optimal auction in that it will maximize efficiency and still give the auctioneer approximately the same revenue as would have been expected from an English auction. Additionally, participating in a Vickrey auction would require each bidder to place a single bid only once. One explanation of online auctioneers is that customers enjoy placing multiple bids, and the entertainment value of the online English auction is a non-negligible component, at least in business-to-consumer markets. The Dutch auction is much harder to implement on the web, which is the main reason for its rare occurrence.

With Internet technology, it is possible to close an auction based on a variety of rules. For example, an auction that closes purely on a time rule would close Monday at noon, regardless of bidding activity. An auction that closes purely on activity could close only when there had been no bids for a specified amount of time. Although there were a wide variety of ways online auctions were conducted, most online auctions in Beam and Segev's sample accepted bids for a standard length of time, and closed the auction at a specific cutoff time. The online auctions tended to close on average about once per week, although 14 of the companies closed auctions every 24 hours or less and 8 of them closed the auctions on a monthly basis. However, there was a wide variation in the auction duration. Some auctions lasted only a few seconds (such as a widely advertised Dutch auction of a popular collectible), while others remained open for several months accepting bids.

5.7.4   Business Models

The two primary business models for Internet auctions are those of merchant sites and listing sites. A merchant site offers its own merchandise for sale, acting as a retailer who happens to conduct its transactions through auction. A listing site acts as an agent for other sellers, allowing them to register their items and running the auctions on their behalf. The sample data described in Lucking-Reiley (1999) found 96 listing sites, 25 merchant sites, and 11 sites offering both. While merchant sites derive their income directly from the sale of their items, listing sites derive their revenues from fees charged to buyers and sellers. In all, 62 out of 107 listing sites charged a seller's commission as a percentage of the final selling price.

The fees tend to be an order of magnitude lower for Internet auctions than they are for traditional auction houses. Sotheby's for example, charges a buyer's premium of 15 percent over the final bid price, and a standard seller's commission of 20 percent of the bid price. In contrast, the total fees at listing sites like eBay are around only 5 percent of the final bid price (Lucking-Reiley, 1999).

An interesting aspect of Internet auctions is the economic competition between the auctioneers. This competition is made even more interesting by the possible presence of network externalities (Varian, 1996c, p. 591): sellers tend to prefer to auction items at the site visited by the most bidders, and vice versa. This phenomenon is particularly important in business-to-consumer and consumer-to-consumer auctions.

5.7.5   Fraud and Strategic Manipulation

So-called listing sites leave the actual transaction up to the seller and the winning bidder. The standard procedure is for the buyer to mail a check or money order to the seller, and wait for the seller to mail the goods in return. This requires a certain level of trust. Many auction sites actively discourage fraud, encouraging users to file formal complaints with the courts. Second, some auction sites implement a feedback and rating system that encourages buyers and sellers to rate each other at the close of a transaction. These ratings and comments are publicly available – when viewing an auction listing, a bidder also sees a numeric feedback rating. Similarly, a seller may see the feedback rating from the bidders in her auction, and always has the option of rejecting bids from any bidder. A single click allows a participant to view the entire history of written comments. A bad rating can also lead to automatic suspension of a user's account. Finally, some auction sites encourage the use of a third-party escrow service, if they fear the possibility of fraud. The buyer sends payment to the escrow agent, who verifies payment before the seller ships the good to the buyer. The buyer then has a short examination period, to make sure that the item meets its description in the auction catalog. After the buyer consents to the transaction, the escrow agent releases the funds to the seller.

Shilling is an attempt by the seller to drive up the price of a product. The concept is that when only one bidder remains in the auction, the seller can try to drive the auction price higher by bidding against this bidder. One difficulty for the seller is the possibility to overbid the high bidder's willingness-to-pay, and, thus, being unable of selling the good at all. Of course, shilling is not allowed on online auctions, but this rule is difficult to enforce.

5.7.6   Minimum Bids and Reserve Prices

Internet auctions usually specify a minimum acceptable bid, below which no bids will be accepted. On listing sites, the individual seller chooses this as a parameter in the auction listing. In addition, many sites feature a secret reserve valuation specified in advance but not revealed to the bidders until after the auction. If the highest bid does not exceed the amount of the reserve valuation, then the item will not be sold. Of the 142 sites reviewed in Lucking-Reiley's (1999) study, practically all used non-zero minimum bid levels, and 55 also allowed the use of reserve valuations. A few English auctions even specified a maximum acceptable bid, or buyout price. The idea is to allow the buyer to buy an early end to the auction by submitting a sufficiently high bid.

The private reserve valuation allows the seller to enter a low minimum bid in hopes of generating interest and bids on their item. However, the seller is not obligated to proceed with the sale until the reserve valuation is met. This procedure at first seems to be positing a kind of irrationality on the part of bidders, who are willing to pay more for the same good, depending on whether the reserve valuation is made public or kept secret. A common value model of bidder values may be able to explain this behavior with a rational model. On the one hand, the low-minimum-bid, high-reserve-valuation auction would give a bidder more opportunity for observing the bidding of others than would the high-minimum-bid auction. On the other hand, many buyers try to avoid auctions with reserve valuations, as it is very upsetting to win an item only to be told that the winning bid was not high enough (Lucking-Reiley, 1999).

An interesting field study of reserve valuations in online auctions can be found in Lucking-Reiley and List (2000). The study presents the results of controlled experimental auctions performed in a field environment. The basic result is that classical auction theory accurately predicts a number of important features from the data: Holding all else constant, implementing reserve valuations reduces the number of bidders increases the frequency with which goods go unsold, and increases the revenues received for the goods, conditional on their having been sold.

5.7.7   Multi-Unit Online Auctions

Internet auction companies frequently have auctions for multiple identical units of a product as the information technology increases the feasibility of ascending-bid multi-unit auctions. In Lucking-Reiley's (1999) sample data from the 120 English auction sites he analyzed, at least 41 included multi-unit auction capability. The multi-unit discriminating-price English auction is also called a Yankee Auction®, which is a trademark of OnSale <http://www.onsale.com>. The multi-unit uniform-price rule is often also called "Dutch auction" on auction sites, which is misleading.

The multi-unit aspect also impacts the design parameters of an online auction. In traditional auctions, the reserve price and the bidding increment are the most important auction design parameters. In multi-unit online auctions the auctioneer also has to set parameters such as the *auction's length*, the *number of items* to be sold, the *price allocation rule* (uniform vs. discriminatory), the *type of information to display*, and *the sharing of information* with all bidders, etc.

Traditional auction theory assumes that the number of bidders is fixed (McAfee and McMillan, 1987), but on the Internet, for example, the auction's duration changes the number of bidders dynamically as more people visit the site. That is, on the Internet, the auctioneer does not know exactly how many bidders there are at any given auction. Therefore, it is important to know what the impact of the minimum bid or auction duration is on the number of bidders who participate in the auction. Using actual bidding transaction data from 324 business-to-consumer online auctions, Vakrat and Seidmann (2000) analyzed the bidders' arrival process during each auction. They used a multi-variable regression on the transaction data in order to learn the impact of duration, minimum initial bid, and quantity available on the equilibrium price. They found that the higher the minimum bid, the fewer the number of bidders attracted to the auction. In addition, as more units were offered more bidders were likely to participate in the auction.

Another empirical result is that longer auctions accumulate more bidders. This means that an auctioneer who keeps the auction open longer is likely to accumulate more bidders and, thus, increase the competitive pressure on the auction's closing price. Vakrat and Seidmann also found that most bidders like to sign on early in the auction. Typically, 70 percent of the bidders sign on during the first half. One reason for this is that many bidders are bargain hunters, so the lower current bid attracts more bidders. As the auction advances, the spot price ascends, and consequently fewer bidders are attracted to place a new bid. For the auctioneer, this has an important implication for the decision about how long she should run the auction, since the marginal benefit of keeping the auction open longer is dependent on the new bidders' arrival rate.

The most immediate conclusion is the obvious one: Online auctions are an extremely dynamic, fast-changing type of electronic commerce which is still in its infancy. The technology has just developed to the point that it is feasible to run an online auction, and new business models are just beginning to serve the tremendous online population of consumers.

5.8   Summary

So far, a variety of alternative market institutions have been compared. Although auctions have gained momentum on the Internet, most deals are not made using auctions. There are goods for which merchants post prices (see section 3.2) and others which people haggle over (see section 5.2).

High-volume securities trading is conducted on organized exchanges, using auction-like rules (see sub-section 5.3.6). These alternatives only scratch the surface of describing the huge variety of terms and institutions that govern trade in the modern world. There is little knowledge about when to use which type of market institution. Nevertheless, some informed guesses can be made.

Posted prices are commonly used for *standardized, inexpensive items* for which there is no need to solicit and compare competing bids. All customers can be served and customers do not find it worthwhile to participate in an auction. In summary, if it is too expensive to gather the competing buyers together and the timing of buyer demands varies, auctions are not a practicable selling institution (Milgrom, 1989). Another alternative to posted prices is one-on-one bargaining. However, bargaining is expensive and time-consuming. In general, bargaining is best avoided when there is enough competition for auctions to be used. Although this may only be true in distributive negotiations, many authors claim that bargaining often results in disagreement and inefficiency. Roth and Schoumaker (1983) show that in bargaining dividing a fixed surplus, with some or all of the surplus being lost if agreement is delayed, there can be a problem of indeterminacy.

When goods are not standardized or when market prices are highly volatile, posted prices work poorly, and auctions are usually preferred. For example, fresh fish is sold at auction so that prices can be responsive to daily variations in the demand. The power of competition in an auction is an important reason for the high efficiency of auction mechanisms. Milgrom (1989) gives a good example of the power of competition in using an auction:

When a seller employs an English auction to sell an item worth US $100 to himself to one of a pair of potential buyers with reservation values of US $170 and US $200, equilibrium theory predicts the sale will occur at a price of US $170. Not only is the result efficient, but the seller gets a good price: By bargaining singly with the US $200 evaluator, the seller can at best hope to split the gains, getting a price of US $150, and the seller may lose some of those gains if the parties fail to reach an agreement.

In summary, *efficiency*, *stability*, and *speed of convergence* are some of the factors that make auctions an excellent negotiation protocol for many contract negotiations in electronic commerce.

6 Experimental Analysis of Multi-Attribute Auctions

> We've suddenly made the interaction cost so cheap, there's no pragmatic reason not to have competitive bidding on everything.
>
> (*Stuart I. Feldman, IBM Institute for Advanced Commerce*)

Subsection 5.2.2 introduced negotiation support systems, which are used to support bilateral negotiations on multiple attributes. This section introduces multi-attribute auctions, a generalization of reverse auctions. Multi-attribute (reverse) auctions combine the advantages of auctions, such as high efficiency and speed of convergence, and permit negotiation on multiple attributes with multiple suppliers in a procurement situation.

6.1 Multi-Attribute Procurement Negotiations

Several authors have analyzed tenders and reverse auctions (Dasgupta and Spulber, 1989; Laffont and Tirole, 1993). Previous game-theoretical models of reverse auctions have generally assumed that the qualitative attributes are fixed prior to competitive source selection – hence, bidding competition is restricted to the price dimension. While such an approach may be appropriate for auctions of homogeneous goods, this assumption does not necessarily apply to most procurement situations.

In reverse auctions, bidders often provide very different kinds of goods and services in their bids. An example is the procurement of large food retailers (Bichler, Kaukal and Segev, 1999). The suppliers in the market consist of large companies as well as a large number of small and medium-sized enterprises (SMEs) such as bakeries and breweries. The buyers are a small number of large food retailers who aggregate the demand and distribute it to the consumer. Purchasing managers have their own preferences for product quality, price, and terms of payment and delivery, and they are looking for the offer that best satisfies these preferences. The overall utility of a deal for the buyer involves not only the price of the item but a combination of the different attributes. In contrast to sales auctions, the bids submitted in tenders often comprise heterogeneous goods or services and the bidtaker has the burden of selecting the "best" bid. When a bid taker procures a standardized item or she can define all the features of the product at the outset, conventional single-attribute auctions are a powerful way of automating negotiations. The negotiation situations which are analyzed in this section describe heterogeneous monopsonies with a single buyer and multiple sellers in which the traded goods have several negotiable attributes and the buyer has certain preferences on these attributes.

The advances in information technology now allow the use of varied and more complex auction mechanisms. Multi-attribute auctions propose a way to take multiple attributes of a deal into account when allocating it to a bidder. In other words, the mechanism automates multilateral negotiations on multiple attributes. However, the design of these mechanisms poses several practical and theoretical problems. The next section will describe a number of multi-attribute auction formats. Based on this description, a number of research questions will be formulated in section 6.3. Section 6.4 will provide a description of the trading with over-the-counter (OTC) financial derivatives, a sample scenario which will be used throughout chapters 7 and 8. IT support is a crucial precondition for multi-attribute auction mechanisms. Therefore, an electronic brokerage system implementing multi-attribute auctions will be outlined in section 6.5. Based on this implementation a series of laboratory experiments were conducted. The results are outlined in section 6.6 and provide a solid idea of how real-world users can cope with this new market mechanism.

6.2   Description of the Analyzed Mechanisms

Laffont and Tirole (1993) describe many of the critical issues in procurement negotiations from an economics point of view and also mention the need for a generalization of auction theory to so-called "multi-dimensional bidding." In multi-dimensional auctions a bid taker negotiates with several bidders over multiple issues/attributes of a contract. Parties engage in the process because they have certain objectives whose achievement depends on the values of the attribute.

Teich, Wallenius and Wallenius (1999) proposed a number of so-called *multi-issue auction algorithms*. In the *leap frog method*, each bid must be an improvement over the previous bid in at least one of the attributes and no worse in any of the attributes. The preferences of the bid taker are not considered at all. In the *auction maker controlled bid mechanism*, the bid taker represents a preference path for a seller in a situation where the seller and the buyers are diametrically opposed in a two-issue space. The bidders then have to follow this preference path (see figure 6.1). In the case of more than

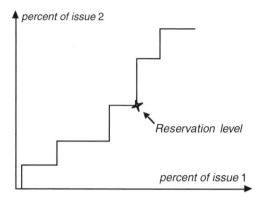

Figure 6.1 Auction maker controlled bid mechanism.
Source: Teich, Wallenius and Wallenius (1999, p. 57).

two negotiable issues it might become difficult for the bid taker to define a preference path.

It is important for a bidder to have explicit instructions on how to improve or optimize the bids. Otherwise, this will lead to unguided bidding and potentially inefficient results. The auction maker controlled bid mechanism is very restricting from the point of view of the bidder in that it permits bidding only along the pre-defined preference path. The presence of two or more attributes raises the possibility of using utility as a measure of offers as well as other mechanisms that have been traditionally used in negotiations.

Multi-attribute auctions[1] assume that the buyer reveals a scoring function to the bidders based on her utility function.[2] That is, a buyer first has to define her preferences for a certain product in the form of a scoring function, which is then made public to all bidders. This might not be feasible or desirable in all cases (e.g. if preferences are highly confidential), but it is a good way to guide bidders towards an efficient solution and to automate the bidding procedure. After soliciting bids from the various suppliers, the mechanism designates the contract to the supplier who maximizes the buyer's preferences – i.e. who provides the highest overall utility score for the buyer.

An important issue in this context is how to model the buyer's preferences in the form of a scoring function. Multi-attribute auctions are based on the concepts of utility theory and decision analysis (see for example

---

[1] I use the term "multi-attribute auction," as "multi-dimensional auction" is also used in the context of combinatorial auctions (Wurman, 1997).
[2] The scoring function and the utility function need not necessarily be the same. However, for now, both functions are assumed to reflect the same preference ordering.

Debreu, 1954; Keeny and Raiffa, 1993; Clemen, 1996). The various approaches prescribe theories for quantitatively analyzing important decisions involving multiple, interdependent objectives (Laux, 1998). For the evaluation of bids, while the price of a product could be important, so could its delivery time. Multi-objective decision analysis techniques are widely used in business and government decision making, and even for product selection in electronic catalogs (Stolze, 1998). The interested reader is referred to the appendix (p. 206), where the basic concepts of utility theory are introduced and the most widespread decision analysis techniques are described.

Multi-attribute utility theory (MAUT) is a suitable and widely accepted methodology to elicit a buyer's preferences and model a scoring function (Bichler, 1998). Almost all reported multi-attribute decision applications assume use of an additive (or linear) function to model a user's preferences, in which the overall utility score is the sum of part utilities (Clemen, 1996, p. 553). An additive scoring function is easy to use and intuitive, but it comes with certain limitations. A crucial pre-condition for the use of an additive function, if certainty of all attribute values in a bid is assumed, is *mutual preferential independence* among all attributes. An attribute x is said to be preferentially independent of y if preferences for specific outcomes of x do not depend on the level of attribute y (Olson, 1995).

Keeny and Raiffa (1993) suggest that if an independence assumption is found to be inappropriate, either a fundamental objective has been overlooked or means objectives are being used as fundamental objectives. Moreover, evidence from behavioral research has shown that it is rarely, if ever, necessary to model more complex scoring functions (Clemen, 1996, p. 593). In very complicated situations, the additive model may become a useful rough-cut approximation, and it often turns out that considering the interactions among attributes is not critical to the decision at hand (Clemen, 1996, p. 585). Section 7.3 will consider a few cases where preferential independence is not given.

The following paragraphs will introduce some terminology and notation. A buyer solicits bids from m suppliers. Each bid specifies an offer of price and multiple quality dimensions, at which a fixed quantity of products with the offered quality levels is delivered. A bid received by the buyer can then be described as an n-dimensional vector Q of relevant attributes indexed by i. Attributes may be either monetary or non-monetary. There is a set B of bids and the m bids are indexed by j. A bid by company i is denoted by a vector $x_j = (x_j^1 \ldots x_j^n)$ where x_j^i is the value of attribute i. In the case of an additive scoring function $S(x_j)$ the buyer evaluates each relevant attribute x_j^i through a scoring function $S_j(x_j^i)$. An individual scoring function, $S: Q \rightarrow \Re$, translates the value of an attribute into "utility scores." The overall utility $S(x_j)$ for a bid x_j is the sum of all individual scorings of the attributes. It is convenient to scale S and each of the single-attribute scoring functions S_i from zero to one, and to weigh the individual attributes. All weights w_i sum up to one. That is, for a bid x_j that has values $x_j^1 \dots x_j^n$ and a scoring function that has weights $w_1 \dots w_n$ on the n relevant attributes, the overall utility for a bid is given by

$$S(x_j) = \sum_{i=1}^{n} w_i S_i(x_j^i) \text{ and } \sum_{i=1}^{n} w_i = 1. \qquad (6.1)$$

The problem a buyer faces is to determine appropriate S_i functions and w_i weights. An optimal auction allocates the deal to the supplier in a way that maximizes the utility for the buyer, that is, to the supplier providing the bid with the highest overall utility score for the buyer. The function

$$\max \{S(x_j)\} \text{ with } 1 \leq j \leq m \qquad (6.2)$$

provides the utility score of the winning bid and can be determined through various auction schemes. The derived scoring function has an ordinal character since a monotonic transformation does not change the preference ordering. It can happen that the utility scores of winning bids are very close. Since the scoring function might be biased, the bid taker is recommended to evaluate the results before the deal is closed and to set a minimum bid increment.

Similar to classic auction theory, open-cry and sealed-bid auctions are distinguished. In a *first-score sealed-bid auction* the winner is awarded a contract containing the attributes x_j of the winning bid. Alternatives with the same overall utility are indifferent and the first of those bids is the winning bid. The *multi-attribute English auction* (also called *first-score open-cry auction*) works in the same way, but all bids are made available to the participants during an auction period and bidders can place multiple bids. In a *second-score sealed-bid auction* the overall utility achieved by the second highest bid S_{max-1} is taken and the gap to the highest score ($S_{max} - S_{max-1}$) is transformed into monetary units. Consequently, the winning bidder can charge a higher price. In the first-score and second-score sealed-bid schemes the auction closes after a certain pre-announced deadline. In a multi-attribute English auction bids are made public and the auction closes after a certain time has elapsed in which nobody submits a bid. A multi-attribute generalization of the Dutch auction is also possible, but this procedure is more difficult to implement in practice (figure 6.2).

The distinction between integrative and distributive negotiations has already been mentioned (see subsection 5.2.2). In many commercial negotiations, exclusive focus on price alone does a disservice to buyers and sellers alike by hiding important attributes from consideration (Teich, Wallenius and Wallenius, 1999). An explicit consideration of multiple attributes as is

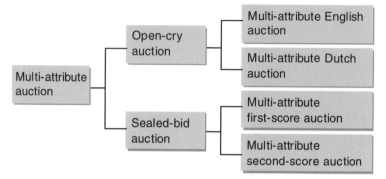

Figure 6.2 Multi-attribute auction formats.

described in this section promises the conversion of distributive negotiations into more integrative negotiations. This is not only useful in the context of multi-person negotiations but also in multi-agent environments. For instance, Vulkan and Jennings proposed a variant of multi-attribute English auctions for automating negotiations among autonomous agents in the ADEPT multi-agent system (Vulkan and Jennings, 2000).

6.3   Research Questions

Before introducing a new market mechanism in the field, it is important to study its economic behavior under certain circumstances. The following sections will try to answer several research questions associated with multi-attribute auctions:

■ *Are multi-attribute auction formats payoff equivalent?*
   One of the most interesting products of classic auction theory is the revenue equivalence theorem (described in subsection 5.3.2). Although this theorem holds only under the conditions of the IPV model, it is interesting to see whether this result can be generalized to the multi-dimensional case.

■ *Are the utility scores achieved in a multi-attribute auction higher compared to single-attribute auctions?*
   A basic question of auction design is which auction format maximizes the bid taker's profit. In a multi-attribute auction, the bidder has several possibilities to improve the value of a bid for the bid taker, sometimes even without increasing her costs and thereby creating joint gains for all parties. The question is whether multi-attribute auctions do in fact achieve a higher utility score than single-attribute auctions with respect to a buyer's scoring function.

■ *Are multi-attribute auctions efficient?*
(Pareto) efficiency can be measured in terms of the percentage of auctions in which the high-value holder wins the item. Many laboratory experiments have analyzed the efficiency of conventional auctions. It is interesting to learn about the efficiency of multi-attribute auctions compared to single-attribute auctions.

The following sections will analyze these questions using a set of tools and methods introduced in chapter 4. They will describe a real-world implementation of multi-attribute auctions and summarize the results of laboratory experiments, game-theoretical and computational analysis. The next section will introduce a sample scenario to be used throughout the following sections.

6.4   Trading Financial Derivatives – A Sample Scenario

The literature on reverse auctions focuses mostly on procurement scenarios in a government or corporate environment. These scenarios involve a multitude of attributes and it is often not known *a priori* what the important attributes are. For the further analysis, a scenario from the financial services industry was chosen which is particularly adept in the use of multi-attribute auctions – so-called over-the-counter (OTC) trading with financial derivatives (Bichler, 2000a). In the OTC market for options several well known attributes (premium, strike price, duration, etc.) are negotiated. The scenario was also chosen because it is easy to model the behavior of a rational bidder in this market. Since participants have different market expectations and different risk attitudes, they value combinations of attribute values differently. This aspect is useful in laboratory experiments as well as in simulations. Based on a few idiosyncratic attributes (such as market expectation and minimum risk premium), a bidder can calculate the optimal combination of attributes in a bid given the preferences of the bid taker.

The following subsections will provide a brief introduction to OTC trading with financial derivatives. This should also provide the necessary background for the laboratory experiments presented in section 6.6. If you are familiar with the trading of financial derivatives, please proceed to section 6.5.

6.4.1   The Basics of Futures and Options

A *forward transaction* is an agreement by which the contracting parties enter into the obligation to buy or sell a determined amount of a commodity at a strike price, both delivery and payment being owing in the future. The spot price is the price paid on the cash market for the immediate delivery of a commodity or a financial instrument. The forward rate fixes the settlement price for the delivery of a commodity (e.g. stocks, coffee, wheat) at a specified future date and usually differs from the spot price, though it follows the same trend. The difference between these prices may be either positive or negative, depending on a variety of factors such as expectations, interest rates, inventories, harvests, etc. The contract or settlement price is the price at which a forward contract is settled at a specified point in time. While the settlement price remains constant, the forward rate and spot price fluctuate. The difference between these two prices will shrink in the course of time. The following paragraphs will introduce the most common types of forward transactions (see Kolb, 2000, for a more detailed introduction).

Futures are contracts in which the purchase or sale of a commodity is fixed at the time the contract is concluded, while delivery and payment are scheduled for a defined future date. The seller of a futures contract agrees to deliver the underlying commodity at a future date at a strike price, while the buyer enters into the obligation to take delivery of the commodity at the strike price. Futures basically serve the purpose of eliminating uncertainty about factors that may influence payments in the future. A good example is the farmer who sells wheat through a futures contract with the aim of minimizing the risk of a future drop in wheat prices. Futures are offered on many markets and may be used for a variety of purposes. In the USA, they are commonly used in the trading of agricultural products. Farmers can, for example, sell wheat through futures, and, thus, secure a certain income level. They are also traded on foreign exchange markets and commodity exchanges.

Forwards are individual, customized agreements between two parties that provide for the delivery and payment of a defined commodity at a later point in time. Since a forward contract is based on an individual agreement between two parties, these parties are at liberty to agree on terms that they consider mutually beneficial. The heterogeneity of contract terms renders forwards applicable to a wide variety of different purposes, at the same time restricting their tradability during their life time. Therefore, they are usually completed upon actual delivery. The chances that the terms agreed on in such a contract will coincide with the requirements of a third trading partner decline with the degree to which the contract is tailored to the individual needs of the original contracting partners. The heterogeneity of the contract terms restricts their tradability and lowers market transparency in forward dealings. Futures contracts, by contrast, are standardized contracts that define the delivery and payment of a specific commodity through a central clearing house. Trading in futures is strongly formalized and subject to strict rules. Thanks to these features, futures contracts, unlike forwards, are easily tradable, even in their maturity.

A *swap* is an agreement between two or more parties to exchange sets of cash flows over a period of time. For example, *A* might agree to pay a fixed rate of interest on US $1 million each year for five years to *B*. In return, *B* might pay a floating rate of interest on US $1 million each year for five years. The two basic kinds of swaps are interest rate swaps and currency swaps.

Options have the same conceptual foundation as do forward contracts. Here, too, the seller has the obligation to fulfill a contract by the end of an agreed period. The right to buy or sell an underlying instrument at a fixed point in time is obtained by paying the option premium upon conclusion of the contract. The risk of the buyer involved in options is restricted to this option premium. Options are traded on a wide variety of commodities and goods. Traders use options to buy or sell wheat, tulip bulbs, precious metals, foreign currency, shares and other securities, to name just a few items. The difference between options traded off-floor (so-called OTC or over-the-counter options) and exchange-traded options is much like that between forwards and futures. Trading in OTC options is not bound to an organizational structure in that supply and demand are concentrated on a centralized trading floor. OTC options are not subject to a standardized trading procedure and are not traded on the exchanges.

The basis of an options contract is the purchase or sale of a right to demand the delivery (call) or the sale (put) of a specified contract size of assets (e.g. shares), over a fixed period of time (maturity) at a strike price. That is, call options involve the right to buy an underlying, put options involve the right to sell it. The holder of a call purchases the right to demand delivery of the underlying contract at the agreed price (strike or exercise price) any time up to the expiration of the options contract. The writer of a call undertakes the obligation to deliver the underlying instrument at the exercise price any time upon (American style) or exactly at (European style) expiration of the call if the holder exercises the right. In contrast, the writer of a put enters into the obligation to take delivery of the underlying contract at the exercise price any time upon or exactly at the expiration date of the put if the holder exercises the right. Options on shares are characterized by standardized agreements. Those contracts are specified with the following criteria:

- type of option (put or call)
- underlying instrument
- style (American or European)
- contract size
- maturity (expiration date)
- strike or exercise price.

Standardization is necessary to safeguard the smooth functioning of secondary market trading. As all market participants trade with options contracts on equal terms, the contracts are easily tradable and exchange-able. This results in lower transaction costs since the parties need not nego-tiate the terms every time a contract is concluded. Today there exist standardized options and futures for shares, stock indices, bonds, and cur-rencies. This book will concentrate on options.

Most options exchanges use a *market maker* system to facilitate trading. A market maker for a certain option is a person who must quote both a bid and an ask price of certain option series. The bid is the price at which the market maker is prepared to buy and the ask is the price at which the market maker is prepared to sell. At the time the bid and the ask are quoted, the market maker does not know whether somebody wants to buy or sell the option. The ask is, of course, higher than the bid, and the difference between ask and bid is referred to as the bid–ask spread. The exchange sets upper limits for the bid–ask spread. The existence of the market maker ensures that buy and sell orders can always be executed at some price without delays. Market makers therefore add liquidity to the market. The market makers themselves make their profits from the bid–ask spread. That means that a market maker has to stand ready to buy or sell a particular option as a dealer for her own account. Each market maker helps maintain a fair and orderly market in at least one security and/or underlying secu-rity's options. For the obligation to quote bid and ask prices, the market maker has the advantage that she has to pay lower fees than the other market participants (customers, brokers).

Firms engaged in buying and selling securities for the public must regis-ter as broker–dealers. Most firms act both as brokers and dealers, but not in the same transaction. *Brokers* are agents that arrange trades for clients and charge commissions. Brokers do not buy shares, but simply arrange trades between buyers and sellers. *Dealers* buy and sell securities for their own accounts, which is often called "position trading." When selling from their inventories, dealers charge their clients markups rather than commis-sions. A markup is the difference between the current inter-dealer offering price and the actual price charged to the client. When a price to a client includes a dealer's markup, it is called the "net price."

6.4.2   Trading Options

There are different reasons for which investors may wish to buy or sell futures and options. Trading in these instruments permits the reconciliation of two seemingly incompatible goals: high profit expectations and the need for insurance. Options and futures are a means of benefiting from upward and downward fluctuations in the price of the underlying. Options also permit speculation on the stable price development of the underlying instrument. At the same time, options and futures are a means of securing

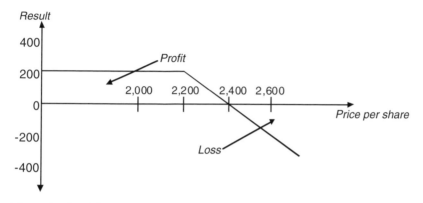

Figure 6.3 Profit/loss example diagram of a short call.

a portfolio against price losses or of hedging a planned purchase against a possible price increase. Hence, the differing risk attitudes of the different market players represent a very important aspect of options trading (see also McLaughlin, 1998, for a detailed description).

A position describes the rights and obligations attached to previously made transactions and may be long or short. A long position is generally a purchase which has not yet been closed out (offset by a counter transaction). A short position, in contrast, is a not yet closed-out sale. An investor who expects the price of an underlying to rise may, instead of buying the share itself, purchase a call on the underlying. Buying the call permits the investor to benefit from the price increase of the underlying instrument without having to purchase it. This position is also called a *long call*. The counter-party to the holder of the call is the writer of the call (option seller). This party's market expectation with regard to the underlying instrument is neutral or slightly bearish. That is, she receives a premium which already represents her maximum profit. The profit/loss diagram depicted in figure 6.3 shows the profit and loss of a *short call* example at different price trends of the underlying share.

If the price of the underlying is below the strike price of the call on the expiration date, the writer will not be required to deliver the underlying, as the holder of the call will abstain from exercising the option. The writer thus books the premium as a profit. However, if the price of the underlying instruments has risen beyond the strike price, the holder will exercise the call and compel the writer to sell the underlying below market value. As soon as the price of the underlying begins to exceed the total strike price plus premium received, the writer starts making a loss. Put options can be regarded in a similar manner.

When the exercise price of a call is lower than the price of the underlying item, the option has an intrinsic value. In the case of a call, the rule is: the higher the value of the underlying relative to the exercise price, the higher the intrinsic value and, thus, the value of the option. When the strike price of a call is lower than the going market price of the underlying, the option has an intrinsic value. The put option has an intrinsic value if the strike price is higher than the going market price of the underlying. Such options are said to be *in-the-money*. The time value is the difference between the premium and the intrinsic value. The time value declines over the life of an option and is always zero on the expiration date.

There are several possibilities for the holder of an option. If she chooses to exercise the option at an options exchange, she has to address an order in writing to a central clearing house through a bank or a broker. The central clearing house then acts as seller if the option holder chooses to buy the underlying and becomes a buyer when the option holder is the party who wrote the option. The clearing house notifies the writer of the option as to which party will buy or sell the underlying security from or to the central clearing house. Every trade through which an option is exercised is subject to a fee. Instead of exercising an option the holder may also hope for cash settlement on the expiration day. If the price of the underlying is above the exercise price, the holder will be credited with the difference between the exercise price and the value of the underlying while the writer of the option will be debited. An option may also be closed out whenever desired by either buying or selling options of the same series (e.g. a holder of a call by writing a call). Finally, an option holder can allow an option to expire. This means that the option loses its entire value and the option holder suffers a loss in the amount of the premium paid.

Writers and holders of options often follow specific trading strategies in order to achieve certain objectives. There are several aspects that come into play in this context, such as the investor's market expectations, the investor's objective, and risk tolerance. When investors buy calls, this implies that they expect prices to develop favorably, which is reflected in an increase in the option's value. On the other hand, a spread refers to the simultaneous selling and buying of one and the same type of option of a different series. For example, a vertical spread (price spread) involves the buying or selling of same-type options with the same expiration date, but differing strike prices. There are numerous different strategies which cannot be discussed in detail in this context. The interested reader is referred to textbooks such as Kolb (1993) or Müller-Möhl (1989).

6.4.3   *Option Pricing Models*

Much research has been done in order to assess the fair value of an option. This section will introduce some of the most widespread option pricing models. There are several factors influencing the price or premium of an option, such as the price of the underlying, the strike price, the life of an option, the volatility of the underlying, interest rates, etc. The option premium, for example, is the higher the more time remains to maturity and the higher the volatility of the underlying. The price of the underlying item has the greatest impact on the option premium. Every change in the price of the underlying is reflected in a change in the option premium. The delta factor is a widespread measure in this context and stands for the absolute change in the price of an option when the underlying changes by one unit. It is calculated:

$$\text{Delta} = \frac{\text{Change in option price}}{\text{Change in underlying}}. \tag{6.3}$$

The delta factor stands for the absolute change in the price of an option when the underlying changes by one unit. A delta factor of one means that a change in the price of the underlying causes the option price to change by exactly the same amount. A delta of zero means that a change in the price of the underlying has no impact whatsoever on the option price.

Older option pricing models use complex risk/reward ratios based on investors' objectives. The basic approach of modern option pricing theory starts out from the concept of market equilibrium price (fair price) and the assumption that there are no arbitrage opportunities in an efficient, well functioning market. Looking at the evaluation of financial instruments, this means that portfolios of equal value at maturity and equal probabilities associated with this value at maturity also have the same price (i.e. no mispricing). If, however, there is a discrepancy, there is an opportunity to lock in a risk-free profit (arbitrage profit). These considerations lead to the assumption of put–call parity: if the combined position of a long call + short put corresponds to a synthetic futures contract, then a position entered by simultaneously selling an actual futures contract and buying a synthetic futures contract should not yield a profit exceeding the risk-free rate of interest attainable on the capital market.

A well known approach is the binomial model of Cox and Rubinstein (1985). Though the binomial model is the more general option valuation model, it was developed later than the Black–Scholes model formulated by Fischer Black and Myron Scholes in 1973, a model which actually represents a more specific version of the binomial model. Black and Scholes (1973) developed their option pricing model under the assumptions that asset prices adjust to prevent arbitrage, that stock prices change continuously, and that stock returns follow a log-normal distribution. Further, they assume that the interest rate and the volatility of the stock remain constant over the life of the option. In the majority of cases, there are virtually no differences between the results derived on the basis of the more specific assumptions Black and Scholes use in their formula and the results obtained with the more general binomial model, but the Black–Scholes model is easier to use. The mathematics they used to derive their result include stochastic calculus which is beyond the scope of this text. This section presents the model and illustrates the basic intuition that underlies it. Expression (6.4) gives the Black–Scholes option pricing model for a call option:

$$c = S_t N(d_1) - X e^{-r(T-t)} N(d_2) \tag{6.4}$$

$$d_1 = \frac{\ln\left(\dfrac{S}{X}\right) + \left(r + \dfrac{\sigma^2}{2}\right) \times (T-t)}{\sigma \times \sqrt{T-t}} \tag{6.5}$$

$$d_2 = d_1 \sqrt{T-t}. \tag{6.6}$$

where:

   c value of the call
   S spot price of the underlying
   X exercise price of the option
   e the base of the natural logarithm
   r short-term risk-free average market rate of interest
   $T-t$ time to expiration
   σ volatility of the underlying
   $N(.)$ cumulative normal distribution function.

$N(d_1)$ states by how many points the value of a call will change if the price of the underlying changes by one point. The first part of the Black–Scholes formula, $S_t N(d_1)$, yields the present value of the underlying in the event the option is exercised. The second part of the formula represents the cash value of the exercise price that has to be paid, $-e^{-r(T-t)} X N(d_2)$. The discount factor $e^{-r(T-t)}$ corresponds to the usual factor $(1+r)^{-t}$ given continuous conversion of compound interest which results from the basic assumption of continuous trading (Kolb, 2000).

The Black–Scholes model is an innovative achievement in so far as options can be evaluated regardless of the personal preferences of market participants (i.e. risk inclination). Rather than being based on such preferences, the model is based on the concept of efficient markets, implying that there cannot be a portfolio that costs nothing at time t and will not with positive probability yield a positive return at some point in time in the future (i.e. no arbitrage). A model can only be as good as its inputs. One of the critical inputs is volatility, σ. Volatility is a measure that helps to determine the fluctuation ranges of stock prices. A reliable estimate of volatility is of the utmost importance in ensuring that the model and the related computer programs produce meaningful results.

6.4.4   OTC Trading of Derivatives

As already shown, several factors influence the price of an option, such as the underlying instrument, the life time, the strike price, the style, and so on. All these factors influence the option premium no matter whether the options are traded on an exchange or OTC. In order to set a certain option premium in the context of its strike price and other parameters, traders often use the so-called *implied volatility*, which indicates the volatility implied by a certain option premium. Thus, the value of a certain premium can be measured independently of the strike price. The lower the implied volatility of an option, the better it is for the buyer of the call. For many traders it has become common practice to quote an option's market price in terms of implied volatility (Kwok, 1998).

On an options exchange all of these attributes are specified in advance and the only negotiable attribute is the price. This makes trading much easier, but it also reduces the number of derivatives traded to a small set of possible products. As a result, the volume of OTC contracts has grown enormously over the past few years (BIZ, 1997). Trading OTC options is not bound to an organizational structure in that supply and demand are concentrated on a centralized trading floor. Potential buyers of OTC options bargain with a number of investment brokers or banks on attributes such as the strike price, the style, the maturity, and the premium of an option. Terms and conditions are usually not made out through auctions, but rather through bargaining. Financial engineers created a whole assortment of different financial OTC products tailored for specific purposes, ranging from plain vanilla options where all important attributes are negotiated during the bargaining process, to exotic derivatives with certain predefined properties (see Kolb, 1993, for different types of options and details of option pricing). Institutional investors have a particular need for special derivative products.

However, traditional OTC transactions have several disadvantages. Bilateral negotiations with banks or investment brokers are conducted via the phone which leads to high transaction costs in each deal. In contrast to electronic exchanges, investors lose their anonymity and must also carry the contractual risk. New approaches are trying to establish efficient, electronic trading systems for OTC derivatives. For example, in 1993 US options exchanges began the development of FLExible Exchange® Options (FLEX Options), an electronic trading system for the trading of index options. Equity FLEX Options (E-FLEX Options) has broadened the concept to encompass listed equity options. Equity FLEXible Exchange Options provide the opportunity to customize key contract terms, including the expiration date, exercise style, and strike price of an equity option. Prices are then determined anonymously by means of single-sided auction mechanisms. Thus, options and futures can be designed to fit an investor's own investment strategies and goals. Both systems have been designed to increase investor access to customized derivative products. They are used on the NASDAQ, the American Stock Exchange, the Chicago Board Options Exchange and the Pacific Stock Exchange.

While systems like this combine many advantages of OTC trading and electronic exchanges, deployed auction mechanisms merely automate negotiations on the price. In contrast, participants in an OTC market also have the possibility to bargain on contract attributes such as strike price, style, contract maturity, or contract size. This gives a participant a much greater degree of freedom during negotiation and provides the potential to achieve a better deal for both parties. The subsequent analysis will utilize multi-attribute auctions to automate such negotiations.

6.5   Implementation of an Electronic Brokerage Service

In order to make multi-attribute auctions more transparent, this section will describe a software implementation as a service of an electronic broker. The implementation is useful for several reasons. First of all, it provides a clear picture of how multi-attribute auctions can be utilized in practice. Information technology is a critical enabler for this new mechanism, as the bidding process would not be feasible without the use of software tools. Second, the implementation was the basis for a series of laboratory experiments.

6.5.1   Overview and Bidding Process

The electronic brokerage service provides several single- and multi-attribute auction mechanisms, as well as a buyer client and a bidder client implemented as Java applets. The server-side application logic (i.e. registration of participants, forwarding of requests for bids, determination of winners, etc.) is implemented in Perl and PL/SQL on top of an Oracle8 database. Messages between buyer client and server, such as bids and requests for bids, are exchanged in a pre-defined XML format using HTTP.

There are numerous ways to implement client–server applications of this type with middleware such as OMG/CORBA or Java RMI (see sub-section 2.3). Fan, Stallaert and Whinston (1999) provide a good example of an Internet marketplace based on distributed object infrastructures. An XML-based approach has been chosen because of its simplicity and flexibility and the fact that one can build on the ubiquitous web infrastructure. The client side runs in most web browsers, the server-side implementation

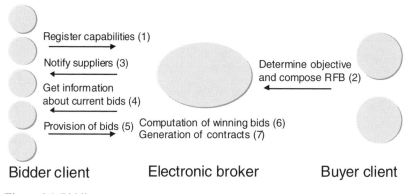

Register capabilities (1)

Notify suppliers (3)

Get information
about current bids (4)

Provision of bids (5)   Computation of winning bids (6)
Generation of contracts (7)

Determine objective
and compose RFB (2)

Bidder client   Electronic broker   Buyer client

Figure 6.4 Bidding process.

does not require additional infrastructure such as, for example, an Object Request Broker, and can be implemented in a variety of programming languages. Therefore, it is possible to conduct the experiments in different computer labs without the installation of additional client-side software. All the transaction data is stored in the Oracle8 database and can be evaluated with standard spreadsheet and statistics packages (see Bichler and Kaukal, 1999, for a detailed description of the implementation). The electronic brokerage service provides a very general framework and can easily be customized to suit different types of products. Figure 6.4 shows the main steps during the bidding process. This process has also been used in the laboratory experiments (see section 6.6).

Suppliers have to register their capabilities with the electronic broker (1). The buyer specifies a request for bids (RFB) and submits it to the trading floor (2). Then the electronic brokerage service notifies suppliers with corresponding abilities (3) and collects their bids. The suppliers can compose a bid out of the RFB (5). A client-side tool helps in composing a winning bid. For this reason the client can query not only the RFB but also information about other bids (4) which is provided anonymously. The auctions can be conducted according to various auction schemes (open-cry, sealed-bid). After the auction closes, it computes the winning bids and aggregates them into a package for the buyer (6). After the winning bids are determined, the brokerage service writes up a digital contract (7).

Unfortunately, current online auctions support negotiations only on price. The rest of the deal is pre-defined at the outset. Using an auction for procurement means that the buyers lose much valuable information about the suppliers. For example, some companies might be able to deliver very high-quality products or others might provide exceptionally good credit terms. Multi-attribute auctions are an alternative and automate negotiations on multiple attributes.

6.5.2   Server-Side Implementation

The server-side implementation of the electronic broker provides several services for the market participants. First of all, it provides a product taxonomy of all the products traded on a particular market. The web-based taxonomy is structured in a hierarchical manner and contains product names and a short description of product features. This makes it easier for buyers and sellers to express their interests or abilities, as they share a common understanding of the terminology they use.

The brokerage facility also manages user profiles of all participants. It provides registration for new buyers and suppliers on the market and admits them to the trading process. During registration, the brokerage service solicits profiles of all suppliers, so that it acquires basic knowledge about capabilities of suppliers available on a market. Registration is performed by means of a conventional web form. The profile management of the brokerage facility is also a means of providing trust, as the broker bans unreliable participants from the market. In most online auctions this simple mechanism provides a reasonable level of trust. High-value, high-volume trading floors, however, require a more sophisticated infrastructure that provides features such as non-repudiation of document exchanges, enforceability of agreements, and dispute resolution for all market participants.

The bidding procedure can be initiated by sending an RFB to the brokerage facility. RFBs contain all the necessary information about the product in question, as well as the preferences for various attributes of a deal. All messages within this marketplace are exchanged as XML-formatted documents via HTTP. As already mentioned, this provides a high degree of flexibility in the implementation of client-side and server-side software. Three different XML DTDs are used in the implementation, namely a request for bids (`rfb.dtd`), a bid, i.e. a response to request for bids (`rrfb.dtd`), and a message containing information about bids submitted for a certain RFB so far (`bid-status.dtd`). Figure 6.5 provides the DTD of an RFB in the marketplace.

After a buyer submits an RFB, the electronic brokerage service parses the document and stores the attributes in the database. Then, the RFB is forwarded to all the suppliers in a specific industry who are able to bid for the special RFB (e.g. quantity wise). Potential bidders receive an e-mail containing a URL from which they can download the particular RFB. At the same time the server starts a certain auction mechanism (as specified in the RFB). Currently, this can be either an English, a first-score, or a second-

```
<!-- RFB.DTD -->
<!ELEMENT rfb (preference*)>
<!ATTLIST rfb
     buyer.id ID #REQUIRED
     prod.name CDATA #IMPLIED
     target.ind CDATA #IMPLIED
     date CDATA #IMPLIED
     taxonomy CDATA #IMPLIED
     auction_type (english | first_score | sec-
     ond_score)
     "english" #REQUIRED
>
<!ELEMENT preference (contattr|disattr)>
<!ATTLIST preference
     name CDATA #REQUIRED
     importance CDATA #REQUIRED
>
<!ELEMENT fixattr EMPTY>
<!ELEMENT disattr (eval*)>
<!ELEMENT eval EMPTY>
<!ATTLIST eval
     attr CDATA #REQUIRED
     value CDATA #REQUIRED
>
<!ELEMENT contattr EMPTY>
<!ATTLIST contattr
     max CDATA #REQUIRED
     min CDATA #REQUIRED
     type (+|-|>|<) "+" #REQUIRED
     step CDATA #IMPLIED
>
```

Figure 6.5 RFB Document Type Definition.

score auction. By means of a bidder client, suppliers are able to compose a
bid from the RFB and submit it to the electronic brokerage service.

Depending on the auction mechanism used, the brokerage system computes the winning bid. The auction mechanisms are controlled by several
parameters such as the bid increment or auction closing (after a certain
elapse time, or at a certain deadline). For example, if the auction is conducted according to the rules of an English auction, a bidder may only bid
a higher utility than the previous bids and the auction closes after a certain
time has elapsed. In a first step, RFB and scoring function can not be

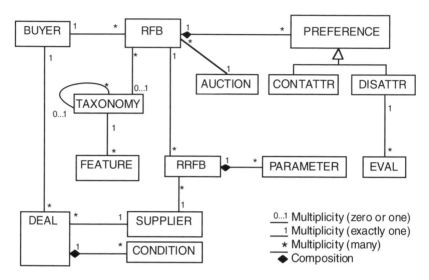

Figure 6.6 UML class diagram of the electronic brokerage service.

altered during the bidding process in order not to jeopardize trust in the system. However, also a more dynamic negotiation process was implemented where the buyer can change his preferences after having received several bids, as well as a tool on the bidders' side which helps the bidder to easily adapt to these changes.

Figure 6.6 shows the database schema of the application following the UML notation for class diagrams (Fowler, 1997). Every RFB in this model has several PREFERENCEs which can be either continuous attributes (subentity CONTATTR) or discrete attributes (subentity DISATTR). An RFB is auctioned off according to a certain type of AUCTION and the products in question can be found in a hierarchical product TAXONOMY. A bid (i.e. RRFB) belongs to a certain RFB and has a set of associated PARAMETERs. The parameters stated in the RRFB and the preferences for certain attributes of the RFB allow the broker to compute the winning bid. After the auction closes the broker computes the final winner and stores the parameters of the winning bid in the CONDITIONs of a particular DEAL.

6.5.3   Client-Side Implementation

Server-side implementation is very similar to what would be expected from the implementation of a conventional online auction. The main difference lies in the way winning bids are computed in the multi-attribute case.

Clients, however, become much more complex. Buyers need an intuitive tool to determine and write down their scoring function in the form of an RFB, whereas bidders need some kind of a decision support tool to formulate a winning bid. The challenge from a system design perspective is how to implement a user interface that is both powerful and easy enough to use for the participants. Owing to space limitations only a very brief outline of the functionality provided by the buyer and the bidder client will be supplied.

6.5.3.1 Buyer Client

This subsection will cover the difficulty of translating buyer preferences and issues into terms which can be meaningfully analyzed, communicated, and bargained in electronic commerce. Many human negotiators do not have clear, well defined utility or scoring functions and values for the various aspects of a deal. Eliciting the buyers' scoring function is one of the key problems that needs to be addressed to make multi-attribute auctions work. The ability to map buyer preferences into coherent scoring functions, as input by a front-end form, is crucial. While preferences are human and, therefore, not completely logical, conflicts within the preferences must be detected.

During an auction period, a buyer specifies her scoring function using the Java applet which can be downloaded over the web (see figure 6.8, p. 162). Eliciting the buyers' preferences is one of the key problems that need to be addressed by the graphical user interface of the applet. The need to acquire "true" data in an appropriate form from the user poses both psychological and theoretical problems in the creation of a suitable interface. The buyer in particular may not have considered her fundamental preferences in sufficient detail and must therefore be prompted with a suitable set of questions. Then the buyer's preferences, as input by the applet, need to be mapped into coherent scoring functions. In the current implementation MAUT and an additive scoring function are used. As already mentioned, the additivity assumption implies that attributes are preferentially independent and there are no interaction effects. Whether this requirement is satisfied depends largely on the type of item traded (see the appendix, p. 220, for details). For instance, the OTC example described in section 6.4 assumes preferential independence of the strike price as well as implied volatility and style of an OTC derivative.

The additive scoring function is composed of two different kinds of elements, scores on individual attribute scales (also called "individual scoring functions"), and weights for these attributes. For the evaluation of bids, the implied volatility is important, but so is its strike price. It is important to determine the relationship and trade-off between the two. The assessment of the individual scoring functions and weights is a core issue when using MAUT. The buyer evaluates each relevant attribute value of a bid x_j^i with

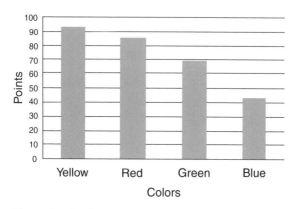

Figure 6.7 Attribute scales.

an individual scoring function $S_i(x_j^i)$ and indicates its relative importance value by a weight, w_i (see section 6.2). A reasonable way to determine the weights for the various attributes is to determine the marginal rate of substitution between one particular attribute and any other attribute. Several other methods are described in Clemen (1996).

Individual scoring functions provide a means of measuring the accomplishment of the fundamental objectives. Some scoring functions are easily defined. If minimizing price is an objective, then, for example, a linear function of the price can be defined that assigns values between one and zero, with some highest acceptable value for the price providing zero utility and a price of zero providing a utility of one. This type of proportional scoring is called a "continuous attribute." The individual utility $S(x_j^i)$ of a continuous attribute can then be computed by:

$$S(x_j^i) = \frac{x_j^i - \text{Worst value}}{\text{Best value–Worst value}}. \tag{6.7}$$

Another way to assess utilities which is particularly appropriate for attributes that are not naturally quantitative is to assess them on the basis of some ratio comparison. This type of attribute is called a "discrete attribute." Suppose that the buyer provides four different colors to choose from (yellow, red, green, blue) for the bidder. Clearly, this is not something that is readily measurable on a meaningful proportional scale. Using a ratio scale, the buyer might conclude that red is twice as good as the color blue, and so on. In the applet the buyer assigns any number of points between 0 and 100 to each possible alternative. In this way, the buyer might, for example, assign 94 points to yellow, 86 points to red, 70 points to green and 44 points to blue (figure 6.7).

These assessments are then scaled so that they range from 0 for the worst alternative to 1 for the best alternative. This can be done by solving two equations simultaneously to compute the constants a and b:

$$0 = a + b(44)$$

$$1 = a + b(94)$$

The utilities of 1 for yellow, 0.84 for red, 0.52 for green, and 0 for blue results. Using these two types of individual scoring functions, the overall utility for a bid is given by the sum of all weighted utilities of the attribute values. For a bid that has values $x_j^1 \ldots x_j^n$ on the n attributes, the overall utility for a bid is again given by (6.1). The bid with the highest overall score is the most desirable under this rule. Similar procedures are used for procurement decisions or in the selection of products from electronic catalogs (Stolze, 1998).

Figure 6.8 shows a screenshot of the Java applet used in the implementation on the buyer side. The user interface consists of several areas. In the upper left area the buyer supplies a unique identifier which she receives upon registration. In the upper text field the buyer can specify a parameter file for a certain product traded on the marketplace. Thus, it is very easy to adapt the applet to any other kind of product by simply changing the parameter file. In this case, calls on the Austrian Trading Index (ATX) are traded (see the scenario described in section 6.4). You will find a list of relevant attributes for the auction below. The negotiable attributes in this case are the "strike price" and the "implied volatility." "Duration" (i.e. maturity) and "style" are fixed in advance. In the lower left panel users can define the individual scoring functions for the negotiable attributes which, as described above, can be either continuous or discrete functions. The scoring function of the strike price (as shown in the screenshot) is determined in a discrete form. From the buyer's input the applet compiles a Request for Bids (RFB) in XML format and sends the RFB via HTTP to the electronic brokerage service. The RFB contains the buyer ID, the product description, and the parameters of the additive scoring function (as can be seen in the XML DTD in figure 6.6). The brokerage service parses the RFB, retains all the relevant data in the database, and informs potential bidders via e-mail.

After the auction has begun, the buyer can query a list of bids submitted on the right-hand side of the applet which are ranked by overall score (third column). By clicking on a certain bid the buyer can see the details of every bid in the form of green numbers on the left-hand side of the applet.

6.5.3.2 Bidder Client

Bidders must also register via a web form in order to receive a bidder ID. Bidders download the RFB from the URL they have received via e-mail to their bidder client (see figure 6.9). This Java applet allows parameters for

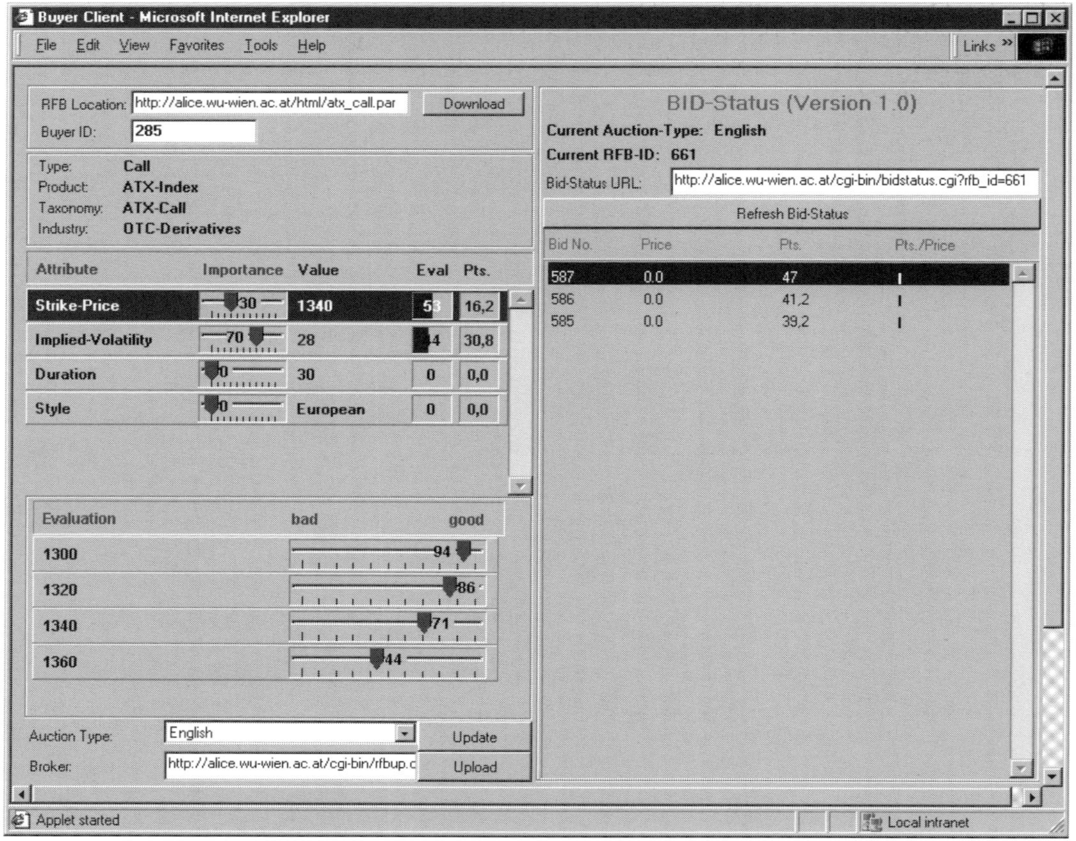

Figure 6.8 Buyer client.

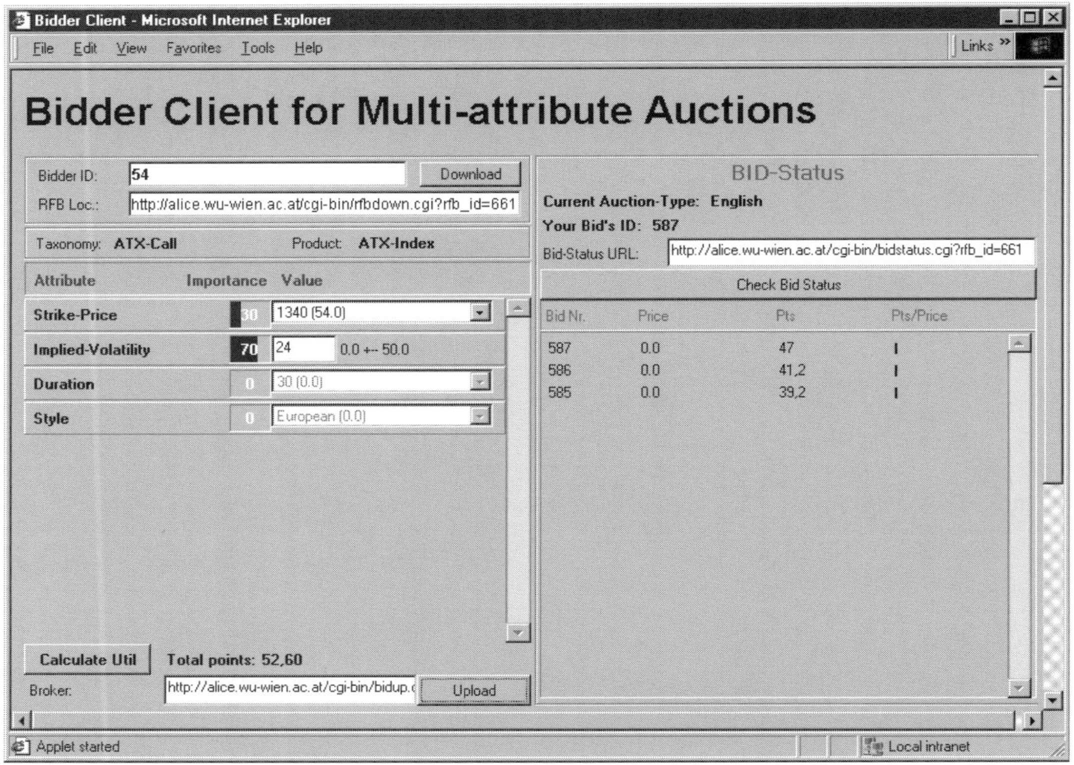

Figure 6.9 Bidder client.

all negotiable attributes to be entered and an XML-formatted bid to be uploaded via HTTP to the brokerage service.

The applet shows important parameters contained in the RFB and allows values to be entered. In the case of a discrete attribute (e.g. the strike price), the bidder can select a value from a drop-down listbox. The numbers in brackets give information about the utility of each value. In the case of continuous attributes the bidder can enter a number in a text field. The numbers must be within a certain range depicted right beside the text field. "0.0 + − 50.0" means that the individual scoring function is downward-sloping, or, in other words, the lower the implied volatility is in a bid, the more utility points are achieved. The "Calculate Util" button on the lower left corner of the applet can be used by the bidder to compute the utilities achieved with different attribute values. In the case of an open-cry auction (e.g. an English auction), the brokerage service reveals information about the bids submitted so far on the right-hand side of the applet.

6.6   Results of a Laboratory Experiment

Based on the electronic brokerage service described in section 6.5, a set of laboratory experiments was conducted (Bichler, 2000a). These experiments provide a good grasp of the dynamics of multi-attribute auctions and the bidders' behavior in a real-world setting. The experiments are particularly useful for learning about the efficiency of multi-attribute auctions and the usability of the overall procedure. Bidding on multiple attributes can be quite complex and it is interesting to evaluate the participants' ability to bid reasonably on multiple attributes and their trust in the mechanism.

Laboratory results are joint outcomes of the characteristics of individual subjects, the laboratory institution, and the environment. Institutions such as the double auction powerfully influence individual behavior so that the final outcomes are relatively insensitive to the characteristics and behavior of individuals (Friedman and Sunder, 1994, p. 57). The final outcomes of multi-attribute auctions are much more sensitive to both the subject's personal characteristics and the environment (e.g. user interface design issues). Therefore, the results of experimental studies provide valuable results for the design and implementation of multi-attribute auctions.

6.6.1   Laboratory Procedures

In the experiments a buyer tried to buy a call on the ATX index of the Vienna Stock Exchange and bidders provided bids in a number of different auction schemes. Every session comprised six different trials in which three

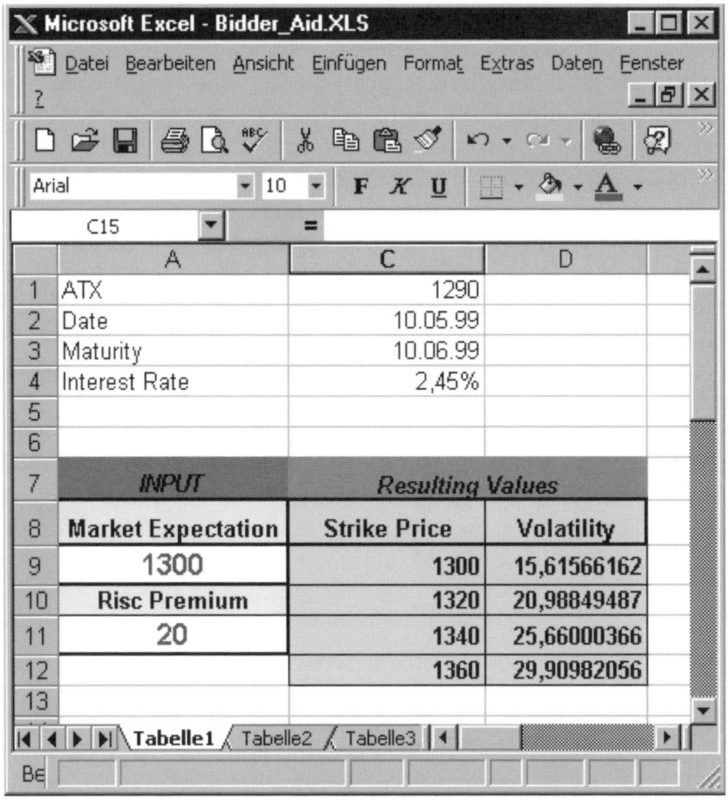

Figure 6.10 Decision support for bidders.

single-attribute and three multi-attribute auctions were deployed (English, first-score, and second-score auction). During an auction period the buyer specifies her preferences in the form of a scoring function (figure 6.10).

As already mentioned, preferential independence of all attributes is a prerequisite for the additive scoring function. Price is not preferentially independent from the strike price. In real-world OTC markets people often negotiate an option's "implied volatility" instead of its price. The volatility measures the "quality" of an option's price and can be viewed independently of its strike price and maturity. Buyers therefore define a scoring function for strike price and implied volatility (see subsection 6.4.4). Bidders provide values for these two attributes and the winner is then calculated based on the rules of the deployed auction scheme. In the single-attribute trials bidders bid only on the volatility; in multi-attribute trials, the buyer additionally provides a list of strike prices for the bidder and bidders can provide bids on both attributes. In some trials bidding on the strike price, implied volatility, and maturity attributes were also tested.

In addition to the bidder client, in the implementation described above, bidders were provided with a decision aid in the form of a spreadsheet calculator helping them to determine values for strike price and implied volatility based on their market expectations and risk attitude. Bidders calculated the implied volatility for a certain strike price depending on the minimum profit they wanted to make (i.e. the risk premium) and their market expectation. Depending on these two parameters they prefer different strike prices which influence the implied volatility. The calculation of implied volatility is not trivial, therefore, the bidders were provided with a decision aid in the form of an Excel spreadsheet (see figure 6.10). Thus, the bidders have only to enter values for their market expectation and the profit they want to make, and the spreadsheet calculates implied volatility values for the various strike prices according to the Newton–Raphson method (Kwok, 1998). This auxiliary tool reduces the complexity of bidding for the bidders and enables less experienced subjects to make reasonable bids after one or two dry runs.

6.6.2   *Experimental Design, Subject Pool, and Reward Mechanism*

In this subsection, the experimental design, subject pool, and reward mechanism used in the experiment will be described. For this purpose, some basic terminology will be introduced. An *experiment* is a set of observations gathered in a controlled environment. A *trial* is an indivisible unit of observation in an experiment, e.g. a single auction or a single round of market trading. Finally, a *session* is a group of trials conducted on the same day, usually with the same set of subjects.

In May and October 1999 sixteen sessions with 64 MBA students were conducted at the Vienna University of Economics and Business Administration. The subjects were students of introductory information systems classes. All subjects had a basic knowledge of economics and financial derivatives. In every session a group of subjects conducted six different trials, namely a first-score sealed-bid auction, a second-score sealed-bid, and an English auction, all of them in their single-attribute and their multi-attribute form. Conducting single-attribute and multi-attribute trials permits comparision of the outcomes of both types of auction formats. A basic question in this context is how many subjects should participate in a single session. Some experimental economists suggest that the number of subjects should be identical to the number observed in real-world settings. According to Friedman and Sunder (1994), two or three subjects in identical situations are sufficient to attain competitive results in a laboratory experiment. In this experiment, four subjects bid in every trial.

An experimental design specifies how variables are controlled within and across a block of trials. The experiments focused in particular on the equilibrium values achieved with the various auction types. Aside from the auction mechanism used in a certain trial, the equilibrium values can be influenced by several variables such as the number of participants in the auction, bidder experience, risk attitudes, as well as other individual or group idiosyncrasies. Ideally, all these variables are controlled either directly or indirectly through appropriate randomization procedures that ensure independence from the focus variables. By keeping the number of subjects constant across all trials an experimenter can control the influence of the number of bidders on the outcome. Since there were different subjects in all sessions, it was possible to randomize individual and group idiosyncrasies such as individual risk attitudes or learning curves.

Before the experiment the scenario was introduced in a 40-minute lecture for all subjects. Subjects were provided with examples of valuations and bids along with profit calculations to illustrate how the auction works. Before each session (approximately 1–1½ hours) two dry runs were conducted in order to familiarize the subjects with multi-attribute bidding and the bidder applet. This was perceived to be sufficient by the participants. All trials of a session used the same scenario. Before a session began, the scenario was repeated and all participants were asked to provide a list of *valuations*, i.e. a minimum implicit volatility value for each strike price. These valuations were used afterwards to analyze the efficiency and strategic equivalence of the different auction schemes. In all sessions each subject's valuations and rewards were kept as private information not available to other subjects.

In order to give the MBA students an incentive to bid reasonably during all auction periods, a reward mechanism had to be introduced. Induced-value theory gives guidelines for establishing control of a subject's preferences in a laboratory economy through appropriate reward mechanisms (Friedman and Sunder, 1994, pp. 12 ff.). A reward mechanism should be dominant, in that it is the only significant motivation for each subject and is the determinant of her actions. The extent of similarities between laboratory and field environments that permits generalization of laboratory findings to field environments is also important. In the trials, the subjects should bid reasonably along the lines of their risk attitude and market expectations. After the maturity of the option expired (after a month), the profits and losses for all winners of an auction were computed based on the market prices of the Vienna Stock Exchange. To participate in a session every subject gained a certain amount of credit points in the final exam. The subjects were ranked by their profits and received additional credit points depending on their profit. If a subject made a loss she also lost part or all of these credit points for the final exam.

6.6.3   Data and Results

The experiments were centered around the three research questions outlined in section 6.3: Are the utility scores achieved in a multi-attribute auction higher compared to single-attribute auctions? Are multi-attribute auctions payoff equivalent? And finally: Are multi-attribute auctions efficient? These questions will be addressed in the following subsections.

6.6.3.1   Comparison of Multi-Attribute and Single-Attribute Auction Formats

A crucial question is whether multi-attribute auctions achieve higher utility scores than single-attribute auctions with respect to the underlying utility function of the bid taker. The scoring function in multi-attribute auctions is assumed to correctly mirror the buyer's utility function and is used to calculate a utility score for the winning bid in single-attribute auctions as well as in multi-attribute auctions. This permits comparison of the three auction schemes in their single-attribute and multi-attribute format. Over time, the ATX changed and different subjects faced slightly different conditions in their session. Therefore, the utility score of the winning bid was computed as a percentage of the highest valuation given by the participants at the beginning of each session. This enabled the comparison of different sessions. In comparing the payoff of different auction formats, the utility scores of the second-best bid in the case of a second-score auction was used.

In the experiment the utility scores achieved in multi-attribute auctions were significantly higher than those of single-attribute auctions for groups of size $n = 4$. Using a t-test with a significance level of $\alpha = 0.05$, the null hypothesis of revenue equivalence between single-attribute and multi-attribute auction formats had to be rejected, but the hypothesis that multi-attribute auctions achieve higher utility scores than single-attribute auctions had to be accepted. According to the empirical data, multi-attribute auctions achieved, on average, 4.27 percent higher utility scores than single-attribute formats. In 72.92 percent of all trials the overall utility achieved in multi-attribute auctions was higher than in single-attribute auctions. Detailed results show that the average utility achieved in multi-attribute first-score auctions was 3.18 percent higher than in single-attribute first-price sealed-bid auctions, the average utility achieved in multi-attribute second-score auctions was 4.25 percent higher than its single-attribute counterpart, and, finally, the average utility achieved in

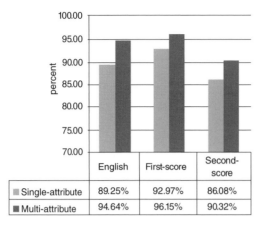

	English	First-score	Second-score
Single-attribute	89.25%	92.97%	86.08%
Multi-attribute	94.64%	96.15%	90.32%

Figure 6.11 Difference between multi-attribute and single-attribute auctions.

multi-attribute English auctions was 5.39 percent higher than in single-attribute English auctions (figure 6.11).

One explanation for these results is that in a multi-attribute auction, a bidder has more possibilities to improve the value of a bid for the bid taker, sometimes without increasing her own costs. Most trials were conducted with two negotiable attributes, some with three negotiable attributes. Here, the difference in achieved overall utility was even higher. However, in the case of a higher number of negotiable attributes, there is a need for bidders to have more sophisticated decision support. It is simply not that easy to find the combination of attributes that achieves the highest utility for the buyer, i.e. the best bid, any more. In most cases, the subjects used all negotiable attributes to improve their bid.

6.6.3.2 Revenue Equivalence of Multi-Attribute Auction Formats
Using a t-test ($\alpha = 0.05$), the null hypothesis of revenue equivalence between the pairs of multi-attribute auction formats had to be rejected. The utility scores achieved in multi-attribute first-score auctions were significantly higher than those in multi-attribute English or second-score auctions. Here, the utility scores of the second-best bid have been used in the case of a second-score auction, i.e. the payoff for the bid taker. In all trials, the utility scores achieved in multi-attribute first-score auctions were on average 1.52 percent higher than those achieved in multi-attribute English auctions and 5.83 percent higher than those achieved in second-score auctions. Figure 6.12 shows that bidders in the experiment used similar strategies in single-attribute as well as multi-attribute auctions, as both histograms follow the same pattern. In the single-attribute trials the equilibrium values achieved

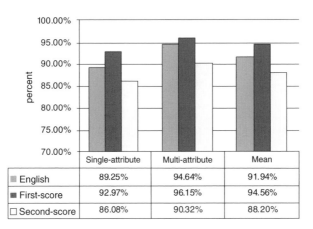

	Single-attribute	Multi-attribute	Mean
English	89.25%	94.64%	91.94%
First-score	92.97%	96.15%	94.56%
Second-score	86.08%	90.32%	88.20%

Figure 6.12 Average equilibrium values below the dominant strategy price.

in first-price sealed-bid auctions were on average 3.72 percent higher than those achieved in English auctions and 6.9 percent higher than those achieved in second-price sealed-bid auctions.

Bidders in the experiment defined their market expectation and risk premium independently of each other and calculated their bids based on these valuations. Therefore, the sealed-bid auctions have many features of a private value model. Of course, this scenario also had a common value element. Because English auctions reveal a lot of information about the other bidders' valuations, the English trials were conducted at the end of each session. In fact, several bidders revised their initial market expectations in these trials and bid above their initial valuation.

The subjects' market expectations in the experiments differed substantially. One reason for this is that during the first set of experiments, the ATX dropped by nearly 100 points. Consequently, the winning bidders in the English auctions often did not have to bid up to their valuation. The higher bidding in first-score auctions is consistent with the assumption of risk aversion in the IPV model. For a bidder, the increment in wealth associated with winning the auction at a reduced bid weighs less than the possibility of losing with such a bid. The results of the second-score auctions depicted in figure 6.12 are those of the second-best bid, and are therefore lower than the other auctions.

6.6.3.3 Strategic Equivalence between Second-Score and English Auctions

A basic assumption of the IPV model is the strategic equivalence of the English and the second-score auction. In both cases, the dominant strategy is to bid up to one's true valuation. In the experiment, the utility scores of the highest bid in multi-attribute second-score auctions were on average 0.4

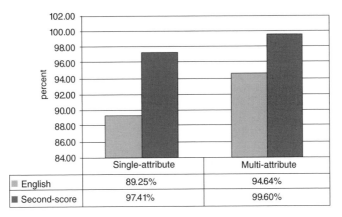

	Single-attribute	Multi-attribute
English	89.25%	94.64%
Second-score	97.41%	99.60%

Figure 6.13 Comparison of the winning bids in English and second-score auctions.

percent below the dominant strategy score. In multi-attribute English auctions, they were on average 5.36 percent below the highest valuation. Using a t-test ($\alpha = 0{,}05$) the null hypothesis of strategic equivalence had to be rejected. The single-attribute trials had similar results. In single-attribute second-price auctions, bids were 2.57 percent below the dominant strategy price, in single-attribute English auctions they were 10.75 percent below. Consequently, the hypothesis of strategic equivalence between English and second-score auctions in both the single-attribute and the multi-attribute cases had to be rejected (figure 6.13).

Bidders in the experiment had a good understanding of bidding strategies in both English and second-score auctions. This is one reason why the best bid in a second-score auction is close to the dominant strategy score. The lower scores in English auctions can again be attributed to the fact that bidders' market expectations and risk attitudes were quite heterogeneous and the bidders with the highest valuation did not have to bid up to their valuation in order to win the auction. Another explanation for the behavioral breakdown of the strategic equivalence of English and second-score auctions is the preference reversal phenomenon where theoretically equivalent ways of eliciting individual preferences do not produce the same preference ordering.

6.6.3.4 Efficiency of Multi-Attribute Auctions
In single-attribute private value auctions efficiency is measured in terms of the percentage of auctions where the high-value holder wins the item. Efficiency has to be computed slightly differently in the case of multi-attribute auctions. Here, the high-value holder is the one with a valuation (containing strike price and volatility) which provides the highest overall

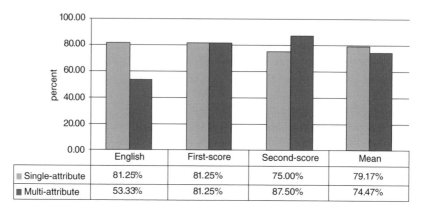

	English	First-score	Second-score	Mean
▨ Single-attribute	81.25%	81.25%	75.00%	79.17%
■ Multi-attribute	53.33%	81.25%	87.50%	74.47%

Figure 6.14 Efficiency of different auction formats.

utility score for the buyer. Subjects had to report these valuations before each session to the experimenters, based on their market expectations. In all trials 79.17 percent of the single-attribute auctions and 74.47 percent of the multi-attribute auctions were efficient. Using a Chi-square test ($\alpha = 0,05$) the null hypothesis that the efficiency of single-attribute and two-attribute auctions is the same had to be accepted (figure 6.14).

A possible explanation for the high efficiency in all auction schemes is that the market expectations in most sessions varied substantially. Kagel and Roth (1995, p. 573) reports that the larger the difference between the highest valuation and the lowest valuation, and the smaller the number of bidders, the higher the average efficiency levels reported. The slightly lower efficiency achieved in multi-attribute auctions is a possible consequence of the bidder's difficulty in determining the "best" bid, that is, the combination of values providing the highest utility for the buyer. Bidders may on occasion accidentally bid below their true valuation. The low efficiency in multi-attribute English auctions is owing to the fact that several bidders revised their initial valuations over the course of an English auction. As already mentioned, in the case of more than two negotiable variables, it is crucial to provide bidders with a decision support tool helping them to determine the "best" bid easily. This can help maintain high efficiency in multi-attribute auctions.

6.6.4   *Discussion of the Results*

The experimental analysis has yielded a number of valuable insights. From the data it can be seen that even with two negotiable attributes, multi-attribute auctions on average delivered significantly higher utility scores (on average 4.27 percent) for the buyer than single-attribute auctions in all of the three auction schemes tested. The efficiency was also measured: The bidder with the highest valuation won in 74.47 percent of the multi-attribute auctions. This is slightly lower than the efficiency measured in single-attribute auctions (79.17 percent) and is also a consequence of the increased complexity of bidding in a multi-attribute auction. In the experiment no evidence was found for the revenue equivalence theorem and strategic equivalence of English and second-score auctions could not be shown. Although these observations are helpful, the analysis could not consider some aspects which might be relevant in the context of multi-attribute auctions.

6.6.4.1 Learning and Bidder Experience

Laboratory experiments of this sort are very time-consuming. This is one reason why the influence of bidder experience could not be tested adequately. There has also been very little study of learning and adjustment processes in standard auction theory (Kagel, 1995). One of the few articles in this field was written by Smith and Walker (1993), who analyzed first-price sealed-bid auctions and reported that more experienced bidders bid significantly higher than inexperienced bidders in auctions with four bidders.

Owing to the inherent complexity of bidding on multiple attributes, there is a correlation between bidder experience and outcome, but decision support on the bidders' side can guide a bidder in finding the "best" bid. One control group conducted four sessions within the period of two weeks. The results of this group were similar to the ones described above and there was no evidence for the impact of bidder experience in the two-dimensional scenario. However, the impact of bidder experience on single- and multi-attribute auctions must be investigated more thoroughly.

6.6.4.2 Information Feedback and Number of Bidders

An interesting issue which was raised in Koppius, Kumar and Van Heck (2000) is the effect of information feedback on multi-attribute open-cry auctions. The information feedback given to the bidders in a multi-attribute auction may include information on their own bid, such as their bid score or bid ranking, but also information on other bidders' bids. For example, an auctioneer could reveal the scores and ranking of all bids, or even the individual attributes and the bidder's identity of all bids. The update may be synchronous, meaning that all bidders have to submit a bid before feedback is given and the next bidding round commences, or it may be asynchronous, in which case it becomes an English auction. The impact on different information feedback policies has yet to be analyzed.

Another open question is how the number of bidders (and consequently information about the number of bidders) influences the equilibrium values achieved in various multi-attribute auction formats. Conventional single-attribute auction theory predicts that increased competition leads to higher equilibrium prices. To the time of writing there is no detailed analysis of the influence of increased competition or uncertainty in the number of bidders on multi-attribute auctions. However, the behavior of bidders is assumed to be similar to the behavior shown in single-attribute auction experiments (see, for example, Battalio, Kogut and Meyer, 1990, or Dyer, Kagel and Levin, 1989).

6.6.4.3 *Number of Negotiable Attributes*

Multi-attribute bidding is rather complex in the OTC scenario, since it is not obvious for the bidder right from the start which combination of attributes provides the highest overall utility for the bid taker. For a bidder, all attributes depend on the risk attitude and market expectation. For this reason, only auctions with one and two negotiable attributes have been evaluated. Such a complex scenario, where a bidder needs to optimize multiple attributes, requires some kind of decision support on the bidder's side (such as the spreadsheet in figure 6.10).

This does not mean that real-world applications must be restricted to two negotiable attributes. One might also imagine scenarios in which determining the best bid is relatively simple. Suppose, for example, a buyer wants to procure pencils, and she has certain preferences in color (e.g. yellow > blue > red > green). For a supplier with yellow and green pencils it is easy to improve her bid without sophisticated calculation by providing a bid for yellow pencils (assuming that yellow pencils are not more expensive than green ones). In summary, an extensive analysis is needed to learn about both the applicability of multi-attribute auctions in a certain domain and the appropriate decision support for buyers and suppliers.

7 Economic Models of Multi-Attribute Auctions

> The mathematical model is a set of assumptions. We know that every assumption is false. Nevertheless, we make them, for our purpose at this point [is] not to make true assertions about human behavior but to investigate consequences of assumptions, as in any simulation or experimental game.
>
> (*Rapoport, 1964*)

The experimental analysis of multi-attribute auctions in chapter 6 provides a good understanding of the relevant issues and causalities. This chapter will focus more on the theoretical underpinnings of multi-attribute auctions. So far, game-theoretical models have focused on cases in which agents' private information is one-dimensional. The consideration of multi-dimensional types poses substantial technical difficulties and results of any generality seem restricted to a few papers. The complications are not merely technical: many economic insights in single-dimensional theory do not necessarily extend in any natural fashion.

Section 7.1 will provide a summary of spare game-theoretical literature in this field. Section 7.2 will compare the results of conventional and multi-attribute auctions using a simulation model. This section will also consider the particularities of OTC trading of financial derivatives, which have been the focus in chapter 6. Up until this stage quantity was assumed to be fixed in advance and all items to be purchased from a single bidder. Section 7.3 will provide a classification framework for multi-attribute auctions where quantity is an issue, and introduce a model which shows the impact of economies of scale on the outcome of multi-attribute auctions. Finally, section 7.4 will introduce a framework of multi-dimensional auction mechanisms, summarizing the earlier chapters.

7.1 Previous Game-Theoretical Analysis

Only a small number of theoretical articles have dealt with procurement negotiations on multiple attributes (Koppius, 1998). In an analysis given by

Thiel (1988), he shows that if the procurer decides on a budget for the project before the auction which becomes known to all agents, and she does not value any savings, the problem of designing optimal multi-attribute auctions will be equivalent to the design of single-attribute auctions. Yet, there is little evidence of this assumption in practice.

Cripps and Ireland (1994) introduced a model in which bid takers set threshold levels for quality and price which are not known to the bidders. They analyzed three different bid evaluation schemes, partially based on the tendering of UK television licenses. First, they assumed a scheme in which price bids are accepted only after quality plans have been submitted and approved. In a second scheme they considered first a price auction, then quality plans submitted in the order of the level of price bids. The first plan to qualify on quality was then accepted. Finally, they investigated the joint submission of a price and a quality bid. The quality test is conducted by the buyer under the assumption that objectively better projects have a greater probability of being accepted. The schemes produce essentially the same results. However, the paper leaves a complete characterization of optimal mechanisms open. Subsection 7.1.1 will concentrate on the analysis of multi-attribute auctions in which the auctioneer designs a scoring rule, as outlined in chapter 6.

7.1.1   *Independent Cost Model*

Che (1993) provides a thorough analysis of the design of multi-attribute auctions. He studied design competition in government procurement with a model of two-dimensional auctions in which firms bid on price and quality. He focuses on an optimal mechanism in cases where bids are evaluated with a scoring rule designed by the procurer. Each bid contains a quality, q, and a price, p, while quantity is normalized to one. The buyer in this model derives a utility from a contract, $(q, p) \in \Re^2_+$:

$$U(q, p) = V(q) - p \tag{7.1}$$

where $V(q)$ is the individual utility function of quality. $V(q)$ is increasing and concave in q. On the other hand, a winning company earns profits from a contract (q, p):

$$\pi_i(q, p) = p - c(q, \theta_i). \tag{7.2}$$

In the cost function $c(q, \theta_i)$, the cost increases both in quality, q, and in cost parameter, θ_i, which is private information. θ_i is assumed to be distributed independently and identically. Losing firms earn zero profits and trade always takes place, even with a very high θ_i.

Che's search for an optimal auction is based on the revelation principle

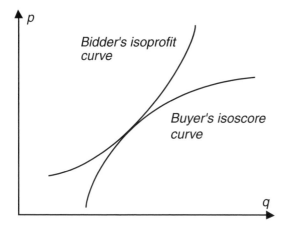

Figure 7.1 Equilibrium in a two-attribute auction.
Source: Che (1993, p. 672).

of mechanism design which says that in order to find the maximum efficient mechanism, it is sufficient to consider only *direct revelation mechanisms* (Gibbard, 1973). In other words, for equilibrium of any arbitrary mechanism there is an incentive compatible direct-revelation mechanism that is essentially equivalent. This means that in Che's model, an optimal multi-attribute auction selects the company with the lowest θ_i. The winning company is induced to choose quality, q, which maximizes $V(q)$ considering the costs.

Che considers three auction rules. In a so-called "first-score" auction, a simple generalization of the first-price auction, each company submits a sealed bid and, upon winning, produces the offered quality at the offered price. In other auction rules, labeled "second-score" and "second-preferred-offer" auctions, the winner is required to match the highest rejected score in the contract. The second-score auction differs from the second-preferred-offer auction in that the latter requires the winner to match the exact quality–price combination of the highest rejected bid while the former has no such constraint. A contract is awarded to the company whose bid achieves the highest score in a scoring rule $S = S(q, p)$. Each auction rule is viewed as a game with incomplete information in which each company picks a quality–price combination as a function of its cost parameter.

Figure 7.1 shows that the bidder's profit is maximized at the tangency point between the isoprofit curve and the buyer's isoscore curve. In a first step, Che assumes the scoring function to resemble the buyer's true preferences, i.e. $S(q, p) = U(q, p)$. In this case, all three schemes yield the same expected utility to the buyer (a two-dimensional version of the *revenue equivalence theorem*).

This model also shows that the equilibrium in the first-score auction is reduced to the equilibrium in the first-price sealed-bid auction if the quality is fixed. The Vickrey auction intuition also applies to the second-score auction: If a company with type θ bids a higher score than one based on θ, it would risk winning at negative profits without increasing its profit conditional on winning. If the company bids a lower score, it would forgo some opportunity of winning at positive profits. Similarly, it can be shown that in a second-preferred-offer auction, each company will bid a score that will earn the company zero profit. However, in the second-preferred-offer auction, a winning company has no control over the quality in the final contract. Che (1993) also tries to discover the *optimal scoring rule* for the buyer. He shows that if the scoring function underrewards quality in comparison to her utility function, first- and second-score auctions implement an *optimal mechanism*. This applies because the true utility function fails to internalize the informational costs associated with increasing quality.

7.1.2   Correlated Cost Model

The costs in Che's model are assumed to be independent across firms. In the context of reverse auctions one might expect the costs of the several bidders not to be independent. Branco (1997) derives an optimal auction mechanism for the case when the bidding firms' costs are correlated, but the initial information of bidders is independent. Bidder i will have some private information about the cost of the project, denoted by the variable θ_i. Bidder i's technology is described in its cost function

$$C_i(q, \boldsymbol{\theta}) = c(q_i, \theta_i, \vartheta(\boldsymbol{\theta})) \tag{7.3}$$

where q_i is the quality provided in the project and $\boldsymbol{\theta}$ is the vector of the bidders' private information about the cost of the project. The underlying $c(\cdot, \cdot, \cdot)$ function shows that each bidder's technology can be interpreted as a special case of a general technology, in which the bidder's efficiency is affected by an idiosyncratic component, θ_i, and a common component, $\vartheta(\boldsymbol{\theta})$. If $\vartheta(\boldsymbol{\theta})$ is a constant function, the model would be reduced to Che's independent cost model.

Branco shows that when the quality of the item is an issue, the existence of correlation among the costs has a significant effect on the design of optimal multi-attribute auctions. Under these conditions, the multi-attribute auctions Che analyzes are not optimal. In Branco's model, optimal quality is a function of the firm's efficiency which depends on parameters not known to the bidder at the time of the auction. This is true because in the correlated cost model, optimal quality is a function of all the bidders' parameters. Therefore, unlike in Che's independent-cost model, optimal quality cannot be achieved through the bidding process alone. As a result, the procurer must use a two-stage mechanism: a first-score or second-score auction, followed by a stage of bargaining on quality between the procurer and the winner of the first stage. Branco shows that both the two-stage first-score auction and the two-stage second-score auction implement the optimal mechanism.

7.2 Comparison of Conventional and Multi-Attribute Auctions

Section 7.1 has shown that under certain conditions the revenue equivalence theorem can be generalized to include multi-attribute auctions. Another interesting question, which was not addressed in previous game-theoretical literature, is whether the utility scores achieved in multi-attribute auctions are higher than those in single-attribute auctions. The difficulty in analyzing multi-attribute auctions lies in the variety of different scoring functions and parameter settings which can be deployed. For this reason, the basic assumptions of game-theoretical models are often kept relatively simple. The models describe two-dimensional auctions (price and quality) and the bidders' behavior is modeled in a rather simple way. Yet, the analytic complexity of these models still poses tight constraints for the modeler. Simulations enable the analysis of complex behavior (see also Galliers, 1994, on methods in IS research) and the impact of various parameters and multiple negotiable attributes on the results (Bichler and Klimesch, 2000). This section will describe the results of a computer simulation which explores the economic behavior of multi-attribute auctions. The following subsections will describe the simulation environment which was used, the model, and the results which were gathered.

7.2.1 Simulation Languages

Since simulation languages with graphical user interfaces have become available, the expression of theories in terms of a computer simulation has become relatively widespread. Faster hardware and improved software have made building complex simulations feasible. Numerous programming languages such as SIMULA, SIMSCRIPT, or GPSS provide support for the construction of simulation models. Swarm is a popular simulation package that was successfully deployed for economic modeling in a number of cases (Stefansson, 1997). It is a library of software components developed by the renowned Santa Fe Institute which allow researchers to construct discrete event simulations of complex systems with heterogeneous agents. Any physical process or social system can potentially be simulated using Swarm, since it imposes no inherent constraints on the model world or patterns of interaction between model elements. The libraries provide objects for analyzing, displaying and controlling simulation experiments and are written in Objective-C. Swarm depends on Unix and the XWindows graphical interface. A number of researchers have used Swarm successfully to simulate supply chains (Fulkerson and Staffend, 1997; Strader, Lin and Shaw, 1998, 1999).

Over the past few years, several Java-based simulation environments have been developed. Java incorporates the language features necessary for simulation, notably objects and threads. Current Java implementations are compiled down to an intermediate byte code which is interpreted. The portability of Java byte code makes it an attractive simulation language. The disadvantage is a lower performance compared to C++. However, Java is a young language, and faster implementations are likely in the future (e.g. by just-in-time compilers). Finally, Java allows animated simulation models in the form of a Java applet in a standard web browser. Several class libraries are available in the form of Java packages that can be used in a Java simulation. For instant, the JavaSim package <http://javasim.ncl.ac.uk/> is a text-only Java version of C++SIM, itself based on SIMULA. JSIM <http://orion.cs.uga.edu:5080/~jam/jsim/> supports a stable graphical environment for displaying queues, and uses a Java database for storing results.

The simulation model described in this section was implemented using the SimJava package which includes several classes for discrete event simulation (Howell and McNam, 1998). SimJava <http://www.dcs.ed.ac.uk/home/hase/simjava/> provides a set of simulation foundation classes useful for constructing and animating discrete event simulation models. The SimJava package has been designed for simulating fairly static networks of active entities which communicate by sending passive event objects via ports. It is actually a collection of three Java packages, `eduni.simjava`, `eduni.simanim`, and `eduni.simdiag`. The `eduni.simjava` package is used for building stand-alone text-only simulations which produce a trace file as the output by default. The `eduni.simanim` package is tightly integrated with the text-only simulation package, and provides a skeleton applet for easily building a visualization of a simulation. Finally, the `eduni.simdiag` package is a collection of classes for displaying simulation results. The extended event handling model of the Java Development Kit (JDK) 1.1 offers a possibility for developing components which can be wired together during runtime. This is ideal for processing simulation results where there is a trace stream which

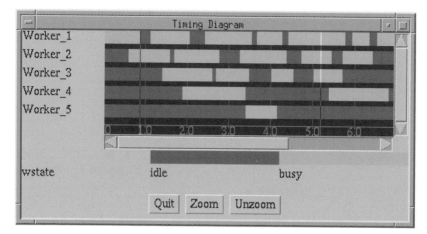

Figure 7.2 Screenshot of the `simdiag` timing diagram bean.

needs to be displayed. For example, the timing diagram bean in figure 7.2 shows how the state of each entity changes over time.

A `simjava` simulation is a collection of entities (`Sim_entity` class), each of which runs in its own thread. These entities are connected by ports (`Sim_port` class) through which they can communicate by sending and receiving event objects (`Sim_event` class). A static `Sim_system` class controls all the threads, advances the simulation time, and maintains the event queues. The progress of the simulation is recorded in the trace messages produced by the entities, and saved in a file. The following section will describe a simulation model used to analyze multi-attribute auctions. Buyers and bidders in this model are entities that send bids and status messages.

7.2.2 Description of the Simulation Model

A buyer solicits bids from m firms. Each bid specifies a price, p, and a certain number of qualitative attributes, x (technical characteristics, delivery schedule, etc.). Quantity is normalized to one, and the buyer never wishes to split the contract to more than one firm. The buyer derives utility from a contract, (x, p). The buyer's scoring function has already been shown in (6.1) (see section 6.2). For the sake of simplicity, the individual utility of all qualitative attributes in the scoring function is assumed to be continuous and ascending. Every bidder, j, in this model has a profit function π in the form of

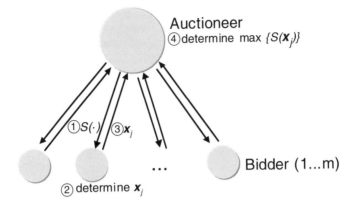

Figure 7.3 Simulation of multi-attribute auctions.

$$\pi\,(x,\,p) = p - \sum_{i=1}^{n-1} \theta x_i. \tag{7.4}$$

where p is the price of the good, θ is the private cost parameter for all attributes x_i, and n is the number of attributes including the price. Losing bidders earn zero profits. $(x,\,p)$ corresponds to the qualitative attributes $x_1 \dots x_{n-1}$ and the price px_n from the buyer's scoring function in (6.1). For the sake of simplicity it will be denoted as vector x in the following.

The cost parameter, θ, is uniformly distributed between $[0,1]$ and describes the efficiency of the bidder in producing the good. The minimum profit a bidder wants to achieve can also be modeled as a uniformly distributed random variable $[\pi_{min},\,\pi_{max}]$ where π_{min} and π_{max} is a lower and upper bound for the minimum profit. This parameter is a proxy for the risk aversion of the bidder. In this model, not all bidders will be able to meet the quality thresholds for the qualitative attributes $x_1 \dots x_{n-1}$. Therefore, the maximum values x_i^* which a bidder can provide are assumed to be uniformly distributed between $[x_{i,min},\,x_{i,max}]$. Thus, each bidder is modeled with the set of independent and uniformly distributed random variables $\{\theta,\,\pi,\,x^*\}$. The data gathered in the laboratory experiments (see section 6.6) indicate that it is reasonable to assume the uniform distribution of these random variables. Given the scoring function $S(\bullet)$, including the weights w_i, each bidder can now determine her price p based on these attribute values:

$$p = \pi + \sum_{i=1}^{n-1} [\theta_i f(x_i^*, w_i)]. \tag{7.5}$$

Bidders optimize the quality of their bids, $f(x_i^*, w_i)$, in the simulation considering the weights w_i from the buyer's scoring function in (6.1) while determining the level of a qualitative attribute x_i. Figure 7.3 depicts the key actors as well as the sequence of steps in this simulation.

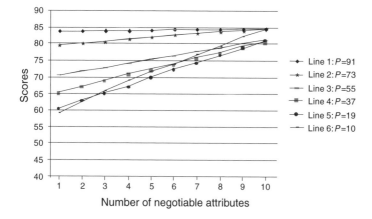

Figure 7.4 Simulation results assuming different scoring functions.

7.2.3 Discussion of the Results

This analysis has assumed 10 relevant attributes of the good, i.e. nine qualitative attributes and the price. Figure 7.4 shows the average results of 60 auction periods. In every auction period 12 virtual bidders posted 10 bids. In the first bid the bidder assumed that all 10 relevant attributes were negotiable. In the second bid the bidder assumed that nine attributes (including the price) were negotiable and one attribute was pre-specified at a level of $(x_{i,max}/2)$ by the buyer, and so forth. Finally, it was assumed all qualitative attributes to be pre-specified and negotiates only on the price. Six different scoring functions were used with varying weights of the attributes, w_i. In addition, a number of uniquely distributed random variables had to be drawn for the bidders in every new auction period, namely the minimum profit π, the cost parameter θ as well as the upper bounds for every qualitative attribute, x_i^*, which a supplier is able to provide. From these initial endowments bidders calculated their optimal bids. In sum, 43,200 bids were evaluated.

Figure 7.4 shows the results of the simulation when different weights are used for price and qualitative attributes in the scoring function $S(x)$ and a different number of negotiable attributes. The number of negotiable attributes on the abscissa ascends from left to right. The ordinate shows the utility scores achieved by the winning bid under the different parameter treatments. A single line is always the result of the same scoring function with a different number of negotiable attributes. For example, in line 1 price is of high importance to the buyer ($w_{price}=91$) whereas all the qualitative attributes have a weight of 1. In contrast in line 6, all attributes including price have a weight of 10.

It can easily be seen that it is optimal to deploy multi-attribute auctions when all attributes are of equal importance (i.e. line 6), simply because the multi-attribute auctions value high achievements in all attributes. That is, if several attributes are important, the multi-attribute mechanism achieves a higher utility score in this model. The more relevant attributes come into play, the higher the difference in the achieved utility scores is. If the buyer's scoring function puts emphasis on the price alone, there is little difference in the outcome, no matter whether a multi-attribute auction or a single-attribute auction is regarded.

If all 10 attributes are of equal importance, the bidder has many more possibilities to comply with the buyer's preferences. She can not only lower the price, but she can improve on several qualitative attributes. In many real-world situations a bidder can even improve a bid without an increase in costs (e.g. to change the color of the good, if the production of the different color poses no additional cost). The simulation is sensitive to changes in basic assumptions such as the initial distributions of attribute values or the cost parameters. However, in all other settings there was a positive correlation between the achieved utility values and the number of negotiable attributes in the auction.

The simulations model rational bidders and a direct revelation mechanism, where bidders simply bid their "best bid" in every auction period. The implementation of an open-cry multi-attribute auction simulation has shown that the results are similar to those achieved in a sealed-bid simulation, but that the simulation takes much longer. This equivalence can be explained with the revenue equivalence theorem described in Che (1993). That is, under certain conditions (perfectly rational bidders, risk neutrality, etc.) the bid elicitation format (open-cry or sealed-bid) can be expected to have no impact on the result of the auction. Of course, these pre-conditions are not necessarily given in a real-world setting. The laboratory experiments described in section 6.6 have already shown that in practice the auction format influences the results considerably. Nevertheless, the results of simulations and game-theoretical analysis provide a good understanding of the economic principles behind a new market mechanism.

7.2.4   *Simulation of OTC Markets for Derivatives*

The results of the general simulation are promising, but it is also interesting to learn whether these results still hold under the more specific assumptions of a market for financial derivatives. This special environment imposes a number of specific assumptions which were not considered in the general simulation. Three relevant attributes on OTC markets are the strike price, the maturity of the option, and the option price. (These three attributes have been chosen because a similar scenario was used in the laboratory experiments.) The buyer's scoring function can now be assumed to be:

$$S(x) = w_{vola}S_{vola}(x_{vola}) + w_{mat}S_{mat}(x_{mat}) + w_{sp}S_{sp}(x_{sp}) \qquad (7.6)$$

In (7.6) the index *vola* is used for the volatility, *mat* for maturity, and *sp* is used as an abbreviation for strike price. In the scoring function the buyer defines a range of allowed values for every attribute. The simulation assumes the individual utility functions for maturity, S_{mat}, and strike price, S_{sp}, to be discrete, i.e. a number of valid attribute values and an associated score achieved by these values were defined. For example, the bidders were allowed to choose from four different maturities, namely 30, 40, 50, and 60 days. Volatility was modeled as a linear, descending utility function $S_{vola}(x_{vola})$, i.e. the lower the volatility values of an option, the better it is for the buyer. A hypothetical volatility of 0 would consequently achieve a score of 100.

In order to calculate the overall utility of a bid, the buyer has to determine the weights of the three attributes. If a buyer is very sensitive about the option price she will be likely to use a high w_{vola} and a low weight for maturity w_{mat} and strike price w_{sp}. In practice this depends heavily on an investor's strategy, risk attitude and market expectation. As in section 7.2.3, it is interesting to learn whether or not it makes sense to negotiate more than one attribute in this context and how different weights affect the outcome of the auction.

In this simulation model, bidders have a certain market expectation β and want to achieve a certain minimum profit π which is a proxy for their risk attitude. The value for the minimum profit π is drawn from a uniform distribution. The market expectation of a bidder is calculated based on the current price of the underlying and the maturity of the option using a linearly ascending or descending function. Market expectation and minimum profit are determined in every auction period for every bidder. Eight bidders try to sell a call option to a single buyer and optimize their offerings based on their market expectation β and minimum profit π. In every auction period a bidder provides four bids, assuming that

1. all three attributes are negotiable
2. volatility and maturity are negotiable
3. volatility and strike price are negotiable, or
4. only the volatility is negotiable.

In a first step, the bidder agent calculates an adequate option price for all possible strike prices and maturities based on her market expectation and minimum profit. This option price is transformed into volatility using an iterative algorithm (see Kwok, 1998, for a detailed description). For the bidder all those offerings achieve the same minimum profit. The buyer,

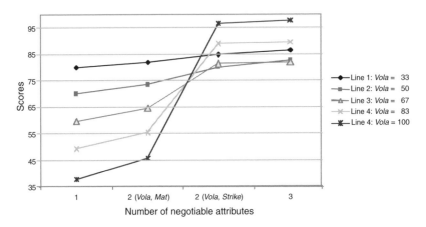

Figure 7.5 Results of the simulation of a financial derivatives market (w_{vola}).

however, has several preferences which are expressed by her scoring function $S(x)$. Consequently, in a second step, the bidder chooses the one combination of attributes that maximizes the buyer's scoring function.

In order to compare the results of the multi-attribute and single-attribute auctions, the scores were measured and compared using the same scoring function $S(x)$. In the case where only one or two of the three attributes are negotiated a fixed value for the other attributes has to be determined in advance. These fixed values are the ones preferred by the buyer, i.e. the ones which achieve a score of 100 in the individual utility function.

Figure 7.5 shows the average scores of the winning bid in 100 auction periods. This analysis uses scoring functions with different weights w_{vola}. Again, the number of negotiated attributes is depicted on the abscissa. "1" shows the results of a conventional reverse auction in which only the volatility (or price) is negotiable. "2 (*Vola, Mat*)" shows the results, when volatility and maturity are negotiable, and so on. The legend describes the different weights of volatility that were used in the scoring function.

Similar to the general simulation described in subsection 7.2.3, there was a positive correlation between the number of negotiable attributes and the average scores achieved in the simulation. However, in contrast to the generic model, the scores are lower if the weights of the three attributes are equal. In other words, the higher w_{vola} was rated, the higher is the utility in the multi-attribute case. This is a consequence of the type of attributes in this derivatives market. The virtual bidders have no restrictions on maturity and strike price and it is relatively easy for them to choose the values with the maximum utility for the buyer. However, it is difficult for them to achieve the maximum score for the volatility which would be a volatility or

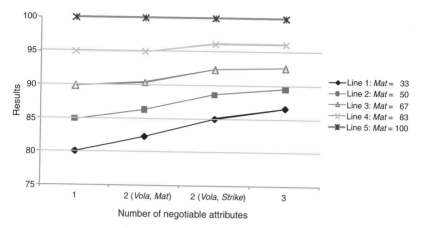

Figure 7.6 Results of the simulation of a financial derivatives market (w_{mat}).

option price of 0. If there is a high w_{vola}, the overall score of a bid is strongly affected by slight improvements of the volatility values. If there is a low w_{vola}, all bidders achieve high scores for maturity and strike price and improvements in the volatility do in fact have little impact. Consequently, the resulting overall scores are relatively similar, no matter whether there are one, two or three negotiable variables.

A similar sensitivity analysis was performed with parameter w_{mat} in which the weight of maturity was changed relative to the weight of volatility and strike price. In reality it will not often be the case that, for example, maturity or strike price are very important relative to volatility and strike price. Nevertheless, it is interesting to analyze the outcomes of the various parameter settings.

The labeling of figure 7.6 is similar to figure 7.5. The legend describes the various parameter settings of (w_{mat}). The weights of strike price (w_{strike}) and volatility (w_{vola}) are calculated as $(1-w_{mat})/2$. Here, the resulting utility values are also higher in the case of more negotiable variables. The impact of w_{vola} is obvious, just as in the setting analyzed in figure 7.4. In cases with a small w_{mat} (and consequently a high w_{vola}) there are big differences among single-attribute and multi-attribute auctions. For example, the slope of line 1 ($w_{mat}=33$) is steeper than in line 4 ($w_{mat}=83$). It is relatively easy for bidders to achieve high scores in maturity. Minimal improvements in volatility have more impact in line 1 than in line 4.

However, in contrast to figure 7.4, resulting utility values are higher, the higher the maturity is weighed. In the case of $w_{mat}=100$ it is relatively easy for bidders to achieve the highest possible utility (though in practice the case in which maturity is the only important attribute is not relevant). In general, as it is easy for bidders in the simulation to provide the best possible value for maturity, it follows that the higher the weight of maturity, the higher are the resulting values. The sensitivity analysis for w_{strike} is similar to the one for w_{mat}.

7.2.5   Discussion of the Results

There are a couple of lessons which can be learned from this simulation. First of all, it makes sense to analyze simulation models that closely reflect the conditions in the target environment. The special nature of attributes in this case (such as the discrete scoring function for maturity and strike price) has an impact on the results. Second, it shows that it is important for a buyer to define the overall scoring function with caution. For example, if the individual utility function for volatility covers values from 0 to 200, but all the incoming bids are within a range of 7 to 30, then the result will be considerably biased. If 0 is the best possible value for volatility, and the best bid achieves a value of 7, then resulting overall utility will be biased downwards. On the other hand, it is not optimal to determine the best achievable value for volatility with 10. This way, a bid with a lower volatility is not valued adequately. Consequently, it is important for a buyer to have a good knowledge about market conditions, in order to define an "appropriate" scoring function. Finally, the scoring function should contain all attributes relevant to the buyer.

Up until now, only qualitative attributes and price have been considered in the negotiations. Evidence has shown that preferential independence holds in most of these situations (Clemen, 1996). Consequently, the additive utility model is reasonable. This assumption might not hold in multi-unit auctions, where quantity is an issue and more than one item is allocated simultaneously. If a buyer encounters preferential dependencies among the attributes, the modeling of preferences can become more complex (Bichler and Werthner, 2000). These situations will be analyzed in the next section.

7.3   Multi-Unit Extensions

The standard game-theoretical auction models focus on single-item negotiations and literature on the sale or purchase of multiple units is much less developed, except for the case in which bidders demand only a single unit each (Maskin and Riley, 1989). There has been much promising research in the field of combinatorial auctions, where multiple heterogeneous goods are put up for sale and buyers supply bids on combinations of goods (Forsythe and Isaak, 1982; Sandholm, 1999a) (see section 5.6). These mechanisms are a promising approach for selling multiple goods and

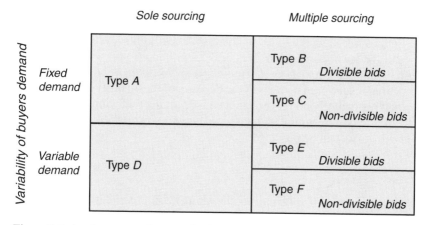

Figure 7.7 Auction types where quality is an issue.

services. However, they are not suitable in a procurement setting in which a buyer has several preferences, but no clear picture of what suppliers are going to bid.

Section 7.2 considered negotiation situations in which price and qualitative attributes were negotiated, but quantity was fixed. A pre-condition for the additive utility function used in the last section was mutual preferential independence of attribute values. Quantity is a special attribute in that it often preferentially depends on price. For example, on financial markets a buyer might be willing to buy 3,000 stocks if the price of a stock is US $29.5, but 6,000 stocks if the price is US $29. This section will analyze how the basic model of multi-attribute auctions can be extended to multi-unit auctions. Although quantity is an important attribute, it will be shown that the buyer has to use a more complex utility function in only a few cases. For the further analysis a classification framework of multi-unit, multi-attribute negotiation situations is introduced (see figure 7.7) which is based on three dimensions:

- *Divisibility of demanded quantity*: Will all the quantity be purchased from a single bidder (i.e. sole sourcing) or from multiple suppliers (i.e. multiple sourcing)?
- *Variability of the demanded quantity*: Does the buyer intend to purchase a fixed quantity of a good or does the buyer's demand depend on the prices offered?
- *Divisibility of bids*: Do bidders accept partial quantities, or do they bid a price for a certain number of items?

The third dimension (i.e. divisibility of bids) is relevant only in the case of multiple sourcing. Therefore, the framework can be depicted in a two-dimensional grid (figure 7.7).

Some of the ideas are based on the work of Dasgupta and Spulber (1989), one of the few theoretical articles dealing with multi-unit reverse auctions. In a game-theoretical model they showed that setting a fixed quantity to be procured is suboptimal and that the decision of the quantity to be procured should instead depend on the received bids. In the following subsections, a more detailed description and potential negotiation protocols for the different categories will be provided.

7.3.1   Type A

Type *A* is a straightforward generalization of the standard (multi-attribute) auction formats on a single item. The bid taker procures multiple items from a single supplier and the quantity is fixed in advance. The classic independent private value model provides a good description of these auctions (McAfee and McMillan, 1987). The buyer optimally selects the quantity to be purchased given a downward-sloping demand curve and an increasing marginal cost for sellers. Considering only price and quantity, the optimal quantity in a theoretical sense is obtained by setting the buyer's marginal value of the good equal to the expected marginal production costs adjusted for information rents obtained by firms and the number of potential bidders (Dasgupta and Spulber, 1989). That is, considering only price and quantity, type *A* auctions are similar to conventional reverse auctions.

7.3.2   Type B *and* C

Type *B* and *C* describe situations in which buyers want to purchase a fixed amount of items from potentially multiple bidders. The critical question is whether price and quantity of an individual bid are preferentially independent for the bid taker or not. Two examples will be considered to analyze the situation in more detail. First, type *B* assumes a tourism marketplace in which a tour operator wants to make reservations for 20 double rooms for a fixed number of nights at a certain destination. The tour operator is of course looking for the lowest possible price. A hotelier provides a bid for six double rooms and US $100 per night. However, the bids are divisible and she is also willing to accept a reservation for only two or three double rooms for exactly the same price. The tour operator prefers one hotelier to be able to supply a large number of rooms, but for the tour operator there is no preferential dependency between price and the number of rooms a hotelier is able to provide. That is, an additive scoring function can be deployed and the auction mechanism is similar to the one described in section 6.2. Similar to single-unit auctions, the first-score auction has two multi-unit generalizations – *discriminatory auctions* in which the bidders who bid the highest scores have to deliver their bid, and *uniform-score auctions* in which all k-successful bidders have to deliver a contract with a score similar to the highest rejected bid. Uniform-score auctions correspond to second-score auctions in the sense that each bidder has a dominant strategy of bidding the private valuation.

A type C situation considers a computer vendor who wants to buy 2,000 hard disks on a business-to-business marketplace. Suppose marginal production costs are decreasing and suppliers consequently encounter considerable economies of scale. On the one hand, price and quantity are preferentially dependent for the bidder and the price of a hard disk is bound to the quantity sold. This preferential dependence for the bidders is important, since they may drop out if they are assigned a partial quantity. On the other hand, the bid taker might have a certain preference for bids of a larger quantity, but for him the price is not preferentially dependent on the level of quantity in a particular bid. The bid taker wants only to purchase a certain overall quantity for a price as low as possible (or, in the multi-attribute case, an overall score as high as possible). That is, an additive utility function can be deployed. However, a basic problem in this second example is that the bid taker wants to purchase an exact amount of items while bids are not divisible.

Teich, Wallenius, Wallenius and Zaitsev (1999) propose a discriminative auction algorithm on price and quantity which can handle situations in which bids are not divisible. Their multiple unit discriminative auction algorithm is as follows: First, the auctioneer specifies quantity for sale, reservation prices, the closing time of the auction and the minimum bid increment (epsilon). Second, the bidder enters an auction by specifying a desired quantity and requesting a price. Third, the auctioneer suggests a price. The suggested price is either at the reservation level if supply has not yet depleted, or is calculated an epsilon above the previous price. Bidders then submit their bid either at the level suggested by the algorithm or above that level, or they drop out. Bids below the suggested level are not accepted. Bidders whose offer is overbid are informed and requested to provide a new bid.

Suppose a seller has 100 units of a homogeneous good to auction, with a reservation price of US $1 per unit and a bid increment of 5 percent. At time 1, bidder 1 enters the auction, specifies a quantity of 80, and requests a price from the auctioneer. Since there are no other bids, the reservation price is suggested. Then bidder 2 enters and specifies a quantity of 40. The supply is depleted and a new price must be calculated at an epsilon percentage above the last price. A price of US $1.05 is suggested to the bidder. Bidder 2 makes this bid and bidder 1 is outbid with a quantity of 20. Bidder 1 can now withdraw from the auction completely, accept a partial quantity, or re-bid. The procedure is repeated until the auction closes. Of course, a bidder can also bid above the suggested price level in order to decrease the probability of being outbid.

Unfortunately, the mechanism was designed for the sale of homogeneous goods when price and quantity are the only negotiable attributes. This auction algorithm can be adapted and combined with multi-attribute auctions in order to negotiate price, quantity, and qualitative attributes in a procurement situation. Again, situations are considered in which bids are not divisible. The following paragraphs propose a multi-unit, multi-attribute auctions conducted in an open-cry manner. The open-cry, multi-unit, multi-attribute auction is as follows:

1. An auctioneer specifies the desired quantity D, the closing time of the auction, the minimum bid increment, and the preferences for certain qualitative attributes in the form of a scoring function $S(x)$.
2. Bidder i submits a bid specified by x_i (including qualitative attributes and price) and a quantity, y_i. The score of this bid has to be higher than the one of the last bid by at least the minimum bid increment.
3. The auctioneer publishes a ranking of all bids indicating the score achieved by every bid. It also notifies bidders whose offers have been overbid. All bidders can now decide to bid again or to drop out.

Suppose a buyer wants to purchase 1,000 units of a good with a reservation score of 30 per unit and a bid increment of 5. At time 1, bidder 1 enters the auction and specifies a quantity of 300 and a score of 40. At time 2, bidder 2 enters and specifies a quantity of 400 and a score of 45. Bidder 3 then enters and bids a quantity of 400 and a score of 50. The demand is depleted and bidder 1 is outbid with a quantity of 100. Bidder 1 can withdraw from the auction completely, accept a partial quantity, or re-bid. The procedure repeats until the auction closes. A bidder can also bid higher than the bid increment in order to decrease the probability of being outbid.

7.3.3   Type D

A type D mechanism dominates the fixed quantity rule by taking into account the information conveyed through the bidding process and is similar to what Dasgupta and Spulber (1989) describe as a type II mechanism. Sole sourcing of this kind allows the buyer to vary the quantity of the good purchased based on bids by competing sellers. This is a realistic scenario on financial markets. Previous analyses have analyzed the market for non-standardized (so called over-the-counter or OTC) financial derivatives

(Bichler and Klimesch, 2000). Products on this market are heterogeneous by definition. For example, buyers in this marketplace want to procure options. Important attributes are the price, the strike price, the maturity (or life time), and the style (American or European) of the option. As price is not preferentially independent from all the other attributes, implied volatility can be used instead which is a proxy variable to price and preferentially independent to all the other variables. As long as quantity is not an issue, a buyer can utilize an additive utility function.

Type A dealt with fixed quantities that have to be assigned to a single bidder. This model can be generalized to a process in which bidders are allowed to bid variable quantities (within a certain range). In this scenario it might also make sense that a buyer wants to purchase all derivatives from a single supplier. The critical question is again whether price and quantity are preferentially independent for the buyer or not. Let us, for the sake of simplicity, reduce the number of negotiable attributes to price and quantity. Suppose a buyer prefers to buy 600 options to 300 options if the price is US $20. The buyer might also prefer to buy only 300 options instead of 600 if the price is US $25. In this case, price, p, is preferentially independent of quantity, y, but quantity is not preferentially independent of price. The utility surface of such a situation is shown in figure 7.8.

It can be shown that such a two-attribute utility function can be specified through either three conditional utility functions, two conditional utility functions and an isopreference curve, or one conditional utility function and two isopreference curves (Keeny and Raiffa, 1993, p. 243). For example, if p is utility independent of y, then

$$U(p,y) = U(p,y_0)[1 - U(p_0,y)] + U(p_0,y_1)U(p_0,y) \tag{7.7}$$

where $U(p,y)$ is normalized by $U(p_0,y_0) = 0$ and $U(p_0,y_1) = 1$. As is evident and expected, the requisite assumptions for these utility functions are more complex than those used earlier. The advantage is clear. This model is more appropriate for the buyer's preference structure. The disadvantage is operational. It is more difficult and less intuitive both to assess the function and to bid reasonably on such a scoring function. This trade-off must inevitably be considered. Of course, another possibility is simply to perform a direct assessment of all possible attribute combinations. Pick the best and worst pairs, assign them utility values of 1 and 0, and then use reference gambles to assess the utility values for other points. OptiMark requires traders to follow a direct assessment technique (Clemons and Weber, 1998). However, this procedure works only in the case of two attributes and a small number of allowed combinations. In summary, type D situations are much harder to automate owing to the complex utility models which have to be utilized.

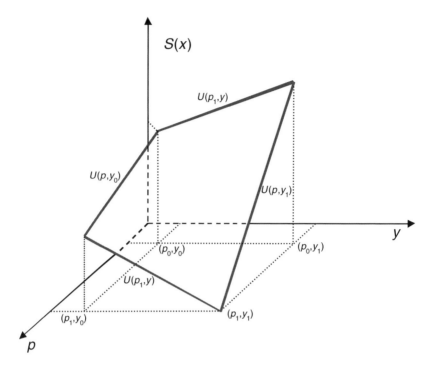

Figure 7.8 Shape of utility function where p is utility independent of y.

7.3.4   *Type* E *and* F

Type E and F situations are similar to type D, but here the buyer is willing to buy from multiple suppliers. In a type E situation bids are divisible – i.e. price and quantity are preferentially independent for the bidder. On the other hand, demand is variable – an indicator that price and quantity are not preferentially independent for the buyer. In a type F situation, price and quantity are preferentially dependent for the bidder and the bid taker.

Since the bid taker is willing to purchase from multiple suppliers, these dependencies need not be modeled in the scoring function (see type B). A buyer in the above scenario is indifferent to an outcome in which she gets one bid of US $20 for 600 options, or in which she gets two bids, with one bid comprising 300 options for US $18 and the second comprising 300 options for US $22. The buyer is interested only in the overall price she has to pay for all items. As the scoring function is a guideline for the individual bids, there is no preferential dependency between price and quantity, and a simple additive scoring function can be modeled. This result extends to the case in which there are additional qualitative attributes. Again, all qualitative attributes and the price are assumed to be preferentially independent from one another. In this example, the dollar amount has to be substituted with scoring points.

As the buyer does not want to buy an exact amount of items, an auction mechanism for a type F situation can be simpler than the one which has been proposed for type C situations. A conventional sealed-bid multi-attribute auction can be conducted in both cases (as shown in section 6.2). In a first step, the buyer defines the scoring function. After suppliers have submitted a bid, the buyer can decide on the quantity, i.e. how many bids she is willing to accept. Of course, setting up an additive scoring function is easier for both the bid taker and the bidder. The bid taker does not have to model a dependency between the attributes in the scoring function, and the bidder gets a scoring function which is easier to follow and easier to understand.

7.3.5   A Model of Multi-Unit Auctions

The impact of quantity can be analyzed with a simple model. Particularly interesting and practically relevant types of multi-unit negotiations are type C and F, in which price and quantity are preferentially dependent for the bidder. This assumption is reasonable in industries with economies of scale. The following model should provide a general understanding for situations in which quantity is an issue.

Again, a buyer solicits bids from m firms. Each bid specifies a price, p, a certain quality, q, and a quantity, y. (Notice that, for reasons of simplicity, in this model quality is reduced to a single dimension, q.) Here, a buyer wants to purchase a fixed amount of goods, bids are non-divisible, and a buyer is willing to source the items from multiple suppliers. The buyer derives utility from a contract, (p, q, y). The price, p, denotes the price of a single item. Consequently, the buyer's scoring function has the following form:

$$S(p,q,y) = w_p S_p(p) + w_q S_q(q) + w_y S_y(y).$$ (7.8)

Let us assume the individual utility of quality, S_q, in the scoring function to be continuous and ascending. The buyer also prefers to buy more of a certain quantity from a single supplier, in order not to have too many suppliers. Consequently, S_y also continuously ascends. The individual utility function of price, S_p, continuously decreases.

Every bidder, j, is modeled with the set of independent and uniformly distributed random variables $\{\pi, q\}$ and a parameter λ that introduces economies of scale in this industry. The bidders calculate a price, p, as follows:

$$p = \pi + c(y,q). \tag{7.9}$$

That is, the price, p, is the sum of the minimum profit, π, and the average cost function $c(y, q)$. The minimum profit a bidder wants to achieve is a uniformly distributed random variable $[\pi_{min}, \pi_{max}]$ where π_{min} and π_{max} is a lower and upper boundary for the minimum profit. The average cost function, $c(y, q)$, measures the cost per unit of output for the bidder's quality, q. Bids are assumed to be non-divisible in this scenario. It is also assumed that every bidder can produce only a single quality, q, which is uniformly distributed between $[q_{worst}, q_{best}]$. That is, the average costs decrease with increased output, y

$$c(y,q) = \left(1 - \frac{\lambda}{y_{\max}} y\right) q. \tag{7.10}$$

The parameter λ determines the rate at which average costs decline with increasing output, y. In other words, λ describes the impact of economies of scale, with $0 \le \lambda \le 1$. A high λ models a high impact of economies of scale, as the cost parameter $(1 - \lambda y/y_{best})$ decreases with increased λ. Suppose bidders can produce any quantity between the minimum and maximum quantity $[y_{min}, y_{max}]$ specified in the scoring function without restrictions. The bidders must then optimize the score of their bid.

This model analyzes different parameter settings and their impact on the outcome of the auction. The main focus is to learn about the impact of varying λs. In addition, a sensitivity analysis of different weights of price is performed. As in many real-world decision analysis situations the individual scoring functions are modeled as linear functions. This means that the score of a certain attribute value x can be calculated as

$$S(x_j) = \frac{x_j - x_{worst}}{x_{best} - x_{worst}}. \tag{7.11}$$

where x_{worst} is the worst possible attribute value and x_{best} the best possible value for the decision maker. However, the basic thought behind the analysis below also applies to cases in which the individual scoring functions are convex or concave, i.e. $\partial^2 S/\partial x^2 > 0$ or $\partial^2 S/\partial x^2 < 0$. If the best value for price, p_{best}, as well as the worst possible values for quality, q_{worst}, and quantity, y_{worst}, are normalized with zero, then each bidder has to optimize

$$S(p,q,y) = \frac{(\pi + q - (\lambda/y_{best})qy)w_p - w_p p_{worst}}{-p_{worst}} + \frac{w_q q}{q_{best}} + \frac{w_y y}{y_{best}}. \tag{7.12}$$

where q is given and p is a function of y. This means that the output, y, is the only variable in a linear function, and this function can be transformed into the following form.

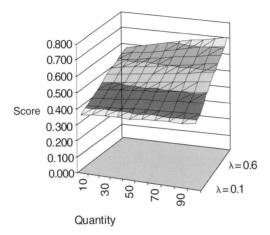

Figure 7.9 Optimal bid for different quantities and λs.

$$S(p,q,y) = \left(\frac{(\lambda/y_{best})qw_p}{p_{worst}} + \frac{w_y}{y_{best}} \right) y - \frac{\pi w_p + qw_p - w_p p_{worst}}{p_{worst}} + \frac{w_q q}{q_{best}}. \quad (7.13)$$

It is obvious that, unless $\lambda = 0$ and $w_y = 0$, the dominant strategy for the supplier in this model is to bid the maximum possible quantity, $y = y_{best}$. Figure
7.9 shows the score of various bids for different λs and different quantities.
Even with a very low λ it is better to bid a higher quantity than a lower
quantity. That is, there is a dominant strategy for a bidder to bid the
maximum quantity in this model.

Up until now an optimal strategy for a single bidder has been derived.
Now, it is interesting to see the result of an auction using different weights
for price, quality, quantity and different λ parameters. A simulation with 12
virtual bidders was implemented in Java similar to the one described in
section 7.2. For every combination of parameters 20 auction periods were
conducted and the average scores were calculated. In sum, 24,000 bids were
evaluated. Figure 7.10 shows the utility scores achieved by the winning bids
using different weights and different λ parameters. The higher the weight of
price (and consequently, the lower the weight of the other attributes), the
more impact high economies of scale have on the outcome. In other words,
if the weight of price is very low, there is little difference, whether strong
economies of scale are encountered or not.

The simulation models yielded several interesting results, but it is also
important to recognize the limitations of these models. Much of the criti-
cism of game-theoretical auction models described in section 5.4 also
applies in this context. Similar to standard game-theoretical auction

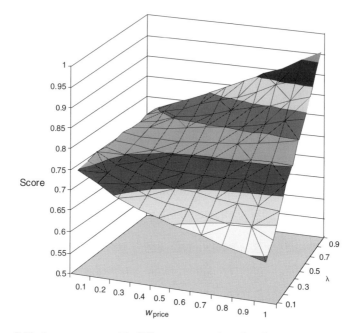

Figure 7.10 Average score with different economies of scale.

models, the simulation models introduced in previous sections describe single, isolated markets and ignore the inter-relations across markets. The models also ignore behavioral deviations of bidders and concentrate on the behavior of purely rational bidders. Although it is worthwhile to incorporate these aspects in future extensions of the simulation models, the basic results described in the previous sections have helped reveal some of the basic principles and causalities of multi-attribute auction mechanisms.

Chapters 5 and 6 analyzed multi-attribute auctions using a variety of different methods. Many of these methods are rather new to economic research. The electronic brokerage implementation provided a good idea of the relevant aspects and the feasibility of multi-attribute auctions in a real-world scenario. In particular, a by-product of the prototype was a detailed system description including all the details which might otherwise have been overlooked. The laboratory experiments enabled us to gather user feedback and statistical data about efficiency and the validity of game-theoretical predictions. Finally, the simulations allowed us to build a model which describes the impact of the various parameter settings. None of these methods is able to cover all the social, economic, and technical aspects of a complex market institution but altogether the results provide a solid knowledge about the economic behavior of the proposed new mechanism.

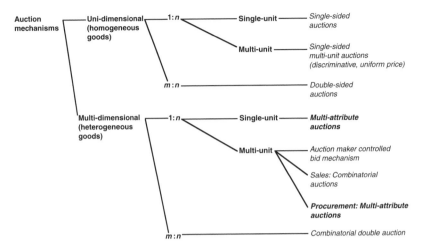

Figure 7.11 Overview of auction mechanisms.

A next step will be the implementation of multi-attribute auctions in a real-world scenario. This will allow the collection and the analysis of field data, another new and particularly exciting possibility for economic research on market mechanisms.

7.4   Summary

A classification framework for auction mechanisms will now be described which places the previous chapters in a context. Figure 7.11 gives a general overview of auction mechanisms and the situations in which they can be used. It distinguishes between uni-dimensional and multi-dimensional auction mechanisms. The theory on conventional uni-dimensional (i.e. single-attribute) auction mechanisms has been described in sections 5.3 and 5.5.

Multi-dimensional auctions automate multilateral commercial negotiations on heterogeneous goods. Section 5.6 provides a broad overview of combinatorial auctions for the sale of multiple heterogeneous goods. Chapters 5 and 6 have described multi-attribute auctions as a very flexible mechanism for the automation of procurement negotiations. The results of a computer simulation and an experiment have shown that the overall utility scores achieved in multi-attribute auctions were significantly higher than in single-attribute auctions. Financial derivatives are a suitable application domain for multi-attribute auctions. These are promising results and, therefore, multi-attribute auction mechanisms have the potential to automate negotiations in many other real-world exchanges such as corporate and governmental procurement.

Up until now, this book has focused on one-sided multi-dimensional auction mechanisms, i.e. one-to-many negotiation situations. An efficient market mechanism supporting the negotiation of many buyers and many sellers on multiple attributes would have a high potential for the automation of many real-world exchanges. The OptiMark system is an interesting example of a many-to-many negotiation protocol in which bidders bid on price and quantity. As described in subsection 5.6.4, OptiMark provides a complicated, multi-step procedure to match multiple buyers and sellers based on price, quantity, and their willingness to trade. Unfortunately, the algorithm works only for bids on price and quantity, and there are still many open questions concerning the efficiency and optimality of the mechanism.

Teich, Wallenius, Wallenius and Zaitsev (1999) propose a simple, many-to-many negotiation protocol for general two-issue negotiations in which quantity is not an issue. The mechanism is based on the "auction maker controlled bid mechanism" introduced in section 6.2 and calculates the closeness of preference paths. This concept also raises a number of questions and is not applicable in the case of more than two attributes. In general, the automation of many-to-many multi-dimensional negotiations is much harder than that of the one-to-many cases.

8 Conclusions and Perspectives

> Given that we are doing the equivalent of evolving monkeys that can type Hamlet, we think the monkeys have reached the stage where they recognize they should not eat the typewriter.
>
> *(Comment by Dallaway and Harvey, accompanying their 1990 entry into the Santa Fe Double Auction Programming Contest, Friedman and Rust, 1993*)

Following Shapiro and Varian (1999), I contend that the Internet does not so much change the fundamental characteristics of the general negotiation process, as the economic principles behind negotiations are still valid. Yet it does enable trading mechanisms to be implemented that were previously unknown or infeasible. This book has analyzed a broad range of negotiation protocols for electronic markets while focusing largely on auction mechanisms.

Auctions have proven to be very *efficient* negotiation protocols that *converge to an equilibrium very quickly*, which is important in situations where transactions need to occur at a rapid rate. Considering political contexts, auctions are also widely *perceived as fair*. In fact, they reflect the general shift of power towards the consumer, as sellers who do not offer some form of negotiation might be in danger of falling behind or being considered consumer-unfriendly. Aside from theoretical arguments, auctions have a number of practical advantages for both seller and buyer:

- An auction mechanism releases the bid taker from having to negotiate with several bidders individually, thus saving time.
- A bid taker can have several bidders compete against each other in an open-cry manner. As shown in subsection 5.4.2, this type of information revelation leads to a sense of competition among bidders which is likely to impact on the equilibrium values in real-world auctions, although this is contrary to game-theoretical predictions.

■ Finally, electronic brokerages of this type also lead to advantages for the bidders. They can participate in negotiations with buyers/sellers they would otherwise never have access to. Moreover, these electronic trading floors enable bidders to learn more easily about their buyers' needs and their competitors' strength.

Current auction mechanisms are simple price finding mechanisms. Considering that product differentiation has become a widespread strategy to defy comparison shopping on electronic markets, there will be a need for more complex negotiation protocols. In particular, for more complex goods and services, multi-attribute negotiations will become an important feature of Internet commerce. Therefore, many experts stress the importance of developing multi-attribute negotiation protocols in electronic commerce (Kersten and Noronha, 1999a; Stroebel, 2000). Multi-attribute auctions are one such protocol – not the only one, but perhaps a very attractive one, given the fashion for single-attribute auctions. They combine the *advantages of auctions* (efficiency, speed of convergence, and fairness) with the *possibility of negotiating on multiple attributes*. That is to say, they also involve many aspects of integrative negotiations which auctions normally do not.

Of course, there are a multitude of integrative negotiation situations in which auctions are of little help. For instance, the negotiations of partners organizing a joint venture need a different kind of negotiation support than is needed in a corporate procurement situation. However, auction-like protocols will play a major role in contexts in which the determination of value is the primary concern. In general, "different business models will need many different kinds of negotiation protocols, some of which will be very complex and rich in human factors" (Kersten and Noronha, 1999a). A detailed analysis of the negotiation situation is the only way to find the "right" type of negotiation protocol.

The following sections will provide some practical guidelines as to when multi-attribute auctions are likely to be the right solution, as well as where the limitations of multi-attribute negotiations lie.

8.1   Applicability and Prerequisites

The application scenario throughout chapter 7 has been the OTC trading with financial derivatives, which has proven to be a suitable application domain for multi-attribute auctions and a very useful test bed for their analysis. This is owing to a number of characteristics:

■ The buyers on financial OTC markets are mostly professionals with a good knowledge of market conditions. All relevant attributes of the product are known in advance, and buyers are able to define a meaningful scoring function.

■ The products traded can be fully described by the attribute values of a bid and there is no need for further evaluation. This feature is given not only in the field of financial services, but in most other types of services (e.g. transportation). However, it might be a critical issue when a buyer wants to purchase physical goods such as a car. Most buyers want to see or test drive a new car in order to get a more complete picture. The "look and feel" is an important additional information which can hardly be communicated via a list of attributes.

■ The relevant attributes in the scenario are preferentially independent and can be described with an additive utility function.[1]

■ The list of relevant attributes is manageable. Multi-attribute utility theory, which is used to elicit the buyer's scoring function, is considered more appropriate for short lists of alternatives (fewer than five–nine) (Olson, 1995).

The first issue focuses on the type of participants on the market, whereas the last three issues are concerned with the type of product traded. These pre-conditions make multi-attribute auctions a suitable negotiation protocol.

If these pre-conditions are given to a lesser extent, this does not mean that multi-attribute auctions are not applicable. For instance, we are in the process of implementing an electronic marketplace for the tourism industry, where several of the above pre-conditions are violated. Here, consumers have a number of preferences for hotel rooms and hotels can provide bids. The most relevant attributes for consumers are price, category, and location, but there are a lot more. The product simply cannot be fully described in advance. For instance, the look and feel of a hotel room depends on the customer's taste and can hardly be captured *a priori* in a scoring function. Moreover, customers often have no clear picture of the market in advance. They do not know the number of suppliers or the prices which can be expected in a certain region.

Considering these circumstances, it is not reasonable to determine the winner automatically. The scoring function might be biased and, therefore, the resulting utility scores are also likely to exhibit a bias. Nevertheless, multi-attribute auctions can also be utilized, but the utility scores can be only a guideline for the selection of the winner. A solution is the introduction of a two-step procedure. Multi-attribute auctions are used in a first step to select the best bids. The bid taker can then browse through the offerings, redefine weights and the bid ranking, and finally determine the winner. This

---

[1] "Preferential independence" is discussed in sections 6.2, 7.3, and in the appendix, (p. 220).

shows that there is no overall solution for all application fields, and a detailed requirements analysis is necessary to define the details of multi-attribute negotiations in different domains.

8.2　The Role of Decision Support

The laboratory experiments have shown that the level of complexity in multi-attribute auctions increases with an increasing number of negotiable attributes for both the buyer and the bidder. On the one hand, the buyer is required to define a meaningful scoring function. On the other hand, bidders have to optimize multiple attributes in their bid given the scoring function.

The *definition of the scoring function* is a crucial step. The simulation (see subsection 7.2.5) has shown that a poorly designed scoring function can lead to inefficient auction results. On the one hand, this concerns the individual scoring functions and their scope. On the other, the weights of the various attributes need to be set appropriately. Therefore, customization is needed as a first step, in order to identify the relevant attributes of the application domain and to model the individual scoring functions and weights of an additive scoring function.

A more fundamental question is whether MAUT is an appropriate technique for eliciting the buyer's preferences, and whether the requirements for an additive utility function are satisfied or not. The procedure described in this book used MAUT, since it is intuitive to most bid takers and it is widely accepted in the literature. However, MAUT can also be replaced by another decision analysis technique such as AHP or conjoint analysis (see the appendix). Most reported multi-attribute decision applications under certainty utilize an additive utility function and it is rarely, if ever, necessary to model more complex scoring functions (Clemen, 1996, p. 593). At least, the additive model is seen as a rough-cut approximation. If preferential independence is not given, the buyer needs to use a more complex utility function that covers the interdependencies between the attributes (see section 7.3).

In a professional environment such as that of corporate procurement or a financial market, buyers will adapt quickly to such a new negotiation protocol. For instance, the OptiMark system requires market participants to define three-dimensional utility landscapes and to adapt to a quite complex matching procedure. This system is already in use on the world's leading stock exchanges. Less experienced buyers, such as consumers in a business-to-consumer market, may not be fully aware of the market conditions and face the danger of biased results. The two-step procedure described in section 8.1 can be a solution to this problem. Yet another approach is the implementation of a multi-round negotiation support tool, which allows buyers to revise their scoring functions several times, based on the bids submitted during the course of an open-cry auction. For example, if a buyer recognizes that all bids achieve very high scores on a certain attribute she can decrease the importance of this attribute. Bidders are informed of a change in the buyer's scoring function and can adapt to these changes. This enables a more dynamic bidding procedure, and a kind of back-and-forth negotiation.

As can be learned from the laboratory experiments, *bidding is also more complex* in multi-attribute auctions. In contrast to conventional single-attribute auctions, it is not obvious for the bidder right from the start which combination of attributes provides the highest overall utility for the bid taker. Thus, an important question is whether bidders can cope with the complexity in such a market. From the point of view of the bidder, financial markets are particularly complex negotiation situations, as all attributes are tightly connected and a change in maturity immediately impacts the option premium. Bidding becomes easier when there are qualitative attributes like color, weight, or size. Nevertheless, appropriate *decision support tools for the bidder* play a crucial role when there are three or more negotiable attributes. In the laboratory experiments bidders were provided with a program that calculated the optimal bids based on market expectation and risk premium. Similar decision support should be provided in other domains.

This book has concentrated on the design of new market mechanisms for electronic commerce. Once the electronic market is in place, it is relatively easy to collect transaction data, which is difficult in a physical marketplace. This creates entirely new possibilities for the analysis of electronic markets. Methods from econometrics play a pivotal role in determining and fine-tuning relevant parameters such as the optimal length of an auction period or the optimal number of items in a multi-unit auction. First steps in this direction have already been taken in the analysis of online auctions (see section 5.7). These methods will also be important for a further understanding of multi-attribute auctions.

Understanding the economics of electronic markets is a core issue for the design of an electronic marketplace. However, it also requires the skills of an experienced software engineer and a talented user interface designer to develop a successful system. Clarity of a web site, ease of navigation, and fast response times are just some of the success factors that must not be overlooked. The design of electronic markets integrates various disciplines from computer science and economics and will remain a challenging research field for the next several years.

Appendix: Utility Theory and Decision Analysis Techniques

> There is a bear dancing on a ball in a circus. We should not criticize the bear that it dances clumsily. Rather, we should marvel that it dances at all.
>
> (*Anonymous*)

Utility theory and decision analysis have a long tradition in microeconomics, operations research as well as in business administration. The following sections will introduce the basic concepts of both disciplines. Understanding these is important to the conceptual design of multi-attribute auctions and to the practical implementation of these mechanisms.

A1   Basic Ideas of Utility Theory

The theory of utility dates back to over a century ago. "Utility" and "value" are synonyms for many researchers, therefore, the term "utility"[1] is used throughout the text. Microeconomists were the first to analyze consumers' preferences and utilities. This research has a long, complicated and controversial history and is as old as economics itself. At the present time economists still do not agree on the real meaning of utility and the way in which it should be defined (Metha, 1998).

A1.1   Existence of a Utility Function

In the nineteenth century economists saw "utility" as an indicator of a person's overall well-being or happiness. The first explicit and systematic use of the concept of utility to explain value of commodities can be found in Jevons' classical *Theory of Political Economy* (1871). Jevons did not, however, distinguish between preference and utility. Pareto (1971) was the

---

[1] Often the term "value" is used when considering decisions under certainty, and "utility" when considering uncertainty.

first to make a distinction between the two concepts. A crucial step was then undertaken in a fundamental paper by Wold (1943). Wold listed axioms for a preference relation and then proved that every preference relation that satisfied the axioms had a real-valued continuous utility representation. Further progress was made by Debreu (1954), who also emphasized the distinction between preference and utility. He developed a rigorous mathematical system reflecting utility and assumed utility to have a number of features, including a monotonically increasing function that is convex and continuous.

Nowadays, consumer behavior is reformulated in terms of *consumer preferences*. The following example will consider a consumer faced with possible consumption bundles in some set X, her consumption set. Concerning choice behavior, all that matters is whether one bundle of goods has a higher utility than another. An important property of a utility assignment is how it orders the bundles of goods. If the magnitude of the utility function is important only insofar as it ranks the different consumption bundles, this kind of utility is referred to as *ordinal utility*. The preferences of the consumer are the description for analyzing choice, and *utility* is simply a way of describing preferences. Preferences should order the set of bundles, so they need to satisfy certain standard properties (bold type denotes a bundle of goods):

■ *Completeness*: For all x and y in X, either $x \geq y$ or $y \geq x$ or both.
■ *Reflexiveness*: For all x in X, $x \geq x$.
■ *Transitiveness*: For all x, y, and z in X, if $x \geq y$ and $y \geq z$, then $x \geq z$.

The first assumption says that any two bundles can be compared, the second assumption is trivial, and the third is necessary for any discussion of preference maximization. Given an ordering $\geq$ describing "weak preference," an ordering $>$ of strict preference can be defined simply by defining $x > y$ to mean not $y \geq x$. Similarly, a notion of indifference is defined by $x \sim y$, if and only if $x \geq y$ and $y \geq x$. Another assumption which is often made is

■ *Continuity*: If y is strictly preferred to z and if x is a bundle that is close enough to y, then x must be strictly preferred to z.

This assumption is necessary to rule out certain discontinuous behavior. In economic analysis it is often useful to summarize a consumer's preferences by means of a *utility function*. A utility function $U: X \rightarrow \Re$ is a way of assigning a number to every possible consumption bundle in which preferable bundles are assigned larger numbers than less-preferred bundles (Varian, 1996c). That is, a bundle (x_1, x_2) is preferred to a bundle (y_1, y_2) if and only if the utility of $x = (x_1, x_2)$ is larger than the utility of $y = (y_1, y_2)$. To denote it more formally:

$$x > y \text{ if and only if } U(x) > U(y).$$

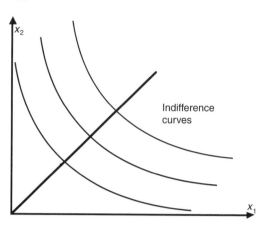

Figure A1 Indifference map.

A typical utility function is assumed to be upward-sloping and concave. An upward-sloping utility curve makes sense and means that more wealth is better than less wealth.

Not all kinds of preferences can be represented by an ordinal utility function. For example, if someone had intransitive preferences so that $a>b>c>a$, then a utility function for these preferences would have to consist of $U(a)>U(b)>U(c)>U(a)$ which is impossible. However, if cases like intransitive preferences are ruled out, it turns out that there will typically be a utility function to represent preferences. There are other assumptions on preferences that are often useful, for example, monotonicity says that more of some good is better:

- *Weak monotonicity*: If $x>=y$ then $x \geqslant y$.
- *Strong monotonicity*: If $x>y$ then $x>y$.

In this context an *indifference curve* indicates bundles that must have the same utility. In the case of two goods, this can lead to an indifference map as given in figure A1. If preferences are assumed to be monotonic, the line through the origin must intersect every indifference curve exactly once and the bundles on higher indifference curves receive higher labels.

Convexity is often used to guarantee proper behavior of consumer indifference curves. It implies that an agent prefers averages to extremes. Convexity is a generalization of the neoclassical assumption of diminishing *marginal rates of substitution* (Gossen, 1853):

- *Convexity:* Given x, y and z in X such that $x \geqslant y$ and $y \geqslant z$, then it follows that $tx+(1-t)y \geqslant z$ for all $0<=t<=1$.
- *Strict convexity:* Given $x \neq y$ and z in X such that $x \geqslant y$ and $y \geqslant z$, then it follows that $tx+(1-t)y>z$ for all $0<t<1$.

It can be shown that if the preference ordering is complete, reflexive, transitive, continuous, and weakly monotonic, there exists a continuous utility function $u: \mathfrak{R}^k_+ \to \mathfrak{R}$ which represents those preferences. This *theorem of existence of a utility function* goes back to Wold (1943).

The most relevant feature of such a utility function is its ordinal character. Since only the ranking of the bundles matters, there can be no unique way to assign utilities to bundles of goods. If $U(x_1, x_2)$ represents a way to assign utility numbers to the bundle (x_1, x_2), then multiplying $U(x_1, x_2)$ by 3 is just as good a way to assign utilities. This is also called a *monotonic transformation*, i.e. a way of transforming one set of numbers into another set of numbers in a way that preserves the order of the numbers. Examples of monotonic transformations are multiplication by a positive number, adding any number, and so on. Consequently, if $f(u)$ is any monotonic transformation of a utility function that represents some particular preferences, then $f(U(x_1, x_2))$ is also a utility function that represents those same preferences. In other words, a monotonic transformation of a utility function is a utility function that represents the same preferences as the original utility function.

Now, consider the example of two perfect substitutes such as blue and red rubber, where the consumer has no preference over the color. A possible utility function would be $U(x_1, x_2) = x_1 + x_2$. This utility function assigns a higher label to more preferred bundles and the indifference curves are constant (along $x_2 = k - x_1$). Of course, this is not the only appropriate ordinal utility function. The monotonic transformation $V(x_1, x_2) = (x_1 + x_2)^2 = x_1^2 + 2x_1x_2 + x_2^2$ will also represent the perfect substitutes' preferences. Another example would be two complements such as a right and a left shoe. In this case, the number of complete pairs is the minimum of the number of right shoes, x_1, and left shoes, x_2: $U(x_1, x_2) = min\{x_1, x_2\}$. So far, all the utility functions have been linear in both goods. A function of the form $U(x_1, x_2) = \ln(x_1) + x_2$ would be labeled a *quasi-linear utility function*, as one of the utilities is not linear. Another special case which is often cited by economists is the *Cobb–Douglas utility function*, $U(x_1, x_2) = x_1^c x_2^d$ which has some nice mathematical properties. One can always take a monotonic transformation of the Cobb–Douglas utility function that makes the exponents sum to 1. This shows that the idea of an ordinal utility function is fairly general and that nearly any kind of reasonable preferences can be represented by such a utility function.

A differentiated utility function is called the marginal utility (MU), i.e. the consumer's utility as she is given a little more of a good. This can be MU_1 if the utility function is differentiated for good 1 or MU_2, if the function is differentiated for good 2 (in the case of only two goods in the consumption bundle). The magnitude of marginal utility depends on the magnitude of utility. Thus, any monotonic transformation has an effect on the marginal utility. Besides, the slope of the indifference curve for a given bundle of goods can be used to express the marginal rate of substitution. This can be interpreted as the rate at which a consumer is willing to substitute a small amount of good 1 for good 2. The marginal rate of substitution (MRS) of two goods can then be expressed as

$$MRS = -MU_1/MU_2. \tag{A1}$$

Microeconomic analysis is mostly based on ordinal utility theory. However, there are also theories that attach a significance to the magnitude of utility. These are known as *cardinal utility theories*. In these theories, the size of the utility difference between two bundles of goods is supposed to have some significance. It is relatively easy to define an ordinal utility function for a person: an analyst can offer a choice between two bundles and see which one is chosen. Then a higher utility will be assigned to the chosen bundle than to the rejected bundle. This provides an operational criterion for determining whether one bundle has a higher utility than another bundle for a certain individual. It is much more complex to define a cardinal utility function. How can somebody tell if a bundle is twice as good as another? The subsequent sections will concentrate on ordinal utility functions.

So far, preferences over product bundles have been considered. Lancester (1966) generalized the theory to cases in which products consist of several features or attributes. If the relevant attributes of a product are denoted with a vector $c = (c_1, ..., c_j)$ then a utility function can be denoted as $U = U(c)$. They assume this utility function to obey the same features as standard utility functions. Maier and Weiss (1990) give an overview of extensions to standard microeconomic utility theory.

A1.2   *Optimal Choice*

So far ordinal utility theory has been discussed. Microeconomic theory uses ordinal utility theory in order to examine optimal choices of consumers. Here, consumers choose the most preferred bundle from their budget sets. Let m be the fixed amount of money available to a consumer, and let $p = (p_1,...,p_k)$ be the vector of prices of goods. The problem of preference maximization can then be written as:

$$max\ U(x) \text{ such that } px <= m \text{ and } x \in X. \tag{A2}$$

This problem can also be restated as the so-called *indirect utility function* or the maximum utility achievable at given prices and income:

$$V(p,m) = max\ U(x) \text{ such that } px = m. \tag{A3}$$

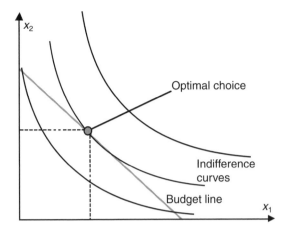

Figure A2 Preference maximization.

The value of x that solves this problem is the bundle demanded by the consumer, and this expresses how much of each good the consumer desires at a given level of prices and income. In the case of convex indifference curves, any point of the budget line that satisfies the tangency condition must be an optimal point. In the case of strictly convex indifference curves, there will be only one optimal choice. Graphically, this is the point at which the slope of the budget line equals the *MRS*. Figure A2 illustrates the procedure of preference maximization in the case of a budget line and two goods.

Economically, the consumer faces a rate of exchange of $-p_1/p_2$, i.e. if she gives up one unit of good 1, she can buy p_1/p_2 units of good 2. At the optimal point, the *MRS* is equal to the rate of exchange. Of course, when prices and income change, the consumer's optimal choice will change.

The function that relates the different values of prices, p, and income, m, to the demanded bundle is called the consumer's *demand function*. In the case of two goods this is denoted as $x_1(p_1, p_2, m)$ and $x_2(p_1, p_2, m)$. The case of perfect complements has already been discussed. The optimal choice must lie on the diagonal where the consumer purchases equal amounts of both goods, no matter what the prices are (figure A3).

In the case of two goods the budget constraint, $p_1x_1 + p_2x_2 = m$, needs to be satisfied. The optimal choices for goods 1 and 2, i.e. the demand function, is then

$$x_1 = x_2 = x = m/(p_1 + p_2) \tag{A4}$$

This is quite intuitive, since the two goods are always consumed together. Similarly, demand functions for various utility curves and budget

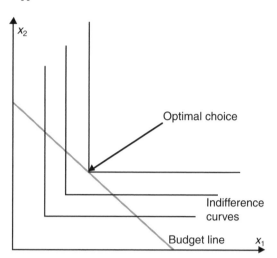

Figure A3 Optimal choice with perfect complements.

constraints can be derived. However, In practice it is often necessary to estimate a demand curve from a given set of empirical data.

A1.3   Certainty vs. Uncertainty

Utility theory and decision analysis (which will be discussed in section A2) distinguish between conditions of certainty and conditions of risk and uncertainty (Kleindorfer, Kunreuther and Schoemaker, 1993, p. 116). Using utility theory under certainty, certain outcomes can be rank-ordered in a way that is consistent with the decision maker's preferences for those outcomes. The other extreme of complete uncertainty concerns cases in which no likelihood can be assigned to the states of nature or outcomes of the alternatives. Decision making under risk implies that there is some probability associated with each state of nature. Expected utility theory incorporates the risk attitudes of the decision maker so that lotteries are rank-ordered in a way that is consistent with this risk attitude.

Different people are willing to accept different levels of risk. Some are more prone to taking risks, while others are more conservative and avoid risk. The objective is to find a way to both represent preferences and incorporate risk attitudes. Concavity in a utility curve implies that an individual is risk-averse. Of course, not everyone displays risk-averse behavior all the time, and so utility curves need not be concave (see figure A4). A convex utility curve indicates risk-seeking behavior. The whole idea of a utility

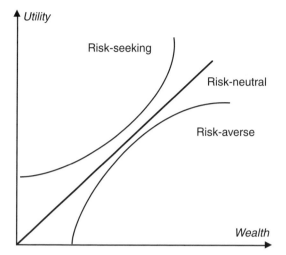

Figure A4 Different shapes for utility functions.
Source: Clemen (1996, p. 552).

function in cases of uncertainty is that it should help a decision maker choose from among alternatives with uncertain payoffs. The decision maker should maximize the expected utility.

Consider the problem of buying a car where the relevant attributes are price and life span. The trade-off between price and advertised life span can be framed as one under certainty. On the other hand, the problem could be reframed and life span can be considered to be uncertain. In this case, a probability distribution over possible life spans needs to be assessed for each car and buyer's risk attitude needs to be incorporated. The decision model would require the decision maker to assess a utility function that covered all of the possible life span outcomes so that the probability distributions for life span that came with each car could be valued appropriately.

The following paragraphs will discuss some of the basic assumptions that form the basis of expected utility. Those assumptions, also called *axioms of expected utility*, go back to von Neumann and Morgenstern's (1944) *Theory of Games and Economic Behavior* in which a set of axioms for choice behavior that leads to the maximization of expected utility is defined. These axioms, relate to the consistency with which an individual expresses preferences from among a series of risky prospects, and, therefore, include decisions under uncertainty which is more demanding than decisions under certainty. In addition to monotonicity, ordering and transitivity, they define:

■ *Continuity*: A decision maker is indifferent to a consequence *A* and some uncertain event involving only two basic consequences *B* and *C* where *B* > *A* > *C*.

■ *Substitutability*: A decision maker is indifferent to any original uncertain event that includes outcome *A* and one formed by substituting *A* for an uncertain event that is judged to be its equivalent.

■ *Invariance*: All that is needed to determine a decision maker's preferences among uncertain events are the payoffs and the associated probabilities.

■ *Reduction of compound uncertain events:* A decision maker is indifferent between a compound uncertain event and a simple uncertain event as determined by reduction using standard probability manipulations.

Even though the axioms of expected utility theory appear to be compelling, people do not necessarily make choices in accordance with them and many decision theorists find some of the axioms controversial. The reasons for the controversy range from introspection regarding particular decision situations to formal psychological experiments in which human subjects make choices that clearly violate one or more of the axioms.

Georgescu-Roegen (1954) considered the assumptions in the theory of utility far too unrealistic. He also discussed the debate on the cardinalist view that utility can be measured in scalar form and the ordinalist view that humans can generally only identify relative preference. Fishburn (1989) concedes that intransitive preferences might not be unreasonable. The substitutability axiom is also a particular point of debate. For some decision makers, the fact of having to deal with two uncertain events can be worse than facing a single one.

Von Winterfeldt and Edwards (1986) describe much intriguing discussion of the axioms from the point of view of behavioral research. Research into the behavioral paradoxes began almost as early as the original research into utility theory itself, and a large amount of literature now exists for many aspects of human behavior under risk and uncertainty. *Framing effects* are among the most pervasive paradoxes in choice behavior. Tversky and Kahneman (1981) show how an individual's risk attitude can change depending on the way the decision problem is posed, i.e. on the "frame" in which a problem is presented. One of the important general principles psychologists have discovered is that people tend to be risk-averse in dealing with gains but risk-seeking in dealing with losses. Consequently, some theorists have attempted to relax the axioms of expected utility in ways that are consistent with the observed patterns of choices that people make. Much of this literature is reviewed in Hogarth (1987).

Practical decision-analysis applications rarely distinguish between certainty and uncertainty as decision makers must primarily understand objectives and trade-offs (Clemen, 1996, p. 553). Although the distinction can be important in theoretical models of economic behavior, it is difficult to determine the extent of a given individual's risk aversion in a practical decision situation. This is the reason why decision making under certainty is employed in the context of multi-attribute auctions. Since many procurement decisions involve little or no uncertainty, decision making under certainty is a useful approximation. The assumption of certainty also keeps the process simple for the buyer.

A2   Multi-Objective Decision Analysis

One of the arguments in subsection A1.3 was that people do not seem to make coherent decisions without some guidance. This does not invalidate the idea that people should still make decisions according to utility theory. The question is whether one should model what people actually do or whether one should help decision makers to adhere to axioms that are compelling but at some times hard to follow. Decision analysis (also called "decision aid") is an approach for making utility theory operational for active decision making in a multi-criteria environment. If a decision maker does wish to make coherent decisions, then a careful decision-analysis approach can help the decision maker look for better decisions. A less rigorous position is that decision analysis should help decision makers learn more about the decision they are facing, so that they can apply the judgment they would normally apply in a more informed way.

The research done in decision analysis has produced a considerable amount of literature on the understanding and improvement of individual, group, and organization decision making. Decision analysis was developed in the 1960s and 1970s at Harvard, Stanford, MIT, Chicago, Michigan, and other major universities. It is generally considered a branch of the engineering discipline of operations research (OR), but also has links to economics, mathematics, and psychology. The theories are widely used in business and government decision making. The literature includes applications such as managing research and development programs, negotiating for oil and gas leases, forecasting sales for new products, corporate procurement, etc.

Multi-objective decision analysis generally prescribes theories for the quantitative analysis of important decisions involving multiple, interdependent objectives (Laux, 1998). In the evaluation of different offers, the price of a product may be important, but so could its delivery time. It is important to determine the relationship and trade-off between the two.

A2.1　General Process

Decision analysis is more than writing down preferences. The principle behind it is that, if alternative performances on concrete, measurable attributes are compared in a rational, unbiased manner, sounder decisions will result. Just as the process of structuring a decision problem can help the decision maker understand the problem better and lead to the recognition of new alternatives for action, so can the assessment process provide a medium in which the decision maker can actually develop her preferences or beliefs. It can also render the decision making process more transparent to third parties, a development particularly desirable in the context of government or corporate procurement decisions.

The essence of decision analysis under certainty is to break complicated decisions down into small pieces that can be dealt with individually and then recombined logically. Decisions are characterized along three dimensions: alternatives, states of nature, and outcomes. A key goal is to make a clear distinction between the choices that you can make (the alternatives), the characteristics of the alternatives (quantified by the measures) and the relative desirability of different sets of characteristics (preferences). These distinctions allow you to clearly separate the objective and subjective parts of your decision and formulate preferences in a formal way.

When many alternatives are present, it is common to reduce the choice set to a more manageable size by first eliminating "inferior" alternatives. Domination and the conjunctive rule are both mechanisms for the identification of "good" alternatives. *Domination* procedures entail the identification of alternatives that are equal to or worse than some other alternative on every single dimension. Let us analyze two alternatives A and B and the associated consequences:

$$x' = (x'_1, ..., x'_i, ..., x'_n) \text{ and } x'' = (x''_1, ..., x''_i, ..., x''_n)$$

x' dominates x'' whenever

$$x'_i \geq x''_i, \text{ for all } i \text{ and } x'_i > x''_i \text{ for some } i.$$

The set of consequences that is not dominated is called the *efficient frontier* or Pareto optimal set. Under a *conjunctive procedure* an alternative is accepted if each dimension meets a set of preset standards or thresholds. The decision maker thereby determines some aspiration levels $x^+_1, ..., x^+_i, ..., x^+_n$ while sorting out all alternatives where

$$x'_i < x^+_i, \text{ for all } i.$$

In the case of heterogeneous product offers those which do not fulfill the minimum requirements in one of the attributes are sorted out. A drawback of the conjunctive rule is that it is non-compensatory. If an alternative barely fails in a given dimension, it cannot be compensated for with surplus elsewhere.

Many complex decision problems involve multiple conflicting objectives. It is often true that no dominant alternative that is better than all other alternatives will exist in terms of all of these objectives. One cannot maximize benefits and at the same time minimize costs. In essence, the decision maker is faced with a problem of trading off the achievement of one objective against another objective. Consequently, after sorting out the inferior alternatives, preference models must be established, i.e. utility functions in order to find the best alternative for a subject. The primary difficulty with these types of decisions lies in creating a function that allows explicit comparisons between alternatives differing in many ways. This requires identifying objectives, arranging these objectives into a hierarchy, and then measuring how well available alternatives perform on each criterion. The following steps describe a general procedure used in most decision analysis methods for multi-objective problems:

1. Identify the alternatives to be ranked
2. Clarify the goals and objectives that should be met
3. Identify measures to quantify how well the alternatives meet the goals and objectives
4. Quantify preferences about different objectives
5. Rank the alternatives.

Keeny and Raiffa (1993) compare the different models. They distinguish between those utility models based on trade-offs of return and risk found in the von Neumann–Morgenstern utility theory and more general value models based on trade-offs among any set of objectives and subobjectives. The following sections will survey some of the most important decision analysis techniques. The terms "criteria," "attribute," and "issue" will be used alternatively, depending on the language used by the different schools of thought.

A2.2   Multi-Attribute Utility Theory

The most widespread heuristic used to decide between alternatives with multiple objectives is the *additive utility function*. The value of an alternative is assumed to consist of measures over the criteria that contribute to worth, all converted to a common scale of utilities. Each alternative's performance on each criterion is assumed to be known. The individual evaluates each relevant attribute x_i through a single-measure utility function $U_i(x_i)$ and indicates its relative importance value by a weight w_i. Once the single-measure utility functions are identified, the value of an alternative can be measured with an overall utility function.

Many authors also use the term *multi-attribute utility theory* (*MAUT*) to refer to this method (Clemen, 1996, p. 532). The basic hypothesis of MAUT is that in any decision problem there exists a real valued function U defined along the set of feasible alternatives which the decision maker wishes to maximize. This function aggregates the criteria $x_1 \ldots x_n$. Besides, individual (single-measure) utility functions $U_1(x_1), \ldots, U_n(x_n)$ are assumed for the n different attributes. The utility function translates the value of an attribute into "utility units." The overall utility for an alternative is given by the sum of all weighted utilities of the attributes. For an outcome that has levels x_1, $\ldots, x_n$ on the n attributes, the overall utility for an alternative i is given by

$$U(x_1 \ldots x_n) = \sum_{i=1}^{n} w_i U(x_i). \tag{A5}$$

The alternative with the largest overall utility is the most desirable under this rule. Each utility function $U(x_i)$ assigns values of 0 and 1 to the worst and best levels on that particular objective and

$$\sum_{i=1}^{n} w_i = 1, \text{ and } w_i > 0. \tag{A6}$$

Consequently, the additive utility function also assigns values of 0 and 1 to the worst and best conceivable outcomes, respectively. Alternatives with the same overall utility are indifferent and can be substituted for one another. Of course, the utility functions and scores are personal attributes which do not carry over to other people. There have been many reported applications of multi-attribute utility theory in fields such as government decision making and corporate procurement, among others. A first example to illustrate the MAUT is given in Olson (1995, p. 21):

The US Department of Energy faced the problem of picking a site to dump nuclear wastes. This was expected to involve an investment of about US $25 to US $250 billion. The National Science Foundation recommended the use of MAUT. Subsequently, the Department of Energy commissioned a MAUT analysis. The measures of value were crucial to determining the relative advantage of alternative sites. The problem involved multiple impacts, with many uncertainties. The measures of value were crucial to determining the relative advantage of alternative sites. The commission included the charge to somehow aggregate the value of alternatives which involved vexing tradeoffs. MAUT was considered appropriate for this application because of its ability to separate facts and values, insuring that hard data did not drive out soft data. Explicit professional judgments could be identified, making rational peer review possible. Fourteen criteria were identified and arranged in a hierarchy. Such criteria should be independent for application of MAUT, so those criteria which overlapped were condensed. Each alternative's value on each criterion were measured with a metric that made sense relative to the decision. For instance, the measure of radiation impact was in expected deaths rather than in rads.

A utility function was developed through interviewing policy makers using market basket tradeoffs. For each criterion, disfunction was measured over a range from 0 to the maximum disbenefit expected from all alternatives. The relative disfunction of public fatalities versus worker fatalities was explored. Additionally, the money value of fatalities was examined through market basket tradeoffs. Four policy makers who conducted the tradeoff analysis tended to share organizational policy, or take on the moral judgements of the agency they worked for. The functions tended to be linear. The researchers concluded that if an issue is important, and involved the public, the function should be linear. They also commented that for important problems, there should not be any noted intransitivity. The analysis started with easy judgments. The disutility aggregation was made the sum of component scores. Each alternative was then ranked on each criterion.

The example shows that this method is appropriate for dealing with uncertainties when many interest groups are involved. MAUT kept the analysis clear and explicit, separating means from ends, thus making it possible to explain the procedure to each interest group. Bunn (1984) formulates a number of theoretical preconditions for MAUT in the case of uncertainty:

- *Structure*: The choices available to the decision maker can be sufficiently described by the payoff values and associated probabilities of those choices. This implies that the value of a choice consists of the choice's measures on factors of value to the decision maker.
- *Ordering*: The decision maker can express preferences or indifference between any pair of trade-offs.
- *Reduction of compound prospects*: Decision makers are indifferent between compound prospects and their equivalent simple prospects.
- *Continuity*: Every payoff can be considered a certainty equivalent for the prospect of some probability p of the worst outcome and the inverse probability $(1-p)$ of the best outcome. This assumption implies that severe outcomes would be risked at small probability.
- *Substitutability*: Any prospect can be substituted by its certainty equivalent.
- *Transitivity of prospects*: Decision makers can express preference or indifference between all pairs of prospects.
- *Monotonicity*: For two options with the same payoffs, decision makers should prefer the option with the higher probability or the better payoff. Cases where this is not demonstrated imply that there is some other factor of value that has not been considered.

Another assumption from the above example is the additivity of the utility function. Utility scores are not necessarily additive, $U(A + B)$ may be unequal to $U(A) + U(B)$. This means that utility functions can curve, which seems entirely reasonable. A precondition for additivity is the *preferential independence* of the attributes. In other words, an attribute x is said to be preferentially independent of y if preferences for specific outcomes of x do not depend on the level of attribute y (Olson, 1995). This can be easily extended to a three-dimensional case: A utility function may be expressed in an additive form

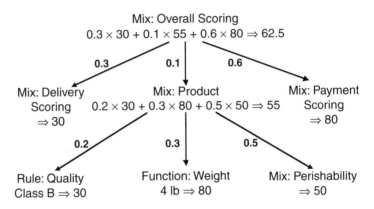

Figure A5 Example of an additive utility function.

$$U(x,y,z) = U_x(x) + U_y(y) + U_z(z) \tag{A7}$$

where U_x, U_y, and U_z are single-attribute value functions, if and only if $\{x,y\}$ is preferentially independent of z, $\{x, z\}$ is preferentially independent of y, and $\{y, z\}$ is preferentially independent of x (Keeny and Raiffa, 1993, p.105). Consequently, in a multi-dimensional space, an additive utility function of the form shown in (A7) can be used if all attributes are mutually preferentially independent, i.e. every subset of these attributes is preferentially independent of its complementary set of attributes. Formal proofs of the theorem can be found in Debreu (1954).

It is fair to say that preferential independence holds for many situations, and the following sections will concentrate on such cases with preferential independence. The idea is that care should be taken to select attributes which are as independent as possible because the analysis of independent attributes is much easier than that of dependent attribute sets. However, interactions between attributes may be modeled. For example, two attributes may be substitutes for one another to some extent. It might also be the case that high achievement in all attributes is worth more than the sum of the values obtained from the individual utilities. In order to express the interdependencies among two attributes, the utility function can be extended (see subsection A2.6 for details).

Figure A5 provides an example of MAUT in the context of purchasing (see Stolze, 1998, for a similar application). This is very similar to the procurement situations which are considered in this book. The first step for a consumer will be to identify the fundamental objectives of the purchase. These objectives are then organized into a hierarchy of clusters, subclusters, and so on in which the lower levels explain what is meant by the higher levels. Individual utility functions can be expressed as *scoring rules* or *scoring functions*. Partially, it shows the computation of a utility score. Scoring rules check to which degree products match a particular objective and compute a base score. Scoring functions also compute base scores, but they usually map a numeric product feature to a scoring. The importance of individual utilities is expressed through *mix rules*. Mix rules combine base scores by creating weighted averages. Again, all weights are positive and add up to 1. More important objectives will receive more weight and will, therefore, contribute more to the overall utility. The weights can, for example, be determined through the pairwise comparison of the objectives. Finally, the overall utility is computed through a hierarchical composition of base scores in the scoring tree.

MAUT is an accepted method for the normative analysis of choice problems. The assessment of the individual utility functions and weights is a core issue when the additive utility function is used. Some kind of subjective judgment forms the basis for the weights, and yet the interpretation of the weights is not always clear. Many different methods exist for assessing the attribute values and weights (Clemen, 1996). One can, for example, try to determine the marginal rate of substitution between several attributes. Decision analysis techniques like the *analytic hierarchy process* and *conjoint analysis* provide more sophisticated approaches. These techniques will be discussed in the following subsections.

A2.3 SMART

The *simple multi-attribute rating technique* (SMART) provides a simple way to implement the principles of multi-attribute utility theory. Edwards (1977) argued that decisions depend on values and probabilities, both subjective quantities. Error can arise in modeling, and can also arise from elicitation. Modeling error arises when a model is applied with simplified assumptions. Elicitation error arises when measures obtained do not accurately reflect subject preference. The more complicated the questions, the more elicitation error there will be. SMART requires no judgment of preference among alternatives because they are assumed to be unreliable and unrepresentative of real preferences. Edwards proposed a ten-step technique for decisions under certainty:

1. Identify the person or organization whose utilities are to be maximized
2. Identify the issue or issues of the decision
3. Identify the alternatives to be evaluated
4. Identify the relevant dimensions of value for evaluation of the alternatives
5. Rank the dimensions in order of importance
6. Rate dimensions in importance, preserving ratios
7. Sum the importance weights, and divide each by the sum

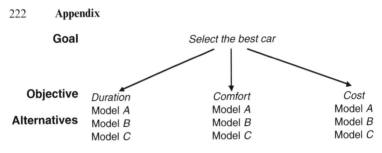

Figure A6 Hierarchical decomposition.

8. Measure the location of each alternative being evaluated on each dimension

9. Calculate utilities for alternatives in the form of $U_k = \Sigma_k w_k u_{jk}$ where U_k is the utility value for alternative j, w_k is the normalized weight for objective k, and u_{jk} is the scaled utility for alternative j on dimension k

10. Decide.

SMART provides a means to apply the principles of multi-attribute utility theory without the need for complex software or lottery trade-off analysis. The method has been applied many times. However, the alternatives must be known with certainty in advance and it is hard to derive a more generic utility function from the process. This is the reason why the technique is not suitable for multi-attribute auctions.

A2.4 Analytic Hierarchy Process

The *analytic hierarchy process* (AHP) became a popular decision analysis technique during the 1990s. AHP was developed in the early 1970s at the Wharton School of Business by Thomas Saaty (1980), one of the pioneers of operations research. AHP has also been used to develop linear utility functions which reflect the relative importance of decision objectives, as well as problem features that have been used for mathematical programming and for ranking alternatives. Cognitive psychology has found that people are poor at assimilating large quantities of information on problems. Saaty used this concept as a principle in AHP. People cope with cognitive overload by employing heuristics that simplify the problem. AHP is composed of several previously existing but unassociated concepts such as:

- decomposition through the hierarchical structuring of complexity
- comparative judgment through pairwise comparisons
- the eigenvector method for deriving weights, and
- hierarchic composition.

Both AHP and MAUT allow decision makers to model a complex problem in a hierarchical structure that shows the relationships of the goal, objectives (criteria), subobjectives, and alternatives (see figure A6).

Table A1. *Pairwise comparison of objectives*

	Duration	Comfort	Cost
Duration	1/1	1/2	3/1
Comfort	2/1	1/1	4/1
Cost	1/3	1/4	1/1

The principle of comparative judgments is applied to construct pairwise comparisons of all combinations of elements in a cluster with respect to the parent of the cluster, in order to get utilities as ratio scale measures. This is a distinguishing feature of the AHP process. Whereas AHP utilizes ratio scales for even the lowest level of the hierarchy, MAUT utilizes an interval scale for the alternatives.

Thus, the resulting priorities for alternatives in an AHP model will be ratio scale measures whereas those in a MAUT model will be interval scale measures. While it is difficult to justify weights that are arbitrarily assigned, it is relatively easy to justify judgments and the basis for the judgments. Table A1 shows an example of a matrix depicting the pairwise comparisons of three objectives.

AHP is based on the mathematical structure of consistent matrices and their associated right-eigenvector's ability to generate true or approximate weights. The eigenvector of the greatest eigenvalue of the matrix in table A1 results in the weights for the different objectives. The results of this method have been tested experimentally and found to be accurate. Finally, the *principle of hierarchic composition or synthesis* is applied to multiply the local priorities of the elements in a cluster by the "global" priority of the parent element, which produces global priorities throughout the hierarchy, and to add the global priorities for the lowest-level elements (usually the alternatives).

A large number of AHP applications have been published (Shim, 1989). A major reason for this popularity is that AHP is relatively easy to understand, and the overall process provides a rational means of approaching a decision that is very easy to explain to others. AHP has also been incorporated in a number of group decision environments.

A2.5   Conjoint Analysis

Conjoint analysis is a versatile marketing research technique (Green and Wind, 1973). Like other decision analysis techniques, it helps to examine the trade-offs that people make when deciding on an alternative and can be used to con-

Table A2. *Example utilities*

Duration	Utility
3 hours	42
5 hours	22

Comfort	Utility
Extra-wide seats	15
Regular seats	12

Cost US$	Utility
400	61
700	5

struct additive utility functions (Kersten and Noronha, 1998). Companies often employ it to determine the optimal features for a product or service.

For instance, a traveler may like the comfort and arrival time of a particular flight, but reject a purchase owing to cost. In this case, cost has a high "utility" value. Utility is defined as a number which represents the value that consumers place on an attribute. In other words, it represents the relative "worth" of the attribute. A low utility indicates less value; a high utility indicates more value. The following figure presents a list of hypothetical utilities for an individual consumer:

The example in table A2 depicts an individual's utilities. Based on these utilities, the following conclusions can be made:

- This consumer places greater value on a 3-hour flight (utility is 42) than on a 5-hour flight (utility is 22).
- This consumer does not differ much in the value that she places on comfort. That is, the utilities are quite close (12 vs. 15).
- This consumer places much higher value on a price of US $400 than a price of US $700.

These utilities also provide information about the extent to which each of these attributes motivates choice of a particular flight. The importance of an attribute can be calculated by examining the range of utilities (that is, the difference between the lowest and highest utilities) across all levels of the attribute. Here, a utility is a numerical expression of the value that consumers place on each level of each attribute. In other words, it represents the relative "worth" of the attribute. That range represents the maximum impact that the attribute can contribute to a product. The absolute values of the utilities have no inherent meaning.

The computation of the relative importance for each attribute depends on the relative range between maximum and minimum level utilities within an attribute. This is based on the assumption that the larger the difference between maximum and minimum level utilities within an attribute, the more determinative and salient the attribute is in the overall evaluation of alternatives. Using the hypothetical utilities presented earlier, the relative importance of each of the three attributes can be calculated. The range for each attribute is given below:

- Duration: *Range* = 20 (42–22)
- Comfort: *Range* = 3 (15–12)
- Cost: *Range* = 56 (61–5).

These ranges give information about the relative importance of each attribute. Cost is the most important factor in the product purchase, as it has the highest range of utility values. Cost is succeeded in importance by the duration of the flight. Based on the range and value of the utilities, it can be seen that seat comfort is relatively unimportant to this consumer. This person will make a purchase choice based mainly on cost and then on the duration of the flight. The relative importance is described in order to reflect its weighted importance across all involved attributes. The calculation of an attribute's relative importance is

$$w_j = \frac{[\max_j(u_{ij}) - \min_j(u_{ij})]}{\sum_{j=1}^{J} [\max_j(u_{ij}) - \min_j(u_{ij})]} . \tag{A8}$$

where w_j is the relative importance of attribute j, max (u_{ij}) is the maximum level utility in attribute j, and min (u_{ij}) is the minimum level utility in attribute j (see also Hu, 1998). The weight of "cost" in our example would be $56/(20 + 3 + 56) = 0.71$.

A2.6 Multi-Attribute Utility Models with Interaction

The models which have been described so far essentially use an additive combination of preferences for individual attributes. Compared to the utility functions used in microeconomic analysis (e.g. a Cobb–Douglas utility function), these are rather simple mathematical formulations of a customer's preferences. However, this is incomplete in some cases because it ignores certain fundamental characteristics of choices among multi-attribute alternatives. The additivity assumption implies that there are no interaction effects between attributes (i.e. preferential independence).

However, two attributes may to some extent be substitutes for one another. It might also be the case that high achievement in all attributes is worth more than the sum of the values obtained from the individual utilities. In order to express these interdependencies among two attributes, an additive utility function can be extended towards a so-called multilinear expression:

$$U(x, y) = w_x U_x(x) + w_y U_y(y) + (1 - w_x - w_y) U_x(x) U_y(y). \qquad \text{(A9)}$$

The product term $(1 - w_x - w_y) U_x(x) U_y(y)$ in this utility function is what permits the modeling of interactions among attributes (Clemen, 1996). Keeny and Raiffa (1993) give an interesting interpretation of the coefficient $(1 - w_x - w_y)$. The sign of this coefficient can be interpreted in terms of whether x and y are complements or substitutes for each other. A positive coefficient means that x and y complement each other, and it will drive up the overall utility for the pair of attributes even more. If the coefficient is negative, then high values on each scale will result in a high product term, which must be subtracted in the multi-attribute preference value. But if one attribute is high and the other low, the subtraction effect is not as strong. Thus, if $(1 - w_x - w_y)$ is negative, the two attributes are substitutes. Suppose, a corporation has two divisions that operate in different markets, and the profits in each division represent two attributes of concern to the president. To a great extent, success by the two divisions could be viewed as substitutes. If profit from one division was down while the other was up, the company would get along fine. The function requires only the individual utility functions and enough information to put them together.

A pre-condition for this kind of multilinear utility function is *utility independence*. An attribute y is considered utility independent of attribute x if preferences for *uncertain* choices involving different levels of y are independent of the value of x. Yet another concept is *additive independence*, which allows us to model an additive utility function in the presence of uncertainty. Utility independence is clearly analogous to preferential independence, except that the assessments are made under conditions of uncertainty. Almost all reported multi-attribute applications assume utility independence (Clemen, 1996, p. 580). If one of the attributes is preferentially dependent, a utility surface can still be modeled (see subsection 7.3.3), although this is already more complicated. If neither x nor y is utility independent of the other, then neither the multilinear nor the additive forms for the utility function are appropriate. In these cases a direct assessment of utility values can be performed for certain alternatives.

In summary, the notion of interaction among attributes is one of the most difficult concepts in multi-attribute utility theory. To use the additive utility function there must be no interaction at all. To use the multilinear utility function, there can be some interaction, but it must be of a limited form (utility independence). Fortunately, evidence from behavioral research suggests that it is rarely necessary to model more complex preference interactions. Keeny and Raiffa (1993) provide a detailed discussion of multi-attribute utility modeling.

Work has also been done to extend AHP to cases of dependence within the hierarchy. The Analytic Network Process (ANP) allows interaction and feedback within clusters in a hierarchy (inner dependence) and among clusters (outer dependence). Using a network approach, it is possible to represent and analyze interactions to incorporate non-linear relations between the elements, and to synthesize mutual effects by a single procedure.

A2.7   Using Software for Decision Analysis

As one can imagine, multiple-objective decisions can become very complex. If these guidelines are implemented in decision analysis software, decision makers can be assisted to adhere to these "rules of clear thinking" (Clemen, 1996, p. 504). Given the ubiquitous nature of multi-objective decisions, it should come as no surprise that many different software programs are available. For example, there is a number of decision analysis tools on the market that help customers decide between different product alternatives. PersonaLogic <http://www.personaLogic.com> is a good example of how software can help a buyer assess a utility function. It leads the user through a multi-step, web-based dialogue in which user preferences and their importance are elicited (see the screenshot in figure A7).

After the interview, this data is used to evaluate the available products and display them in a rating-sorted list. Given a set of constraints on product features, PersonaLogic filters products that do not meet the given hard constraints and prioritizes the remaining products using the given soft constraints. The tool is used by different companies to compare complex products such as cars, camcorders, bicycles, mutual funds, and travel packages. Several researchers have tried to use decision analysis techniques in order to build more sophisticated query interfaces for electronic catalogs (see, for example, Stolze, 1998).

Decision analysis tools such as ExpertChoice <http://www.expertchoice .com> and LogicalDecisions <http://www.logicaldecisions.com> provide even more sophisticated solutions for the general decision making process. LogicalDecision uses multi-attribute utility theory, whereas ExpertChoice uses AHP. Apart from pure analysis functionality, the tools include support for decision problem structuring and the eliciting of probabilities, utility functions, weights, and risk preferences.

A2.8   Summary

So far, this section has concentrated on techniques used to select the best choice. Other techniques are meant to focus the decision maker's attention on a short list of alternatives from an initial large set. For example, *outranking techniques* (ELECTRE and PROMETHEE) seek to eliminate

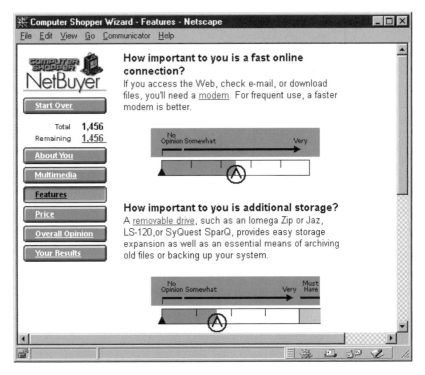

Figure A7 Screenshot of PersonaLogic.

alternatives dominated according to a set of weights which is assumed to be given (Roy, 1981). ELECTRE is an acronym for elimination and a choice translating algorithm. Given a set of alternatives on K-objectives, this algorithm seeks to reduce the size of the non-dominated set. It assumes that the decision maker will provide a set of weights reflecting the relative importance of the objectives. The fundamental idea is that alternatives can be eliminated which are dominated by other alternatives to a specific degree. The method uses a concordance index to measure the relative advantage of each alternative over all other alternatives. These techniques have not been considered further, since they are not directly applicable in multi-attribute auctions.

The decision analysis techniques all seek to help decision makers select multi-attribute choices that best match their preference function. The procedure of decomposing the overall goal into a hierarchy of objectives and subobjectives, quantifying scores and preferences for each objective, and finally composing it again, is similar to all of the techniques. However, the methods vary in the types of problems they deal with, and their underlying assumptions are discussed at length by proponents of the different schools of thought.

The previous analysis concentrated on techniques which enable a decision maker to derive a utility function that can be used to determine the best choice in a subsequent evaluation of bids. In principle, MAUT, AHP, and conjoint analysis are all suitable for this task. All three techniques are considered more appropriate for short lists of alternatives (less than five–nine). In contrast, outranking methods require a large list of alternatives before their implementation can make sense. AHP and its related methods have an exponential growth in the number of required comparisons with more criteria. The number of pairwise comparisons required grows exponentially with the number of criteria, as well as the number of categories upon which each criterion is graded. Moreover, the eigenvector method used in AHP has been questioned by several researchers. Conjoint analysis is used by some researchers in the field of negotiation support systems (Kersten and Noronha, 1998). MAUT is the most theoretically accepted approach for decision analysis (see Olson, 1995, for a comparison). This is also the reason why MAUT is used for the implementation of multi-attribute auctions in this book (described in section 6.5).

References

Alty, J. L., Griffiths, D., Jennings, N. R., Mamdani, E. H., Struthers, A. and Wiegand, M. E. (1994). *ADEPT – Advanced Decision Environment for Process Tasks: Overview and Architecture.* Paper presented at the BCS Expert Systems 94 Conference (Applications Track), Cambridge, UK

Alzon, P., Tothesan, P., Hubert, M., Athanassiou, E. and Hoang, V. (1998). *ABS Broker Business Model.* ABS. Available: <http://b5www.berkom.de/ABS/D23.htm>, August 12

Arrow, K. J. (1959). Toward a theory of price adjustment. In M. Abramovitz (ed.), *The Allocation of Economic Resources*, pp. 41–51. Stanford: Stanford University Press

Arrow, K. J., Block, H. D. and Hurwicz, L. (1959). On the stability of competitive equilibrium II. *Econometrica, 27*, 82–109

Aumann, R. J. and Hart, S. (1992). *Handbook of Game Theory*, I. Amsterdam *et al.*: North-Holland

Axelrod, R. (1984). *The Evolution of Cooperation.* New York: Basic Books

Bailey, J. P. and Bakos, Y. (1997). An exploratory study of the emerging role of electronic intermediaries. *International Journal of Electronic Commerce, 1*(3)

Bakos, Y. (1991). A strategic analysis of electronic marketplaces. *MIS Quarterly, 15*(3), 295–310

(1998). The emerging role of electronic marketplaces on the Internet. *Communications of the ACM, 41*(8), 35–42

Bakos, Y. and Brynjolfsson, E. (1993). Information technology, incentives and the optimal number of suppliers. *Journal of Management Information Systems, 10*(2), 37–53

(1999). Bundling information goods: pricing, profits and efficiency. *Management Science, 45* (12)

Balakrishnan, P., Sundar, V. and Eliashberg, J. (1995). An analytical process model of two-party negotiations. *Management Science, 41*(2), 226–43

Banks, J., Carson, J. S. and Nelson, B. L. (1999). *Discrete-Event System Simulation,* 2nd edn. New York *et al.*: Prentice-Hall

Banks, J. S., Ledyard, J. O. and Porter, D. P. (1989). Allocating uncertain and unresponsive resources: an experimental approach. *RAND Journal of Economics, 20*, 1–23

Battalio, R. C., Kogut, C. A. and Meyer, D. J. (1990). The effect of varying number of bidders in first-price private value auctions: an application of a dual market bidding technique. In L. Green and J. H. Kagel (eds.), *Advances in Behavioral Economics*. Norwood, NJ: Ablex Publishing

Bazerman, M. H. and Samuelson, W. F. (1983). I won the auction but don't want the price. *Journal of Conflict Resolution, 27*, 618–34

Beam, C. (1999). *Auctioning and Bidding in Electronic Commerce: The Online Auction*. Unpublished Dissertation, University of California, Berkeley

Beam, C., Bichler, M., Krishnan, R. and Segev, A. (1999). On negotiations and deal making in electronic markets. *Information Systems Frontiers, 1*(1 and 2)

Beam, C. and Segev, A. (1997). Automated negotiations: a survey of the state of the art. *Wirtschaftsinformatik, 39*(3), 263–7

(1998). *Auctions on the Internet: A Field Study* (98–WP-1032). University of California, Berkeley: Haas School of Business

Berners-Lee, T. (1990). *World-Wide Web: Proposal for a HyperText Project* <http://www.w3.org/Proposal.html>. Geneva, CERN. Available

Bernhardt, D. and Scoones, D. (1994). A note on sequential auctions. *American Economic Review, 84*, 653–7

Bernstein, P. A. (1996). Middleware: a model for distributed system services. *Communications of the ACM (CACM), 39*(2), 86–98

Berthold, M. and Hand, D. (1999). *Intelligent Data Analysis*. Berlin *et al.*: Springer

Bichler, M. (1997). *Aufbau unternehmensweiter WWW-Informationssystem*. Braunschweig *et al.*: Vieweg

(1998). *Decision Analysis – A Critical Enabler for Multi-attribute Auctions*. Paper presented at the 12th Electronic Commerce Conference, Bled, Slovenia

(2000a). An experimental analysis of multi-attribute auctions. *Decision Support Systems, 29*(3)

(2000b). *A Roadmap to Auction-based Negotiation Protocols for Electronic Commerce*. Paper presented at the 33rd Hawai'i International Conference on Systems Sciences (HICSS), Maui

Bichler, M., Beam, C. and Segev, A. (1998a). An electronic broker for business-to-business electronic commerce on the Internet. *International Journal of Cooperative Information Systems, 7*(4), 315–31

(1998b). *OFFER: A broker-centered Object Framework for Electronic Requisitioning*. Paper presented at the IFIP Conference Trends in Electronic Commerce (TrEC), Hamburg

(1998c). Services of a Broker in electronic commerce transactions. *International Journal of Electronic Markets, 8*(1), 27–31

Bichler, M. and Hansen, H. R. (1997). Elektronische Kataloge im WWW. *Information Management, 12*(3), 47–53

Bichler, M. and Kaukal, M. (1999). *Design and Implementation of A Brokerage Service for Electronic Procurement*. Paper presented at the DEXA '99 Workshop on Electronic Commerce, Florence

Bichler, M., Kaukal, M. and Segev, A. (1999). *Multi-Attribute Auctions for Electronic Procurement*. Paper presented at the First IBM IAC Workshop on Internet Based Negotiation Technologies, Yorktown Heights, NY, March 18–19

Bichler, M. and Klimesch, R. (2000). Simulation multivariater Auktionen – Eine Analyse des Handels mit Finanzderivaten. *Wirtschaftsinformatik, 42*(3)

Bichler, M. and Loebbecke, C. (2000). Pricing strategies and technologies for on-line delivered content. *Journal of End User Computing 12*(3)

Bichler, M. and Segev, A. (1998a). A brokerage framework for Internet commerce. *Journal of Distributed and Parallel Data-bases, 7*(2), 133–48

(1998b). *InfoLink: A Case Study and an Analysis of Object Web Infrastructures.* Paper presented at the DEXA Workshop on Network-Based Information Systems, Vienna

Bichler, M., Segev, A. and Zhao, L. J. (1998). Component-based E-Commerce: assessment of current practices and future directions. *ACM SIGMOD Records, 27*(4)

Bichler, M. and Werthner, H. (2000). *A Classification Framework for Multidimensional, Multi-Unit Procurement Negotiations.* Paper presented at the DEXA Workshop on E-Negotiations, Greenwich, UK

Binmore, K. (1985). Bargaining and coalitions. In A. E. Roth (ed.), *Game Theoretic Models of Bargaining.* Cambridge, MA: Cambridge University Press

Binmore, K. and Vulkan, N. (1999). Applying game theory to automated negotiation. *Netnomics, 1*(1), 1–9

BIZ (1997). *67th Annual Report.* Basel, Switzerland: Bank for International Settlements

Black, F. and Scholes, M. (1973). The pricing of options and corporate liabilities. *Journal of Political Economy, 81*

Blair, G., Gallagher, J., Hutchinson, D. and Shepard, D. (1991). *Object-oriented Languages, Systems and Applications.* Horwood, NY: Halsted Press

Blair, G. S. and Stefani, J.-B. (1997). *Open Distributed Processing and Multimedia.* New York *et al.*: Addison-Wesley

Booch, G. (1991). *Object-oriented Design with Applications.* Redwood City, CA: Benjamin Cummings

Branco, F. (1997). The design of multidimensional auctions. *RAND Journal of Economics, 28*(1), 63–81

Browning, E. K. and Zupan, M. A. (1999). *Microeconomic Theory and Applications,* 6th edn. New York *et al*: Addison-Wesley

Bulow, J. I. and Roberts, D. J. (1989). The simple economics of optimal auctions. *Journal of Political Economy, 97,* 1060–90

Bunn, D. W. (1984). *Applied Decision Analysis.* New York: McGraw-Hill

Camerer, C. (1990). Behavioral game theory. In R. M. Hogarth (ed.), *Insights in Decision Making: A Tribute to Hillel J. Einhorn,* pp. 311–336. Chicago: University of Chicago Press

Chatterjee, K. and Samuelson, W. F. (1983). Bargaining under incomplete information. *Operations Research, 31,* 835–51

Chavez, A. and Maes, P. (1996). *Kasbah: An Agent Marketplace for Buying and Selling Goods.* Paper presented at the First International Conference on the Practical Application of Intelligent Agents and Multi-Agent Technology (PAAM '96), London

Che, Y.-K. (1993). Design competition through multidimensional auctions. *RAND Journal of Economics, 24*(4), 668–80

Chen, J., Kacandes, P., Manning, D., Meltzer, B. and Rhodes, T. (1999). *eCo Framework Project*. Palo Alto: CommerceNet, Inc.

Choudhury, V., Hartzel, K. S. and Konsynski, B. R. (1998). Uses and consequences of electronic markets: an empirical investigation in the aircraft parts industry. *MIS Quarterly, 22*(4), 471–507

Clarke, E. H. (1971). Multipart pricing of public goods. *Public Choice, 11*, 17–33

Clemen, R. T. (1996). *Making Hard Decisions: An Introduction to Decision Analysis*. Belmont, CA: Wadsworth Publishing

Clemons, E. K. and Reddi, S. P. (1994). *The Impact of IT on the Degree of Outsourcing, the Number of Suppliers and the Duration of Contracts*. Paper presented at the 26th Hawai'i International Conference on Systems Science (HICSS), Maui

Clemons, E. K. and Weber, B. W. (1998). Restructuring institutional block trading: an overview of the OptiMark system. *Journal of Management Information Systems, 15*, 41–60

Coase, R. H. (1937). The nature of the firm, *Economica 4*, 386–405; reprinted in R. H. Coase, *The Firm, the Market and the Law*. Chicago: University of Chicago Press (1988)

CommerceNet (1995). *CommerceNet Catalog Working Group – Catalog Requirements* (Internal Memorandum Report). Palo Alto: CommerceNet, Inc.

Cortese, A. E. and Stepanek, M. (1998). Good-bye to fixed pricing. *Business Week*, May 4

Cox, J. and Rubinstein, M. (1985). *Option Markets*. Englewood Cliffs, NJ: Prentice-Hall

Cox, J. C., Roberson, B. and Smith, V. L. (1982). Theory and behavior of single object auctions. In V. L. Smith (ed.), *Research in Experimental Economics*. Greenwich, CT: JAI Press

Cox, J. C., Smith, V. L. and Walker, J. M. (1983). Tests of a heterogeneous bidder's theory of first price auctions. *Economics Letters, 12*, 207–12

(1994). Theory and behavior of multiple unit discriminative auctions. *Journal of Finance, 39*, 983–1010

Cripps, M. and Ireland, N. (1994). The design of auctions and tenders with quality thresholds: the symmetric case. *The Economic Journal, 104*, 316–26

Crowston, K. (1997). *Price Behavior in Electronic Markets*. Paper presented at the 18th International Conference on Information Systems (ICIS '97), Atlanta

Dasgupta, S. and Spulber, D. F. (1989). Managing procurement auctions. *Information Economics and Policy, 4*, 5–29

Dataquest. (1999). *The E-Market Maker Revolution*. Stamford, CT: Gartner Group

Davenport, T. H. (1993). *Process Innovation: Reengineering Work through Information Technology*. Boston, MA: Harvard Business School Press

Debreu, G. (1954). Representation of a preference ordering by a numerical function. In R. Thrall and R. Davis (eds.), *Decision Processes*, pp. 159–66. New York: Wiley

Domschke, W. and Drexl, W. (1998). *Einführung in Operations Research.* Heidelberg: Springer

Dworman, G. O., Kimbrough, S. O. and Laing, J. D. (1993). *On Automated Discovery of Models using Genetic Programming in Game Theoretic Contexts* (Research Report). The Wharton School, University of Pennsylvania

Dwyer, F. R. and Walker, O. C. (1981). Bargaining in an asymmetrical power structure. *Journal of Marketing, 45*(1), 104–115

Dyer, D., Kagel, J. H. and Levin, D. (1989). Resolving uncertainty about the number of bidders in independent private-value auctions: an experimental analysis. *Rand Journal of Economics, 20,* 268–79

Edgeworth, F. Y. (1881). *Mathematical Psychics.* London: Kegan Paul

Edwards, W. (1977). How to use multiattribute utility measurement for social decisionmaking. *IEEE Transactions on Systems, Man and Cybernetics SMC, 7*(5), 326–40

Engelbrecht-Wiggans, R. (1989). On a possible benefit to bid takers from using multi-stage auctions. *Management Science, 34*(9), 1109–20

Fan, M., Stallaert, J. and Whinston, A. B. (1999). A web-based financial trading system. *IEEE Computer, 32*(4), 64–70

Fayad, M. E. and Schmid, D. C. (1997). Object-oriented application frameworks. *Communications of the ACM (CACM), 40*(10), 32–8

Field, S. and Hoffner, Y. (1998). VIMP – a virtual market place for insurance products. *Journal of Electronic Markets, 8*(4)

FIPA (1997). *Specifications.* Geneva: Foundation for Intelligent Physical Agents

Fishburn, P. C. (1989). Foundations of decision analysis: along the way. *Management Science, 35,* 387–405

Fisher, F. M. (1983). *Disequilibrium Foundations of Equilibrium Economics.* Cambridge, MA: Cambridge University Press

Fisher, R. and Ertel, D. (1995). *Getting Ready to Negotiate.* Harmondsworth: Penguin

Foroughi, A. (1995). A survey of the user of computer support for negotiation. *Journal of Applied Business Research, Spring,* 121–34

Forsythe, R. and Isaak, R. M. (1982). Demand-revealing mechanisms for private good auctions. In V. L. Smith (ed.), *Research in Experimental Economics.* Greenwich, CT: JAI Press

Fowler, M. (1997). *UML Distilled – Applying the Standard Object Modeling Language.* Reading, MA: Addison-Wesley

Franklin, M. K. and Reiter, M. K. (1996). The design and implementation of a secure auction service. *IEEE Transactions on Software Engineering, 22*(5), 302–12

Friedman, D. and Rust, J. (eds.) (1993). *The Double Auction Market – Institutions, Theories and Evidence.* Reading, MA: Addison-Wesley

Friedman, D. and Sunder, S. (1994). *Experimental Methods: A Primer for Economists.* Cambridge, UK: Cambridge University Press

Fudenberg, D. and Tirole, J. (1991). *Game Theory.* Boston, MA: MIT Press

Fulkerson, B. and Staffend, G. (1997). Decentralized control in the customer focused enterprise. *Annals of Operations Research, 77,* 325–33

Galliers, R. (1994). *Information Systems Research – Issues, Methods and Practical Guidelines.* Maidenhead, UK: McGraw-Hill

Gebauer, J., Segev, A. and Färber, F. (1999). Internet-based electronic markets. *International Journal of Electronic Markets, 9*(3)

Georgescu-Roegen, N. (1954). Choice, expectations and measurability. *Quarterly Journal of Economics, 468*(4), 503–34

Gibbard, A. (1973). Manipulation of voting schemes: a general result. *Econometrica, 41*, 587–602

Gilbert, N. and Troitzsch, K. (1999). *Simulation for the Social Scientist.* Buckingham: Open University Press

Gode, D. K. and Sunder, S. (1993). Allocative efficiency of markets with zero intelligence traders. *Journal of Political Economy, 101*, 119–37

Gomber, P., Schmidt, C. and Weinhardt, C. (1996). Synergie und Koordination in dezentral planenden Organisationen. *Wirtschaftsinformatik, 38*(3), 299–307

(1998a). Efficiency, incentives and computational tractability in MAS-coordination. *International Journal of Cooperative Information Systems, 8*(1), 1–15

(1998b). *Auctions in Electronic Commerce – Efficiency versus Computational Tractability.* Paper presented at the International Conference on Electronic Commerce (ICEC) '98, Seoul

Gossen, H. H. (1853). *Entwicklung der Gesetze des menschlichen Verkehrs und der daraus fließenden Regeln für menschliches Handeln,* 3 (Berlin 1927)

Graham, D. and Marshall, R. C. (1987). Collusive bidder behavior at single-object second-price and English auctions. *Journal of Political Economy, 95*, 1217–39

Green, P. E. and Wind, Y. (1973). *Multiattribute Decision in Marketing: A Measurement Approach.* Hinsdale, IL: The Dryden Press

Gresik, T. and Satterthwaite, M. A. (1989). The rate at which a simple market converges to efficiency as the number of traders increases: an asymptotic result for optimal trading mechanisms. *Journal of Economic Theory, 48*, 304–32

Groves, T. (1973). Incentives in teams. *Econometrica, 41*, 617–31

Gurbaxani, V. and Whang, S. (1991). The impact of information systems on organizations and markets. *Communciations of the ACM, 34*(1), 59–73

Guttman, R. and Maes, P. (1998). *Agent-mediated Integrative Negotiation for Retail Electronic Commerce.* Paper presented at the Workshop on Agent Mediated Electronic Trading (AMET '98), Minneapolis, November 22

Guttman, R., Moukas, A. and Maes, P. (1998). Agent-mediated electronic commerce: a survey. *Knowledge Engineering Review, 13*(3)

Hansen, H. R. (1995). A case study of a mass information system. *Information and Management, 28*(2)

Hansen, R. G. (1988). Auctions with endogenous quantity. *Rand Journal of Economics, 19*, 44–58

Harkavy, M., Kikuchi, H. and Tygar, J. (1998). *Electronic Auctions with Private Bids.* Paper presented at the 3rd USENIX Workshop on Electronic Commerce, Boston, MA

Harsanyi, J. C. and Selten, R. (1972). A generalized Nash solution for two-person bargaining games with incomplete information. *Management Science, 18*(5), 80

Hayek, F. A. (1945). The use of knowledge in society. *American Economic Review*, *35*, 519–30

Hof, R. D., Green, H. and Judge, P. (1999). Online auctions: going, going, gone. *Business Week*, April 12

Hogarth, R. (1987). *Judgment and Choice*, 2nd edn. New York: Wiley

Holler, M. and Illing, G. (1996). *Einführung in die Spieltheorie*, 3rd edn. Berlin *et al.*: Springer

Howell, F. and McNam, R. (1998). *Simjava: A Discrete Event Simulation Package for Java with Applications in Computer Systems Modeling*. Paper presented at the First International Conference on Web-based Modeling and Simulation, San Diego, CA

Hu, C. (1998). *The Basics of Conjoint Analysis* (WWW). Available: <http://www.nevada.edu/~huc/html/doca.html>, December 12

Hurwicz, L. (1973). The design of mechanisms for resource allocation. *American Economic Review*, *63*, 1–30

Isaak, R. M. and Walker, J. M. (1985). Information and conspiracy in sealed bid auctions. *Journal of Economic Behavior and Organization*, *6*, 139–59

Jevons, W. S. (1871). *The Theory of Political Economy*, 1st edn. London *et al.*: Macmillan

Johnston, J. (1991). *Econometric Methods*, 3rd edn. Auckland *et al.*: McGraw-Hill

Kagel, J. H. (1995). Auctions: a survey of experimental research. In J. H. Kagel and A. E. Roth (eds.), *The Handbook of Experimental Economics*, pp. 501–87. Princeton: Princeton University Press

Kagel, J. H. and Levin, D. (1985). Individual bidder behavior in first-price private value auctions. *Economics Letters*, *19*, 125–8

(1991). The winner's curse and public information in common value auctions. *American Economic Review*, *81*, 362–9

(1993). Independent private value auctions: bidder behavior in first-, second- and third-price auctions with varying numbers of bidders. The *Economic Journal*, *103*, 868–79

Kagel, J. H., Marstad, R. M. and Levin, D. (1987). Information impact and allocation rules in auctions with affiliated private values: a laboratory study. *Econometrica*, *55*, 1275–1304

Kagel, J. H. and Roth, A. E. (1995). *The Handbook of Experimental Economics*. Princeton: Princeton University Press

Kalakota, R. and Whinston, A. B. (1996). *Frontiers of Electronic Commerce*. Reading, MA: Addison-Wesley

Kaukal, M. and Werthner, H. (2000). *Integration of Heterogeneous Information Sources*. Paper presented at the 7th ENTER Conference 2000, Barcelona

Keenan, V. (1998). *The Keenan Report – Exchanges in the Internet Economy*. Keenan Vision. Available: <http://www.keenanvision.com/html/content/exchange/internet_exchange.html>, January 14, 2000

Keeny, R. L. and Raiffa, H. (1993). *Decision Making with Multiple Objectives: Preferences and Value Tradeoffs*. Cambridge, UK: Cambridge University Press

Kendrick, D. (1991). *Research Opportunities in Computational Economics*. Austin, TX: Center for Economic Research, University of Texas at Austin

Kephart, J. O., Hanson, J. E. and Sairamesh, J. (1998). Price-war dynamics in a free-market economy of software agents. *Artificial Life, 4*(1)

Kersten, G. E. (1997). Support for group decisions and negotiations. In J. Climaco (ed.), *Multicriteria Analysis*, pp. 332–346. Heidelberg: Springer

(1998). *Negotiation Support Systems and Negotiating Agents.* Paper presented at the Modèles et Systèmes Multi-Agents pour la Gestion de l'Environment et des Territoires, Clermont-Ferrand

Kersten, G. E. and Noronha, S. J. (1998). *Negotiation and the Internet: Users' Expectations and Acceptance.* Carleton University. Available: <http://interneg .carleton.ca/interneg/research/interneg/inspire_users/>, May 8

(1999a). *Are All E-Commerce Negotiations Auctions?* Paper presented at the 4th International Conference on the Design of Cooperative Systems (COOP '2000), Sophia-Antipolis

(1999b). *Negotiations in Electronic Commerce: Methodological Misconceptions and a Resolution.* Paper presented at the 29th Atlantic Schools of Business Conference, Halifax, Canada

Kleindorfer, P. R., Kunreuther, H. C. and Schoemaker, P. J. H. (1993). *Decision Sciences: An Integrative Perspective.* Cambridge, UK: Cambridge University Press

Klemperer, P. (1999). Auction theory: a guide to the literature. *Journal of Economic Surveys*, forthcoming; also published in *Journal of Economic Surveys, 13* (3) (1999) and reprinted in S. Dahiya (ed.), *The Current State of Economic Science, 2*: (1999)

Kolb, R. W. (1993). *Financial Derivatives.* Englewood Cliffs, NJ: New York Institute of Finance

(2000). *Futures, Options and Swaps*, 3rd edn. Oxford: Blackwell

Koopmans, T. C. (1957). Allocation of resources and the price system. In T. C. Koopmans (ed.), *Three Essays on the State of Economic Science*, pp. 1–126. New York: McGraw-Hill

Koppius, O. R. (1998). *Electronic Multidimensional Auctions: Trading Mechanisms and Applications.* Paper presented at the Edispuut Workshop '98: E-Commerce – Crossing Boundaries, Rotterdam

Koppius, O., Kumar, M. and Van Heck, E. (2000). *Electronic Multidimensional Auctions and the Role of Information Feedback.* Paper presented at the 8th European Conference on Information Systems (ECIS 2000), Vienna

Kumar, M. and Feldman, S. (1998a). *Business Negotiations on the Internet.* Paper presented at the inet '98, Geneva, July 21–23

(1998b). *Internet Auctions.* Paper presented at the 3rd USENIX Workshop on Electronic Commerce, Boston, MA

Kwok, Y.-K. (1998). *Mathematical Models of Financial Derivatives.* Berlin *et al.* <http://www.springer.de/cgi-bin/search_book.pl/isbn=981-3083-25-57>

Laffont, J.-J. and Tirole, J. (1993). *A Theory of Incentives in Procurement and Regulation.* Cambridge, MA: MIT Press

Lancester, K. J. (1966). A new approach to consumer theory. *Journal of Political Economy, 74*, 132–57

Lassila, O. and Swick, R. R. (1999). *Resource Description Framework (RDF) Model and Syntax Specification* (W3C Recommendation). WWW Consortium <http://www.w3.org/RDF/>

Laux, H. (1998). *Entscheidungstheorie*, 4th edn. Berlin: Springer

Ledyard, J. (1986). The scope of the hypothesis of Bayesian equilibrium. *Journal of Economic Theory, 39*, 59–82

Lee, H. G. (1998). Do electronic marketplaces lower the price of goods? *Communications of the ACM, 41*(1), 73–80

Lewandowski, S. M. (1998). Frameworks for component-based client/server computing. *ACM Computing Surveys, 30*(1)

Lindemann, M. A. and Runge, A. (1998). *Electronic Contracting within the Reference Model for Electronic Markets* (Research Report). St. Gallen HSG

Linhart, P. B. and Radner, R. (1992). Minimax-regret strategies for bargaining over several variables. In P. B. Linhart, R. Radner and M. A. Satterthwaite (eds.), *Bargaining with Incomplete Information*, pp. 215–41. San Diego, CA: Academic Press

Linhart, P. B., Radner, R. and Satterthwaite, M. A. (1992). *Bargaining with Incomplete Information*. San Diego, CA: Academic Press

Lucking-Reiley, D. (1999a). *Auctions on the Internet: What's Being Auctioned and How?* Available: <http://www.vanderbilt.edu/Econ/reiley/cv.html>, February 1, 2000

  (1999b). Using field experiments to test equivalence between auction formats: magic on the Internet. *American Economic Review, 89*(5), 1063–80

Lucking-Reiley, D. and List, J. (2000). Demand reduction in multi-unit auctions: evidence from a Sprotscard field experiment. *American Economic Review,* September

Ma, C., Moore, J. and Turnbull, S. (1988). Stopping agents from "cheating." *Journal of Economic Theory, 46*, 355–72

Maes, P. (1997). *Modeling Adaptive Autonomous Agents* (Working Paper). Cambridge, MA: MIT Media Laboratory

Maier, G. and Weiss, P. (1990). *Modelle diskreter Entscheidungen*. Wien *et al.*: Springer

Malhotra, A. and Maloney, M. (1999). *XML Schema Requirements* (W3C Note). WWW Consortium <http://www.w3.org/RDF/>

Malone, T. W., Yates, J. and Benjamin, R. I. (1987). Electronic markets and electronic hierarchies. *Communications of the ACM, 30*(6), 484–97

Mansfield, E. (1996). *Microeconomics*, 9th edn. New York *et al.*: W. W. Norton

Marimon, R., McGrattan, E. and Sargent, T. J. (1990). Money as a medium of exchange in an economy with artificially intelligent agents. *Journal of Economics, Dynamics and Control, 14*, 329–73

Maskin, E. S. and Riley, J. G. (1984). Optimal auctions with risk averse buyers. *Econometrica, 52*, 1473–1518

  (1989). Optimal multi-unit auctions. In F. Hahn (ed.), *The Economics of Missing Markets, Information and Games*, pp. 312–35. Oxford: Oxford University Press

  (1993). *Asymmetric Auctions* (Working Paper). Boston, MA: Harvard University and UCLA

McAfee, R. and McMillan, P. J. (1987). Auctions and bidding. *Journal of Economic Literature, 25*, 699–738

McCabe, K., Rassenti, S. and Smith, V. (1991). Smart computer-assisted markets. *Science, 254*, October, 534–8

(1993). Designing a uniform price double auction: an experimental evaluation. In D. Friedman and J. Rust (eds.), *The Double Auction Market: Theories, and Evidence.* Reading, MA: Addison-Wesley

McConnell, S. (1997). *The OMG/CommerceNet Joint Electronic Commerce Whitepaper* (Research Report). Needham, MA: OMG

McLaughlin, R. M. (1998). *Over-the-Counter Derivative Products.* New York *et al.*: McGraw-Hill

McMillan, J. (1994). Selling spectrum rights. *Journal of Economic Perspectives, 8*(3), 145–62

Meltzer, B. and Glushko, R. (1998). XML and electronic commerce: enabling the network economy. *SIGMOD Record, 27*(4), 21–5

Mertens, P. and Höhl, M. (1999). *Wie lernt der Computer den Menschen kennen? Bestandsaufnahme und Experimente zur Benutzermodellierung in der Wirtschaftsinformatik.* Paper presented at the Wirtschaftsinformatik '99, Saarbrücken, March 3–5

Metha, G. B. (1998). Preference and utility. In S. Barbera, P. J. Hammond and C. Seidl (eds.), *Handbook of Utility Theory*, 1, pp. 2–40. Dordrecht *et al.*: Kluwer Academic Publishers

Milgrom, P. R. (1987). Auction theory. In T. Bewley (ed.), *Advances in Economic Theory: Fifth World Congress.* Cambridge, UK: Cambridge University Press

(1989). Auctions and bidding: a primer. *Journal of Economic Perspectives, 3*(3), 3–22

Milgrom, P. R. and Weber, R. J. (1982). A theory of auctions and competitive bidding. *Econometrica, 50*, 1089–1122

Moessenboeck, H. (1996). Trends in object-oriented programming. *ACM Computing Surveys, 28A*(4)

Müller-Möhl, E. (1989). *Optionen.* Stuttgart: Schäffer Verlag

Myerson, R. B. (1981). Optimal auction design. *Mathematics of Operations Research, 6*, 58–73

Myerson, R. B. and Satterthwaite, M. A. (1983). Efficient mechanisms for bilateral trade. *Journal of Economic Theory, 29*, 265–81

Nash, J. (1950). The bargaining problem. *Econometrica, 18*, 155–62

(1953). Two-person cooperative games. *Econometrica, 21*, 128–40

Neslin, S. A. and Greenhalgh, L. (1986). The ability of Nash's theory of cooperative games to predict the outcomes of buyer–seller negotiations: a dyad-level test. *Management Science, 32*(4), 480–98

Nwana, H. S. and Ndumu, D. T. (1997). An introduction to agent technology. In H. S. Nwana and N. Azarmi (eds.), *Software Agents and Soft Computing. Towards Enhancing Machine Intelligence; Concepts and Applications*, pp. 3–26. Berlin: Springer

OECD (1997). *Measuring Electronic Commerce* (OECD/GD(97)185). Paris: OECD

(1998). *The Economic and Social Impacts of Electronic Commerce.* OECD. Available: <http://www.oecd.org/subject/e_commerce/summary.html>, August 12, 1999

Oliver, J. R. (1996). A machine learning approach to automated negotiation and prospects for electronic commerce. *Journal of Management Information Systems, 13*(3), 83–112

(1997). *On Automated Negotiation and Electronic Commerce.* Unpublished Dissertation, University of Pennsylvania, Philadelphia

Olson, D. L. (1995). *Decision Aids for Selection Problems.* New York *et al.*: Springer

OMG (1997). *CORBA Services Specification: Trading Object Service Specification* (Technical Specification). Boston, MA: Object Management Group

Orfali, R. and Harkey, D. (1997). *Client/Server Programming with Java and CORBA.* New York: John Wiley

OSM (1999). *OMG Negotiation Facility Submission.* OSM Consortium. Available: <http://www.osm.net/about/negotiation.html>, February 19

Ostrom, T. (1988). Computer simulation: the third symbol system. *Journal of Experimental Social Psychology, 24*, 381–92

OTP (1999). *OTP Standard v 0.9.* OTP Consortium. Available: <http://www.otp.org>, June 12

Page, F. H. (1993). *Optimal Auction Design with Risk Aversion and Correlated Information* (Discussion Paper RePEc:dgr:kubcen:1994109). Tilburg: Tilburg University, Center for Economic Research

Parameswaran, M., Stallaert, J. and Whinston, A. B. (1999). *Electronic Markets and the Logistics of Digital Products.* Paper presented at the First IAC Workshop on Internet-based Negotiation Technologies, Yorktown Heights

Pareto, V. (1971). *Manual of Political Economy.* New York: A.M. Kelley

Pauwels, W. (2000). *Pricing Digital Information Goods and Services on the Net.* Paper presented at the 8th European Conference on Information Systems (ECIS 2000), Vienna

Perkins, W. C., Hershauer, J. C., Foroughi, A. and Delaney, M. (1996). Can a negotiation support system help a purchasing manager? *International Journal of Purchasing and Materials Management, Spring*, 37–45

Picot, A., Bortenländer, C. and Heiner, R. (1995). The automation of capital markets. *Journal of Computer-Mediated Communication, 1–3* (Special Issue on Electronic Commerce)

Picot, A., Bortenländer, C. and Roehrl, H. (1997). Organization of electronic markets: contributions from the new institutional economics. *The Information Society, 13*, 107–23

Pigou, A. C. (1920). *The Economics of Welfare.* London: Macmillan

Poulter, K. (1998). *The Role of Shared Ontology in XML-Based Trading Architectures.* Available: <http://www.ontology.org/main/papers/cacm-agents99.html>, October 20, 1999

Pree, W. (1997). *Komponenten-basierte Softwareentwicklung mit Frameworks.* Heidelberg: dpunkt

Raiffa, H. (1982). *The Art and Science of Negotiation.* Cambridge, MA: Belknap Harvard Press

Rapoport, A. (1964). *Strategy and Conscience.* New York: Harper

Rassenti, S., Smith, V. L. and Bulfin, R. L. (1982). A combinatorial auction mechanism for airport time slot allocations. *Bell Journal of Economics, 13*, 402–17

Riley, J. G. and Samuleson, J. G. (1981). Optimal auctions. *American Economic Review, 71*(3), 381–92

Robinson, M. S. (1985). Collusion and the choice of auction. *Rand Journal of Economics, 16,* 141–5

Robinson, W. N. and Volkov, V. (1998). Supporting the negotiation life cycle. *Communications of the ACM, 41*(5), 95–102

Rosenschein, J. S. and Zlotkin, G. (1994). *Rules of Encounter: Designing Conventions for Automated Negotiation Among Computers.* Cambridge, MA: MIT Press

Rosenthal, R. W. (1993). Rules of thumb in games. *Journal of Economic Behavior and Organization, 22*(1), 1–13

Roth, A. (1995). Bargaining experiments. In J. H. Kagel and A. E. Roth (eds.), *The Handbook of Experimental Economics,* pp. 253–348. Princeton: Princeton University Press

Roth, A. and Schoumaker, F. (1983). Expectations and reputations in bargaining: an experimental study. *American Economic Review, 73,* 362–72

Roth, A. E. (1999). *Game Theory as a Tool for Market Design.* Available: <http://www.economics.harvard.edu/~aroth/alroth.html>, September 21

Rothkopf, M. H. (1977). Bidding in simultaneous auctions with a constraint on exposure. *Operations Research, 25,* 620–9

Rothkopf, M. H. and Harstad, R. M. (1994). Modeling competitive bidding: a critical essay. *Management Science, 40*(3), 364–84

Rothkopf, M. H. and Pekec, A. (1998). *Computationally Manageable Combinatorial Auctions.* Paper presented at the Maryland Auction Conference, Maryland, May 29–31

Roy, B. (1981). Multicriteria analysis: survey and new directions. *European Journal of Operational Research, 8,* 207–18

Rubinstein, A. (1982). Perfect equilibrium in a bargaining model. *Econometrica, 50*(1), 97–109

Rumbaugh, J., Blaha, M., Premerlani, W., Eddy, F. and Lorensen, W. (1991). *Object-oriented Modeling and Design:* Englewood Cliffs, NJ: Prentice–Hall

Rust, J., Miller, J. H. and Palmer, R. (1993). Behavior of trading automata in a computerized double auction market. In J. Rust and D. Friedman (eds.), *The Double Auction Market: Institutions, Theories and Evidence,* pp. 153–96. Reading, MA: Addison-Wesley

Saaty, T. L. (1980). *The Analytic Hierarchy Process.* New York: McGraw Hill

Samuelson, P. A. (1947). *Foundations of Economic Analysis.* Cambridge, MA: Harvard University Press

Sandholm, T. (1993). *An Implementation of the Contract Net Protocol Based on Marginal Cost Calculations.* Paper presented at the Eleventh National Conference on Artificial Intelligence, Washington DC

(1999a). Approaches to winner determination in combinatorial auctions. *Decision Support Systems, 28*(1), 165–76

(1999b). Automated negotiation. *Communications of the ACM, 42*(3), 84–5

Satterthwaite, M. A. and Williams, S. R. (1989). The rate of convergence to efficiency in the buyer's bid double auction as the market becomes large. *Review of Economic Studies, 56,* 477–98

Schmid, B. and Lindemann, M. (1997). *Elemente eines Referenzmodells Elektronischer Märkte* (Research Report). St. Gallen: HSG

Schwarzhoff, K. (1997). *An Appartment Marketplace* (CommerceNet Research Report 97–14). Mountain View, CA: CommerceNet

Sebenius, J. K. (1992). Negotiation analysis: a characterization and review. *Management Science, 38*(1), 18–38

Sedgewick, R. (1992). *Algorithms*. Bonn *et al.*: Addison-Wesley

Segev, A. and Bichler, M. (1999). Component-based electronic commerce. In M. Shaw, R. Blanning, T. Strader and A. Whinston (eds.), *Handbook on Electronic Commerce*. New York *et al.*: Springer

Segev, A., Dadong, W. and Beam, C. (1995). *Designing Electronic Catalogs for Business Value: Results from the CommerceNet Pilot* (Working Paper 95–WP-1005). Berkeley: Haas School of Business, University of California at Berkeley

Shapiro, C. and Varian, H. R. (1999). *Information Rules: A Strategic Guide to the Network Economy*. Boston, MA: Harvard Business School Press

Shim, J. P. (1989). Bibliographical research on the analytic hierarchy process (AHP). *Socio-Economic Planning Sciences, 23*(3), 161–7

Sierra, C., Faratin, P. and Jennings, N. R. (1997). *A Service-Oriented Negotiation Model between Autonomous Agents*. Paper presented at the Proceedings of the 8th European Workshop on Modeling Autonomous Agents in a Multi-Agent World (MAAMAW-97), Ronneby

Singh, N. P., Genesereth, M. R. and Syed, M. (1995). A distributed and anonymous knowledge sharing approach to software interoperation. *International Journal of Cooperative Information Systems, 4*(4), 339–67

Smith, C. W. (1989). *Auctions: The Social Construction of Value*. Los Angeles: University of California Press

Smith, H. and Poulter, K. (1999). *The Role of Shared Ontology in XML-Based Trading Architectures* (White Paper). <http://www.ontology.org/>

Smith, R. G. (1980). The ContractNet protocol: high-level communication and control in a distributed problem solver. *IEEE Transactions on Computers* (C-29)

Smith, S. A. and Rothkopf, M. H. (1985). Simultaneous bidding with a fixed charge if any bid succeeds. *Operations Research, 33*, 28–37

Smith, V. L. (1982). Microeconomic systems as an experimental science. *American Economic Review, 72*, 923–55

Smith, V. L. and Walker, J. M. (1993). Rewards, experience and decision costs in first price auctions. *Economic Inquiry, 31*, 237–44

Stefansson, B. (1997). *Swarm: An Object Oriented Simulation Platform Applied to Markets and Organizations*. Paper presented at the Evolutionary Programming VI. Proceedings of the Sixth Annual Conference on Evolutionary Programming, P. J. Angeline, R. G. Reynolds, J. R. McDonnell and R. Eberhart (eds.), *Lecture Notes in Computer Science*, 1213. Berlin *et al.*: Springer Verlag

Stolze, M. (1998). *Soft Navigation in Product Catalogs*. Paper presented at the European Conference on Digital Libraries, Heraklion, 19–23 September

Strader, T. J., Lin, F. and Shaw, M. J. (1998). Simulation of order fulfillment in divergent assembly supply chains. *Journal of Artificial Societies and Social Simulation, 1*(2)

(1999). The impact of information sharing on simulation of order fulfillment in divergent differentiation supply chains. *Journal of Global Information Management, 7*(1)

Stroebel, M. (2000). *Effects of Electronic Markets on Negotiation Processes.* Paper presented at the 8th European Conference on Information Systems (ECIS 2000), Vienna

Stubblebine, S. and Syverson, P. (1999). *Fair On-line Auctions Without Special Trusted Parties.* Paper presented at the Financial Cryptography 1999 Anguilla

Sycra, K. (1991). Problem restructuring in negotiations. *Management Science, 37*(10), 1248–68

Sydow, J. (1992). On the management of strategic networks. In H. Ernste and V. Meier (eds.), *Regional Development and Contemporary Industrial Response: Extending Flexible Specialisation,* pp. 114–29. London *et al.*: Belhaven Press

Teich, J., Wallenius, H. and Wallenius, J. (1999). Multiple-issue auction and market algorithms for the world wide web. *Decision Support Systems, 26,* 49–66

Teich, J. E., Wallenius, H., Wallenius, J. and Zaitsev, A. (1999). A multiple unit auction algorithm: some theory and a web implementation. *Electronic Markets: International Journal of Electronic Commerce and Business Media, 9*(3), 1–7

Tesauro, G. J. and Kephart, J. O. (1998). *Foresight-based Pricing Algorithms in an Economy of Software Agents.* Paper presented at the International Conference on Information and Computation Economies, New York

Tesfatsion, L. (1997a). How economists can get a life. In B. Arthur, S. Drulauf and D. Lane (eds.), *The Economy as an Evolving Complex System.* Reading, MA: Addison-Wesley

(1997b). A trade network game with endogenous partner selection. In H. Amman, B. Rustem and A. Whinston (eds.), *Computational Approaches to Economic Problems.* Dordrecht: Kluwer Academic Publishers

(1998). Agent-based computational economics: a brief guide to the literature. In J. Mitchie (ed.), *Reader's Guide to the Social Sciences.* London: Fitzroy-Dearborn

Tesler, L. G. (1994). The usefulness of core theory in economics. *Journal of Economic Perspectives, 8*(2), 151–64

Thiel, S. E. (1988). Multidimensional auctions. *Economics Letters, 28,* 37–40

Thompson, C., Linden, T. and Filman, B. (1997). *Thoughts on the OMA-NG: The Next Generation Object Management Architecture* (OMA-NG Green Paper). San Francisco: OMG

Troitzsch, K. (1999). Social science simulation – origins, prospects, purposes. In R. Conte, R. Hegselmann and P. Terna (eds.), *Lecture Notes in Economics and Mathematical Systems – Simulating Social Phenomena,* 456, pp. 41–54. Berlin *et al.*: Springer

Turban, E. (1997). Auctions and bidding on the Internet: an assessment. *International Journal of Electronic Markets, 7*(4), 7–11

Tversky, A. and Kahneman, D. (1981). The framing of decisions and the psychology of choice. *Science, 211,* 453–58

Uschold, M. and Gruninger, M. (1996). Ontologies: principles, methods and applications. *Knowledge Engineering Review, 11*(2)

Vakrat, Y. and Seidmann, A. (2000). *Implications of the Bidders' Arrival Process on the Design of Online Auctions.* Paper presented at the 33rd Hawai'i International Conference on Systems Sciences, Maui

Van Heck, E., Koppius, O. and Vervest, P. (1998). *Electronic Web-Based Auctions: Theory and Practice.* Paper presented at the 6th European Conference on Information Systems (ECIS '98), Aix-en-Provence

Varian, H. (1992). *Microeconomic Analysis*, 3rd edn. New York *et al.* W. W. Norton

(1995). *Economic Mechanism Design for Computerized Agents.* Paper presented at the Usenix Workshop on Electronic Commerce, New York

(1996a). Differential pricing and efficiency. *First Monday (online journal)*, *1*(2)

(1996b). Pricing electronic journals. *D-lib Magazine,* July

(1996c). *Intermediate Microeconomics*, 4th edn. New York: W. W. Norton

(1997). *Versioning Information Goods.* Paper presented at the Internet Publishing and Beyond: Economics of Digital Information and Intellectual Property, Cambridge, MA

Vickrey, W. (1961). Counterspeculation, auctions and competitive sealed tenders. *Journal of Finance, 3,* 8–37

Vidal, J. M. and Durfee, E. H. (1997). *Agents Learning about Agents: A Framework and Analysis.* Paper presented at the AAAI Workshop on Learning in Multi-Agent Systems, Providence, RI

von Neumann, J. and Morgenstern, O. (1944). *Theory of Games and Economic Behavior.* Princeton: Princeton University Press

von Winterfeldt, D. and Edwards, W. (1986). *Decision Analysis and Behavioral Research.* Cambridge, UK: Cambridge University Press

Vulkan, N. and Jennings, N. R. (2000). Efficient mechanisms for the supply of services in multi-agent environments. *Decision Support Systems, 28*(1), 5–19

Walras, L. (1874). *Elements of Pure Economics.* London: Allen & Unwin

Walton, R. E. and McKersie, R. B. (1965). *A Behavioral Theory of Labor Negotiations.* New York: McGraw-Hill

Watson, J. (1998). Alternating-offer bargaining with two-sided incomplete information. *Review of Economic Studies, 85,* 573–94

Weber, R. J. (1983). Multiple-object auctions. In R. Engelbrecht-Wiggans, M. Shubik and J. Stark (eds.), *Auctions, Bidding and Contracting*, pp. 165–91. New York: New York University Press

Weld, D. (1995). The role of intelligent agents in the national infrastructure. *AI Magazine* (Fall), 45–64

Werthner, H. and Klein, S. (1999). *Information Technology and Tourism – A Challenging Relationship.* Vienna *et al.*: Springer

Wiederhold, G. (1992). Mediators in the architecture of future information systems. *IEEE Computer, 3,* 38–49

Wigand, R. T. and Benjamin, R. I. (1993). Electronic commerce: effects on electronic markets. *Journal of Computer Mediated Communication, 1*(3)

Williamson, O. E. (1975). *Markets and Hierarchies.* New York: Free Press

(1981). The modern corporation: origin, evolution attributes. *Journal of Economic Literature, 19,* 1537–68

Wilson, R. (1977). A bidding model of perfect competition. *Review of Economic Studies, 44*, 511–18

(1979). Auctions of shares. *Quarterly Journal of Economics, 93*, 675–89

(1985). Incentive efficiency of double auctions. *Econometrica, 53*, 1101–15

(1992). Strategic analysis of auctions. In R. J. Aumann and S. Hart (eds.), *Handbook of Game Theory*, I, pp. 227–71. Amsterdam *et al.*: North-Holland

(1999). *Market Architecture*. Stanford, CA: Stanford University Press

Wold, H. (1943). A synthesis of pure demand analysis. *Skandinavisk Actuarietidskrift, 26*, 85–118

Wolfstetter, E. (1996). Auctions: an introduction. *Journal of Economic Surveys, 10*(4), 367–420

Wrigley, C. (1997). Design criteria for electronic market servers. *International Journal of Electronic Markets, 7*(4), 12–16

Wurman, P. R. (1997). *Multidimensional Auction Design for Computational Economies: A Dissertation Proposal*. Unpublished Dissertation Proposal, University of Michigan

Wurman, P. R., Walsh, W. E. and Wellman, M. P. (1998). Flexible double auctions for electronic commerce: theory and implementation. *Decision Support Systems, 24*, 17–27

Wurman, P. R., Wellman, M. P. and Walsh, W. E. (1998). *The Michigan Internet AuctionBot: A Configurable Auction Server for Human Software Agents*. Paper presented at the Second International Conference on Autonomous Agents (Agents '98), Minneapolis

(2000). A Parametrization of the auction design space. *Games and Economic Behavior*, forthcoming

Zelewski, S. (1998). Auktionsverfahren zur Koordinierung von Agenten auf elektronischen Märkten. In M. Becker, J. Kloock, R. Schmidt and G. Wäscher (eds.), *Unternehmen im Wandel und Umbruch*, pp. 305–37. Stuttgart: Schäffer Poeschel Verlag

Zeng, D. and Sycara, K. (1998). Bayesian learning in negotiation. *International Journal of Human-Computer Studies, 48*, 125–41

Index